Where to Wear 2004

THE INSIDER'S GUIDE TO
LONDON SHOPPING

Fairchild & Gallagher

NEW YORK • LONDON

PUBLISHERS
Jill Fairchild & Gerri Gallagher

WRITER
Daisy Finer

PREVIOUS WRITER
Erica Youngren

COPY EDITOR
John Graham

INTERN
Elizabeth Duff

DESIGN / PRODUCTION ARTIST
Jeff Baker

COVER DESIGN
Richard Chapman

CARTOGRAPHER
Candida Kennedy

DISTRIBUTION, SALES AND MARKETING
The Julie Craik Consultancy

Where to Wear, London, 2004 Edition
ISBN 0-9720215-3-1

Printed and bound in the United Kingdom.

For information, contact Where to Wear in New York or London at:

666 Fifth Avenue
PMB 377
New York, NY 10103
TEL 212-969-0138
TOLL-FREE 1-877-714-SHOP (7467)
FAX 212-315-1534
E-MAIL wheretowear@aol.com

10 Cinnamon Row, Plantation Wharf, London SW11 3TW
TEL 020 7801 1381
E-MAIL wheretowear@onetel.net.uk

www.wheretowear.com

Table of Contents

Introduction

Dear London Shopper,

Welcome to *Where to Wear*, the world's most detailed and authoritative directory of clothing and accessory stores. At *Where to Wear* we annually update our collection of global guides, making your travels through the world's fashion cities a breeze. We pioneered in 1999 with *Where to Wear New York*, and we have since added London, Paris, Los Angeles, San Francisco and *Where to Wear Italy* which includes Florence, Milan and Rome.

The 2004 edition of *Where to Wear London* has all the information you'll need to look and feel great. We describe over 600 different clothing and accessories stores, ranging from the globally famous names of Bond Street and Sloane Street to out-of-the-way treasure-houses. *Where to Wear* shows visitors where to begin and Londoners where to go next. If you want the best vintage value or the bonniest baby boutique, you'll find them using *Where to Wear*.

These are the only shopping guides written by teams of top fashion journalists. We have our fingers on the pulse of the ever-changing fashion world. We've tromped through each and every store to discover what's fabulous, functional, frumpy, fancy or frightful in them this season. We tell you what the store and its merchandise are all about and who its target customer is, and we list the address, phone number and opening hours. We've marked those stores that merit special consideration with a star (☆), and occasionally we have something sweet (or not so sweet) to say about the staff's helpfulness or attitude. Please let us know if you disagree.

And to make your life even simpler we have included ten pages of user-friendly maps and two separate indexes grouping the stores both by category and by location. Shopping has never been easier! In addition, you'll find the best addresses for beauty treatments, fitness studios, day spas, couture dry cleaners, shoe repair shops, specialty stores (for beads, ribbons, etc) and much else.

Life is not all shopping, of course, so you will also find a list of in-store restaurants and other delightful lunch spots. It's an eclectic list, chosen by our experts for your fun and convenience.

So rev up your credit card and get going, and make sure to keep *W2W* in your handbag, briefcase or backpack.

—Jill Fairchild & Gerri Gallagher

Jill Fairchild Melhado, daughter of fashion world legend and *W* magazine founder John Fairchild, worked as an intern at *Glamour* magazine, *GQ* and *Vogue*. Ms Fairchild has also worked for Ailes Communications, a television production company, and in the late Eighties she founded and ran her own accessories company.

Gerri Gallagher is a Condé Nast editor who has lived in Europe for 15 years. She was the managing editor of Fairchild Publication's *W Europe* from 1990 to 1993 and is currently associate editor of *Tatler* magazine in London.

Julie Craik, *Where to Wear* partner and director of sales, marketing and distribution has worked in publishing for 20 years. Before joining *W2W* she was associate publisher of *Tatler* magazine and had previously worked for the National Magazine Company.

Where to Wear 2004

Best Picks

In-Store Restaurants

Restaurants

Size Conversion Chart

Best Picks

9 London
Accessorize
Agent Provocateur
Anya Hindmarch

Brioni
Brora
Browns
Butler & Wilson

Chloé
Connolly
The Cross
Egg

Emma Hope
Ermenegildo Zegna
Fenwick
Harrods

Harvey Nichols
Heidi Klein
Henry Poole & Co

Hilditch & Key
Huntsman
Jimmy Choo

John Lobb
Joseph
Kilgour French Stanbury
Koh Samui

Liberty
Lulu Guinness
Matches
MiMi

Olivia Morris
Paul Smith
Richard James
Selfridges

Semmalina
Souvenir
SpaceNK
Steinberg & Tolkien

Stella McCartney
Top Shop
Tricker's

Turnbull & Asser
Whistles
Zara

In-Store Restaurants

All are recommended, but a star (☆) indicates that they are our particular favorites.

Fifth Floor Restaurant at Harvey Nichols **020 7235 5250**
109-125 Knightsbridge, SW1

Fifth Floor Café at Harvey Nichols **020 7823 1839**
109-125 Knightsbridge, SW1

☆ **Nicole's at Nicole Farhi** **020 7499 8408**
158 New Bond Street, W1

☆ **202 Restaurant at Nicole Farhi** **020 7727 2722**
202 Westbourne Grove, W11

DKNY Bar at DKNY **020 7409 7473**
27 Old Bond Street, W1

Emporio Armani Caffè **020 7581 0854**
191 Brompton Road, SW3

☆ **The Fountain at Fortnum & Mason** **020 7734 8040**
181 Piccadilly, W1
also The Patio, and the St. James Restaurant on the 4th floor

Iguacu at Selfridges **020 7318 3937**
44 Duke Street, W1

Premier at Selfridges **020 7318 3155**
400 Oxford Street, W1
also YO! Sushi on 020 7318 3944 and 12 others—they have restaurants on every floor

The Georgian at Harrods **020 7730 1234**
87-135 Brompton Road, SW1
they have more than 20 restaurants, on every floor except the 5th

☆ **Joe's Restaurant at Fenwick** **020 7495 5402**
63 New Bond Street, W1
*also *Carluccio's 020 7629 9161*

☆ **Joe's Café at Marni** **020 7235 9869**
16 Sloane Street, SW1

Joe's Restaurant at Gigi **020 7225 2217**
126 Draycott Avenue, SW3

Restaurants

The following is a select list of restaurants perfect for lunching during your shopping spree.

N1 (ISLINGTON)

Frederick's **020 7359 2888**
Camden Passage
modern European

Granita **020 7226 3222**
127 Upper Street
Mediterranean

NW1 (PRIMROSE HILL)

Fresh & Wild **020 7428 7575**
49 Parkway
high-class food store but you can eat here as well

☆ **Lemonia** **020 7586 7454**
89 Regent's Park Road
the most popular Greek restaurant in London

Lucca **020 7485 6864**
63 Parkway
hugely friendly family-run Italian

Odette's **020 7586 5486**
130 Regent's Park Road
modern British

NW3 (HAMPSTEAD)

Byron's **020 7435 3544**
3a Downshire Hill
French/modern British

ZeNW3 020 7794 7863
83 Hampstead High Street
Chinese

NW8 (ST. JOHN'S WOOD)

L'Aventure 020 7624 6232
3 Blenheim Terrace
French; outside terrace for fine days

La Casalinga 020 7722 5959
64 St. John's Wood High Street
Italian; outside tables for fine days

Rosmarino 020 7328 5014
1 Blenheim Terrace
Italian; outside terrace for fine days

SW1 (KNIGHTSBRIDGE/BELGRAVIA)

Boxwood Café 020 7235 1010
The Berkeley Hotel
Wilton Place
(opening as we went to press, but they aim to be a "New York-style café")

☆ **Drones** 020 7235 9555
1 Pont Street
French/Mediterranean; celebrity favorite

Isola 020 7838 1044
145 Knightsbridge
Italian

☆ **Olivo** 020 7730 2505
21 Eccleston Street
Italian

Oriel 020 7730 4275
50-51 Sloane Square
brasserie for café society, very popular rendezvous

Signor Sassi 020 7584 2277
14 Knightsbridge Green
Italian

Simply Nico 020 7896 9909
12 Sloane Square
Franco-Mediterranean

☆ **Zafferano** 020 7235 5800
15 Lowndes Street
Italian

SW1 (ST. JAMES'S)

☆ **Le Caprice** 020 7629 2239
Arlington Street
modern British; A-list clientele

Quaglino's **020 7930 6767**
16 Bury Street
International

The Avenue **020 7321 2111**
7 St. James's Street
modern European; airy, spacious, stylish

SW3 (CHELSEA, SOUTH KEN, FULHAM ROAD)

Area **020 7589 7613**
162 Brompton Road
Italian

Bacio **020 7351 9997**
386 King's Road
a nostalgic throwback to the vibrant Italian trattorias of the Seventies

Benihana **020 7376 7799**
77 King's Road
Japanese

☆ **Bibendum Oyster Bar** **020 7589 1480**
81 Fulham Road
seafood; worth visiting for the Michelin building alone

Bluebird **020 7559 1000**
350 King's Road
northern European

Brasserie St. Quentin **020 7589 8005**
243 Brompton Road
French; with a recommended wine list chosen by Charles Sandeman of high-rep vintners Lea & Sandeman

Carpaccio **020 7352 3433**
4 Sydney Street
Italian

El Gaucho **020 7376 8514**
125 Sydney Street
Argentinian, i.e. serious red meat

Floriana **020 7838 1500**
15 Beauchamp Place
Italian; celebrity favorite

Itsu **020 7590 2400**
118 Draycott Avenue
Japanese

☆ **La Brasserie** **020 7584 1668**
272 Brompton Road
traditional brasserie; favorite with the beau monde

Le Colombier **020 7351 1155**
145 Dovehouse Street
French

Picasso 020 7352 4921
127 King's Road
traditional coffee bar, evergreen favorite; no one can remember a time before Picasso

Pucci Pizza 020 7352 2134
205 King's Road
Pizzas, pasta, steaks

Racine 020 7584 4477
239 Brompton Road
French classics

☆ **San Lorenzo** 020 7584 1074
22 Beauchamp Place
Italian; celebrity favorite

Scalini 020 7225 2301
1-3 Walton Street
Italian classics

☆ **Tartine** 020 7589 4981
114 Draycott Avenue
modern European, but always tartines

☆ **The Admiral Codrington** 020 7581 0005
17 Mossop Street
modern British; heartland of the beau monde

Thierry's 020 7352 3365
342 King's Road
traditional French; a rare King's Road survivor from the Sixties

SW6 (FULHAM)

Blue Elephant 020 7385 6595
3 Fulham Broadway
Thai; wonderful rainforest decor

Jim Thompson's 020 7731 0999
617 King's Road
Oriental

Mao Tai 020 7731 2520
58 New King's Road
Chinese

Megan's Delicatessen 020 7371 7837
571 King's Road
French, Italian, organic, home-made… and you can eat in the garden

The Salisbury Tavern 020 7381 4005
21 Sherbrooke Road
modern British, surprisingly good wines; sister of the Admiral Codrington

SW7 (KNIGHTSBRIDGE)

Zuma **020 7584 1010**
5 Raphael Street
Japanese

SW10 (FURTHER OUT THE FULHAM AND KING'S ROADS)

Aubergine **020 7352 3449**
11 Park Walk
French

La Famiglia **020 7351 0761**
7 Langton Street
Italian

Randall & Aubin **020 7823 3515**
329-331 Fulham Road
Continental

Vama **020 7351 4118**
438 King's Road
North Indian

Vingt-Quatre **020 7376 7224**
325 Fulham Road
Contemporary English for the smart set, open 24 hours

W1 (MAYFAIR & MARYLEBONE)

Alloro **020 7495 4768**
19-20 Dover Street
Italian

Cecconi's **020 7434 1500**
5a Burlington Gardens
Italian

☆ **Hush** **020 7659 1500**
8 Lancashire Court, New Bond Street
brasserie downstairs, French restaurant upstairs, tables out in the courtyard on fine days

Kaspia **020 7493 2612**
18 Bruton Place
French; serious caviar specialists

Mosaico **020 7409 1011**
13 Albemarle Street
Northern Italian

☆ **Nobu** **020 7447 4747**
The Metropolitan, 19 Old Park Lane
Japanese, about as up-market as you can go

The Providores **020 7935 6175**
109 Marylebone High Street
fusion, one of the better pub conversions

Sketch **0870 777 4488**
9 Conduit Street
lunch in the Library, not in the Gallery (which is the UK's most expensive restaurant)

☆ **Sotheby's Café** **020 7293 5077**
34-35 New Bond Street
International, very social

Truc Vert **020 7491 9988**
42 North Audley Street
delightful grocery store and all-day diner; the name means "green thing"

Wagamama **020 7292 0990**
10a Lexington Street
noodle specialists

W8 (KENSINGTON)

☆ **Clarke's** **020 7221 9225**
124 Kensington Church Street
modern British/Mediterranean, with excellent American wines (and a wonderful shop attached)

Ken Lo's Memories of China **020 7603 6951**
353 Kensington High Street
Chinese

Kensington Place **020 7727 3184**
201-209 Kensington Church Street
modern European

The Ark **020 7229 4024**
122 Palace Gardens Terrace
Italian

The Terrace **020 7937 3224**
33c Holland Street
modern British/Mediterranean

W9 (LITTLE VENICE)

Green Olive **020 7289 2469**
5 Warwick Place
Italian, a little-known gem

Raoul's Café **020 7289 7313**
13 Clifton Road
international, sidewalk tables on fine days

W10/11/W2 (NOTTING HILL, WESTBOURNE GROVE)

192 **020 7229 0482**
192 Kensington Park Road
modern British, beau monde hang-out

Beach Blanket Babylon **020 7229 2907**
45 Ledbury Road
modern British

Dakota **020 7792 9191**
127 Ledbury Road
modern European

☆ **E&O** **020 7229 5454**
14 Blenheim Crescent
pan-Asian, and very very fashionable

☆ **Electric Brasserie** **020 7908 9696**
191 Portobello Road
modern British, and the Notting Hill rendezvous

Four Seasons **020 7229 4320**
84 Queensway
Chinese, where the Chinese themselves eat

Fresh & Wild **020 7229 1063**
210 Westbourne Grove
high-class food store but you can eat here as well

Livebait **020 7727 4321**
175 Westbourne Grove
fish and seafood

Mediterraneo **020 7792 3131**
37 Kensington Park Road
Italian, favourite Euro haunt

☆ **Notting Hill Brasserie** **020 7229 4481**
92 Kensington Park Road
good enough for Joan Collins's pre-wedding party

Rotisserie Jules **020 7221 3331**
133 Notting Hill Gate
spit-roast chicken and lamb

☆ **Tom's Café** **020 7221 8818**
226 Westbourne Grove
popular café/deli

Zucca **020 7727 0060**
188 Westbourne Grove
modern Italian

WC2 (COVENT GARDEN)

☆ **Bertorelli's** **020 7836 3969**
44 Floral Street
modern Italian

Café des Amis du Vin **020 7379 3444**
11 Hanover Place
Mediterranean

Café Pacifico 020 7379 7728
5 Langley Street
Mexican; Margarita heaven

Christopher's 020 7240 4222
18 Wellington Street
modern American and very stylish

J.Sheekey 020 7240 2565
28-32 St. Martin's Court
fish, part of the Ivy/Caprice group

☆ **Joe Allen** 020 7836 0651
13 Exeter Street
europeanised American, perennial favorite

Manzi's 020 7734 0224
1-2 Leicester Street
fish

Mon Plaisir 020 7836 7243
21 Monmouth Street
classic French

Neal Street Restaurant 020 7836 8368
26 Neal Street
Italian

Prospect Grill 020 7379 0412
4-6 Garrick Street
Anglo-American, anything grilled

West Street 020 7010 8600
13-15 West Street
Italian/modern European, intensely fashionable

CITY

Caravaggio 020 7626 6206
107 Leadenhall Street, EC3
Italian

Le Coq d'Argent 020 7395 5002
1 Poultry, EC2
French

Perc%nto 020 7778 0010
26 Ludgate Hill, EC4
Italian

Prism 020 7256 3888
147 Leadenhall Street, EC3
modern British

Sweetings 020 7248 3062
39 Queen Victoria Street, EC4
fish & seafood, famous old City favorite

Clothing & Shoe Size Equivalents

Children's Clothing

American	3	4	5	6	6X
Continental	98	104	110	116	122
British	18	20	22	24	26

Children's Shoes

American	8	9	10	11	12	12	1	2	3
Continental	24	25	27	28	29	30	32	33	34
British	7	8	9	10	11	12	13	1	2

Ladies' Coats, Dresses, Skirts

American	3	5	7	9	11	12	13	14	15
Continental	36	38	38	40	40	42	42	44	44
British	8	10	11	12	13	14	15	16	17

Ladies' Blouses and Sweaters

American	10	12	14	16	18	20
Continental	38	40	42	44	46	48
British	32	34	36	38	40	42

Ladies' Hosiery

American	8	8.5	9	9.5	10	10.5
Continental	1	2	3	4	5	6
British	8	8.5	9	9.5	10	10.5

Ladies' Shoes

American	5	6	7	8	9	10
Continental	36	37	38	39	40	41
British	3.5	4.5	5.5	6.5	7.5	8.5

Men's Suits

American	34	36	38	40	42	44	46	48
Continental	44	46	48	50	52	54	56	58
British	34	36	38	40	42	44	46	48

Men's Shirts

American	14	15	15.5	16	16.5	17	17.5	18
Continental	37	38	39	41	42	43	44	45
British	14	15	15.5	16	16	17	17.5	18

Men's Shoes

American	7	8	9	10	11	12	13
Continental	39.5	41	42	43	44.5	46	47
British	6	7	8	9	10	11	12

Alphabetical Store Directory

The 1920s–1970s Crazy Clothes Connection

Situated in the heart of vintage-mad Notting Hill, Crazy Clothes Connection is one of London's best-known secondhand shops. Specialists in designer clothing, they've even supplied exhibition pieces for the Victoria & Albert Museum, and they're more than a little taken with their own PR—just look at the walls, plastered with pictures of customers from Kate Moss to Robbie Williams and countless press clippings about the store. But back to the clothes—fur-trimmed coats, leather jackets, evening gowns...all the vintage bits you could hope for. www.crazyclothes.co.uk

020 7221 3989 **tube: Ladbroke Grove**
134 Lancaster Road Tues-Sat 11-7
London W11

☆ 9 London

At last stylish maternity wear has come to London. Adela King and Emily Evans opened their basement boutique in Knightsbridge last year and they've filled it with the sort of fashionable gems soon-to-be-mums are desperate to find: Diane von Furstenberg wrap dresses, Juicy Couture maternity jeans, Maternelle bras by Elle Macpherson and swimwear by Melissa Odabash. They also stock a range of pregnancy pieces by Marc Jacobs, Matthew Williamson and Liz Lange. No wonder Kate Moss and Claudia Schiffer paraded their bumps proudly after shopping here. To top it off, a brilliant customizing service means if you still want to wear your favorite pair of pre-pregnancy trousers the girls will make it possible; just cut off the waist-band, take out the zip, put in an elastic panel and hey presto! There is no excuse for looking frumpy any more.

020 7838 0703 **tube: Knightsbridge**
4 Beaufort Gardens (by appointment)
London SW3

40 Savile Row

It's a block steeped in sometimes heavy tradition, but the striking window display and prominent magazine clips give this (relative) newcomer to Savile Row a trendy, youthful feel. Their confident no-frills service offers handmade bespoke suits for men and women from £1,800 and laser-cut made-to-measure suits for men from a very-good-value £595. The cut is traditional English, the fabrics wide-ranging and up-to-the-minute and the details engaging and quirky. www.40savilerow.co.uk

020 7287 6740 **tube: Piccadilly Circus/Oxford Circus**
40 Savile Row Mon-Fri 10-6:30, Sat 10-6
London W1

295

This vintage shop is one of many buried behind the bustle of Portobello market. The selection leaves much to be desired in terms of designer labels, but it's not expensive

and there's a little bit of everything, from men's tailored jackets and button-down shirts to dainty, breezy dresses and deconstructed blouses for women. You'll also find a rack of shoes and handbags to dig through and lovely evening dresses hanging from the ceiling.

(no phone) **tube: Ladbroke Grove**
295 Portobello Road Fri-Sat 8:30-5
London W10

à la mode

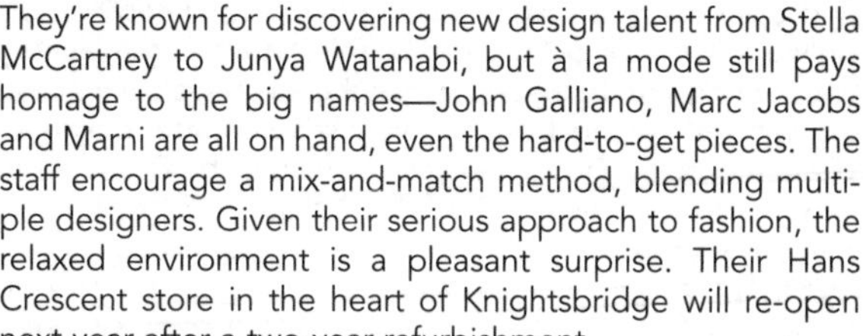

They're known for discovering new design talent from Stella McCartney to Junya Watanabi, but à la mode still pays homage to the big names—John Galliano, Marc Jacobs and Marni are all on hand, even the hard-to-get pieces. The staff encourage a mix-and-match method, blending multiple designers. Given their serious approach to fashion, the relaxed environment is a pleasant surprise. Their Hans Crescent store in the heart of Knightsbridge will re-open next year after a two-year refurbishment.

020 7730 7180 **tube: Sloane Square**
10 Symons Street Mon-Sat 10-7
London SW3

☆ Accessorize

If you miss this store the first time, don't worry—you're bound to come across another. It's one of the handiest and most fun chains in all of London. Pop in and spruce up a bland wardrobe with bohemian handbags and stripy hats, colorful scarves with intricate patterns and evening bags as sweet as they are useful. Each store is small and organized by color scheme, making it easy to match things up. All are jam-packed with accessories to suit every generation, from tweenies to seniors, but the jewelry—beaded bracelets, trinket necklaces and flower hairpins—could make anyone feel little-girly.

020 7240 2107 **tube: Covent Garden**
22 The Market Mon-Fri 9-8, Sat 10-8
London WC2 Sun 11-7

020 7937 1433 **tube: High Street Kensington**
123a Kensington High Street Mon-Sat 9-7 (Thurs 9-8)
London W8 Sun 11-7

020 7591 0049 **tube: Sloane Square**
102 King's Road Mon-Sat 9:30-7
London SW3 Sun 12-6

020 7581 3972 **tube: Knightsbridge**
61 Brompton Road Mon-Sat 9:30-7:30, Sun 12-6
London SW3

020 7629 0038 **tube: Oxford Circus**
293 Oxford Street Mon-Sat 9:30-7:30 (Thurs 9:30-8)
London W1 Sun 11-6:30

020 7491 9424 **tube: Oxford Circus/Bond Street**
386 Oxford Street Mon-Sat 9:30-7:30
London W1 (Thurs 9:30-8), Sun 11-6

020 7494 0566
1 Piccadilly Circus
London W1

tube: Piccadilly Circus
Mon-Sat 10-9:45, Sun 11-9

020 7727 3406
237 Portobello Road
London W11

tube: Ladbroke Grove
Mon-Sat 10-6, Sun 11-5

Ad Hoc

Punk, glam, and rock 'n' roll...fashion's strongest style influences thrive on here. Having lost much of its eclecticism and color since its Sixties heyday, the King's Road harbors only a few remaining places like this. Overhead, a laundry line is hung with baby tees, while the space below is bursting with fishnet stockings in every shade, glitter make-up, diamanté belts, PVC shirt dresses, feather boas and neon wigs. Part Elvis Presley, part Dame Edna.

020 7376 8829
153 King's Road
London SW3

tube: Sloane Square
Mon-Sat 10-6:30
(Wed 10-7), Sun 12-6

020 7287 0911
10-11 Moor Street
London W1

tube: Leicester Square/ Tottenham Court Road
Mon-Sat 11-7:30

Adolfo Dominguez

The style of this Spanish label and the snoozy store ambience certainly won't quicken your pulse, but the two floors of merchandise will cover you top to toe, from outerwear to shoes. For shoppers who seek solace in the classics (cotton T-shirts, pinstriped suits, beaded eveningwear and simple knits) this well-tailored women's and menswear might just suffice. Fashion followers could skip this stop. www.adolfodominguez.com

020 7494 3395
129 Regent Street
London W1

tube: Piccadilly Circus
Mon-Sat 10-7, Sun 12-6

020 7836 5013
15 Endell Street
London WC2

tube: Covent Garden
Mon-Sat 10:30-7, Sun 12-6

Aftershock

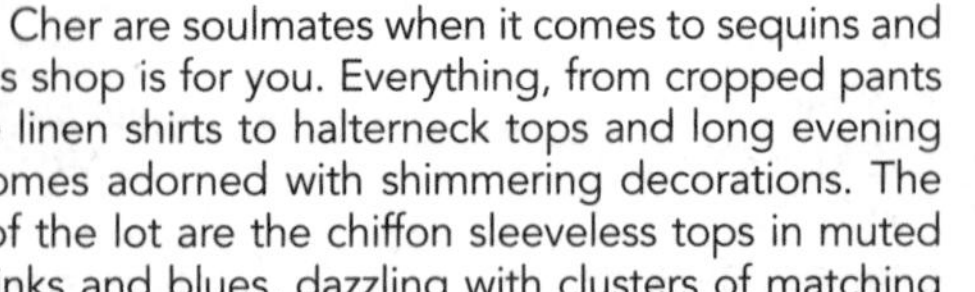
If you and Cher are soulmates when it comes to sequins and beads, this shop is for you. Everything, from cropped pants and loose linen shirts to halterneck tops and long evening gowns, comes adorned with shimmering decorations. The prettiest of the lot are the chiffon sleeveless tops in muted greens, pinks and blues, dazzling with clusters of matching sequins. If the total ensemble is a bit too much, choose carefully and you could go home with your next party outfit.

020 7499 2858
12 South Molton Street
London W1

tube: Bond Street
Mon-Sat 10:30-7, Sun 12-6

020 7352 7353
194 King's Road
London SW3

tube: Sloane Square
Mon-Sat 10-6:30, Sun 12-6

☆ Agent Provocateur

More X-rated than Victoria's Secret, this English lingerie lair brings a new naughty dimension to panties and bras. Vampish satin, silk and lace creations—plus everything from jeweled manacles to their own heady fragrance—are presented with sex-kitten kitsch. But the strait-laced should be prepared—window mannequins bent in racy poses may make you blush. www.agentprovocateur.com

020 7235 0229 **tube: Knightsbridge/Sloane Square**
16 Pont Street Mon-Sat 10-6
London SW1

020 7439 0229 **tube: Oxford Circus**
6 Broadwick Street Mon-Sat 11-7
London W1

Directory

agnès b.

The French, with their uncanny knack for looking effortlessly chic, have an ideal fashion ambassador in agnès b. The collection is sheer heaven for women who favor understated femininity infused with youth, including fine cotton tops, tailored skirts, pants and knits. Even men will appreciate the sleek tailoring of the sports jackets, pants and button-down shirts. Some accessories are also available. www.agnesb.fr

020 7379 1992 **tube: Covent Garden**
35-36 Floral Street Mon-Sat 10:30-6:30
London WC2 (Thurs 10:30-7), Sun 1-6

020 7225 3477 **tube: South Kensington**
111 Fulham Road Mon 11-6, Tues-Sat 10-6 (Wed 10-7)
London SW3 Sun 12-5

020 7431 1995 **tube: Hampstead**
58-62 Heath Street Mon-Sat 10-6
London NW3 Sun 12-6

020 7935 5556 **tube: Baker Street/Bond Street**
40-41 Marylebone High Street Mon 11-6
London W1 Tues, Fri-Sat 10-6, Wed-Thurs 10-7

020 7792 1947 **tube: Notting Hill Gate**
233-235 Westbourne Grove Mon 10:30-6:30
London W11 Tues-Sat 10-6:30

020 7730 2255 (M) **tube: Sloane Square**
31-32 Duke of York Square Mon-Wed 10-6,
London SW3 Thurs-Sat 10-7, Sun 12-5

Aimé

It all began when two sisters, Val and Venda Heng Vong, grew nostalgic for their native France. Rather than go home, they brought home to Notting Hill, with French fashion's best and brightest labels: Barbara Bui, Sonia Rykiel, Les Prairies de Paris, Claudie Pierlot and Isabel Marant. In addition to clothing, their sleek boutique houses handbags and shoes, Asian-style crockery, candles, glassware and an assortment of CDs that changes every two weeks.

020 7221 7070 | **tube: Notting Hill Gate**
32 Ledbury Road | Mon-Sat 10:30-7
London W11

Ajanta

Even before it opened, the headlines were buzzing with Ajanta—not about the clothing but about the ill-fated partnership between Lady Victoria Hervey and owner Sybil Stanislaus. Hervey is out, and expensive eastern-style holidaywear is in, from colorful caftans to sequined tie-dyed dresses to batik sarongs with matching bikinis. There are also beaded slippers, soft silk scarves, Indian bracelets and bathing suits by Missoni. www.ajantadesign.com

020 7235 1572 | **tube: Knightsbridge**
21 Motcomb Street | Mon-Sat 10-6
London SW1

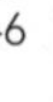

Alberta Ferretti

Ferretti's demure, sophisticated collection stays just this side of frilly femininity. Her fabrics are soft and sheer, while the cuts are body-conscious but not clinging. Dresses, skirts, sleek suits and blouses are the staples, in colors that range from brooding blue to baby pink, some with girlish patterns. Philosophy, her lovely diffusion line, is housed upstairs. www.aeffe.com

020 7235 2349 | **tube: Knightsbridge**
205-206 Sloane Street | Mon-Sat 10-6 (Wed 10-7)
London SW1

Aldo

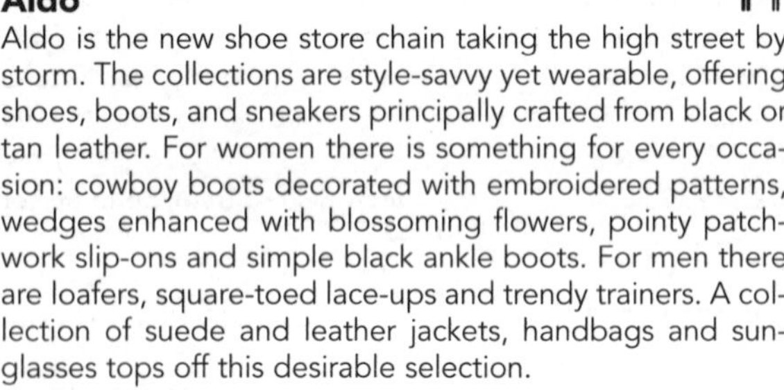

Aldo is the new shoe store chain taking the high street by storm. The collections are style-savvy yet wearable, offering shoes, boots, and sneakers principally crafted from black or tan leather. For women there is something for every occasion: cowboy boots decorated with embroidered patterns, wedges enhanced with blossoming flowers, pointy patchwork slip-ons and simple black ankle boots. For men there are loafers, square-toed lace-ups and trendy trainers. A collection of suede and leather jackets, handbags and sunglasses tops off this desirable selection.

020 7499 4348 | **tube: Oxford Circus/Bond Street**
309 Oxford Street | Mon-Sat 10-8 (Thurs 10-9)
London W1 | Sun 12-6

020 7836 7692 | **tube: Covent Garden**
3-7 Neal Street | Mon-Sat 10-7 (Thurs 10-8)
London WC2 | Sun 12-6

Alexander McQueen

He's back, with a new location, new perfume and a raunchy new collection. McQueen is London's reigning bad boy of fashion and was nicknamed "enfant terrible" by the French press. His clothes are outlandish works of art infused with attitude, decorative impact and theatrics. They frequently make a fashion headline, which is why Gucci was so keen to snap up the company although McQueen remains creative director. His spectacular fashion shows are legendary, so too is his brutally sharp and accurate tailoring. His signature silhouette comprises sharp shoulders, stiff collars and reed-slim pants, but when he gets romantic he is equally effective. A recent catwalk featured an incredible jacket constructed of white tulle pom-poms that looked like a gathering of snowballs.

020 7355 0080 **tube: Green Park**
4 Old Bond Street Mon-Sat 10-6 (Thurs 10-7)
London W1

Alice Berrill

If you live in Clapham you should probably pop into this boutique but if you're not local don't pay money to get here. The selection is nice enough—embroidered pashminas, cropped gingham pants, leather loafers from Italy and plenty of colorful baskets—but you are unlikely to find anything truly inspiring or original. If you are looking for a gift you may be in luck—there are photo frames and albums, baby grows, silver key rings, painted china boxes and bath products by Cath Collins.

020 7228 1281 **tube: Clapham Common**
31 Lavender Hill Mon-Sat 10-6
London SW11

Allegra Hicks

She first made a name for herself as a textile designer but Allegra Hicks has now turned her hand to holiday wear—and there's no looking back. Her tiny shop is a calm oasis of casual, comfortable clothing. There's a strong emphasis on the caftan, the ultimate chill-out attire. Loose and floaty, they come in an array of summer colors from pale lilac to flaming orange. Hicks's eye for detail is ever-present in the delicately embroidered patterns of simple shapes and flowers. You'll also find a selection of bohemian handbags and chunky semi-precious jewelry. Underwear by Elle Macpherson rounds out the collection and makes this store a perfect stop-off before your departure.

020 7589 2323 **tube: Sloane Square/South Kensington**
4 Cale Street Mon-Sat 10-6
London SW3

Amanda Wakely

For a first ball, a formal wedding or a night at the opera this store offers women what they most want: beautiful, sexy evening dresses. Light materials and a loose fit make them as comfortable as everyday wear, while the modern cuts (and slits up the thigh) add a naughty edge. In perennial colors like black, gold and lipstick red you're bound to wear them more than once, making the investment even more worthwhile. The dresses are the belles of the boutique, although the skirts and suits are worth a look, as is the bridalwear.

020 7590 9105 **tube: South Kensington**
80 Fulham Road Mon-Sat 10-6 (Wed 10-7)
London SW3

American Classics

The name suggests bland Ralph Lauren style for the boy next door, but the reality is quite a bit cooler. Loads of Levi's, Hawaiian shirts and baseball caps emblazoned with motorcycle motifs all suggest Reality Bites-style suburban ennui. Durable Lee pants and workboots by Redwing recall the early Nineties, when highschoolers liked to slum it in John Deere caps and Texaco T-shirts. Skater-style Stüssy and Vans sneakers are also on hand.

020 7352 2853 **tube: Sloane Square**
398 King's Road Mon-Sat 10-6:30, Sun 12-5
London SW10

Ananya

For a taste of authentic Indian fashion hotfoot it to this Aladdin's cave in Knightsbridge. Designer Anu Mirchandin's boutique is crammed with eye-catching, boldly shimmering pieces, all in beautiful textiles from her native India. You'll find hand-beaded trousers and appliqué jeweled skirts, funky little embroidered tops and comfortable cotton caftans with matching trousers. Far from looking like fancy dress, the delicately detailed clothing is Bollywood cool and has been spotted on the likes of Claudia Schiffer, Rachel Hunter and Jemma Kidd. Other bits on offer include raffia bags depicting the Indian gods, paste jewelry and antique mirrored photo frames.

020 7584 8040 **tube: Knightsbridge**
4a Montpelier Street Mon-Sat 10-6
London SW7

Anderson & Sheppard

Here is a Savile Row institution that has resisted any modernization. The relatively spacious interior is dominated by vast rolls of cloth and has a distinctly late-Fifties feel. Renowned for their tact, A&S politely discourage contact with the press, although it is common knowledge that Prince Charles and Calvin Klein are fans of their signature cut, which is softer and less sculpted than elsewhere on the Row. They also sell a limited range of covetable cashmere sweaters.

020 7734 1420 **tube: Piccadilly Circus/Green Park**
30 Savile Row Mon-Fri 8:30-5
London W1

Anello and Davide

The company began in 1922 as a theatrical and dance footwear provider and has since expanded to include handmade everyday and special occasion shoes. Non-dancers can expect to find high heels, mules and strappy slingbacks. On the pricier side there are bridal shoes and a couture collection.

020 7225 2468 **tube: Knightsbridge/South Kensington**
47 Beauchamp Place Mon-Sat 10-6 (Wed 11-6)
London SW3

Angela Stone

Duchesse satin, silk crepe and chiffon are favorite fabrics at Angela Stone, where the understated eveningwear and bridal gowns are virtually indistinguishable. Light and fluid, some of the dresses are more suited to a barefoot beach ceremony than a traditional church wedding. Simple styles say second wedding—they're not quite special enough for the bride who's been dreaming of her big day since she was a girl. To match, there's a spectrum of accessories from underwear to suede sandals to veils. www.angelastone.com

020 7371 5199 **tube: Parsons Green**
257 New King's Road Mon-Fri 9-6, Sat 9:30-6
London SW6

Angels

Medieval damsels, can-can dancers, comic book heros—if you've been invited to a fancy dress party, there's no better place to kit yourself out than Angels. This for-hire costume shop has dressed Jerry Hall, Elton John, and Mick Jagger from their time-traveling racks. Selection dates from 1066 to the 1970s and comes with all the trimmings—gold masks, powdered wigs, feather boas and make-up. Quality is top-notch so expect to pay accordingly. www.fancy-dress.com

020 7836 5678 **tube: Leicester Square**
119 Shaftesbury Avenue Mon-Fri 9-5:30
London WC2 (last fitting at 4:30)

Ann Harvey

On a block bursting with big names, small-scale Ann Harvey features large clothing with style—exclusively for the size 16-28 set. From evening dresses to suits to jeans and accessories the selection is diverse, though tinged with middle-age undertones. Still, the friendly atmosphere and reasonable prices give this modest plus-size shop a firm following.

020 7408 1131 **tube: Oxford Circus**
266 Oxford Street Mon-Sat 10-7
London W1 (Thurs 10-8), Sun 12-6

Ann Wiberg

This Danish designer offers affordable daywear with a dash of bohemian detail. Though everyone is doing boho this season, Wiberg has been at it for some time—a billowing gypsy top, a layered chiffon skirt, a pink sleeveless T-shirt with a diagonal lace ruffle are some staples of her collection. The overall effect is pleasingly handmade and one-off-ish (though Ann Wiberg is a chain in Scandinavia), with unusual highlights like a tattered suede bustier and a dress with a halterneck made from a man's silk tie. The whitewashed interior, strewn with dried rosebuds, enhances the romance of the designs. www.annwiberg.dk

020 7229 8160 **tube: Notting Hill Gate**
63a Ledbury Road Mon-Sat 10:30-6
London W11

Anna

The Appleton Sisters, Kate Winslet, Sadie Frost and a host of trendy North London ladies flock to this small, cozy boutique for their fashion fix. A smattering of hot designer labels—Fake London, Alice Temperley, Maharishi, Velvet and Saltwater—sit alongside some trusty old favorites—Whistles, Nicole Farhi, Cashmere Studio and 120% Linen. Avoid Saturdays—the crowds drift in when Campden market gets too much for them. www.shopatanna.co.uk

020 7483 0411 **tube: Chalk Farm**
126 Regent's Park Road Mon-Sat 10-6, Sun 12-5
London NW1

Anna Molinari Blumarine

Behind the best entrance on Bond Street—between a pair of gold mosaic lady's legs—rests this small shop with turquoise tiled walls, suggesting an empty swimming-pool (a tiled Zeus watches the action from the ceiling). The few clothing racks feature Molinari's floaty dresses, bias-cut skirts and ruffled blouses, as well as the latest collection from Blumarine, the slightly less-expensive diffusion line.

020 7493 4872 **tube: Green Park**
11a Old Bond Street Mon-Sat 10-6 (Thurs 10-7)
London W1

Anne Fontaine

Most designers would rather die than get bored recreating the same piece over and over. Not Anne Fontaine, a Brazilian based in France who is taking the basic white shirt to fashionable frontiers. Select a simple button-down for winter or one embellished with lighthearted ruffles for spring. Superior quality, creative cuts and seasonal details keep the selection fresh. Every collection comes with the occasional touch of color and a bit of basic black. www.annefontaine.com

020 7584 7703 **tube: South Kensington**
151 Fulham Road Mon-Sat 10-6:30, Sun 12-6
London SW3

020 7408 2280 **tube: Bond Street**
30 New Bond Street Mon-Sat 10-6:30 (Thurs 10-7)
London W1

Anthony J. Hewitt/Airey & Wheeler

Established Savile Row tailors Anthony J. Hewitt took over Airey & Wheeler a few years ago, revamping the famous tropical clothing range and putting the accent on high-quality linen suits, pinfeather cotton suits and super-100

(the finest worsted) wool suits. The Anthony J. Hewitt side of the business continues to concentrate on handmade bespoke suits but has also introduced an innovative made-to-measure service in Dormeuil fabrics. With prices starting around £600, this offers outstanding value to first-time Savile Row customers.

020 7734 1505 **tube: Piccadilly Circus/Oxford Circus**
9 Savile Row Mon-Fri 9-5:30, Sat 9-12:30
London W1

The Antique Clothing Shop

There's a century of fashion, hanger by hanger, in this large vintage shop where the unique selection of period costumes and accessories dates from the 1860s to the 1960s. Though some pieces look too costume-drama to be worn down Madison Avenue, the lacy Victorian blouses and billowing ballgowns could make good wearable fun. A great place to find clothes with a soul and a story.

020 8964 4830 **tube: Ladbroke Grove**
282 Portobello Road Fri-Sat 9-6
London W10

Antoine et Lili

This Paris import adds a colorful hippy vibe to World's End with hanging fairy lights, bright woven mats and stripy cushions. The designs, as vibrant as the decor, are Asian in their simplicity but French-bohemian in their brilliant hues. Raw silk wrap-skirts with bustles in cotton-candy pink and crisp cotton shirts trimmed with ruffles give old-fashioned feeling to the gypsy look. Meanwhile Moroccan slippers and plastic floral bags are dotted about, giving the store a funky street-market feel.

020 7349 0033 **tube: Sloane Square**
404 King's Road Tues-Sat 10-7
London SW10

☆ Anya Hindmarch

This iconic British handbag designer injects as much whimsy into a basic black leather wallet as into her sequined evening bags or Fifties-print beach satchels. The trademark tiny bow is the stamp of her classic design sense, which has broadened to cover a small selection of stretch tops, cashmere knits and footwear in quirky prints.

020 7838 9177 **tube: Knightsbridge/Sloane Square**
15-17 Pont Street Mon-Sat 10-6 (Wed 10-7)
London SW1

Aquaint

This small new boutique offers a fresh, feminine selection of womenswear from promising (and pricey) young designers Ashley Isham, Lanvin, Emma Cook and Boyd. Geek-chic pinafores and plaid skirts, pin-tucked trousers with slits at the ankles, and silk floral halter dresses so light they float.

Everything here has been carefully crafted right down to the details like silk-covered buttons and striking stitching. In the window, hats by Naomi Goodsir featuring peacock feathers will draw you into the shop, where soothing orchid plants and a friendly staff will make you want to linger.

020 7240 9677 **tube: Covent Garden/Leicester Square**
38 Monmouth Street Mon-Sat 10-6 (Thurs 10-7)
London WC2 Sun 12-5

Aquascutum

Intrinsically English, Aquascutum is aiming for an image overhaul to catch up with rival Burberry. But at 150 years old the company is still the place for classic, conservative cashmere and cotton and vicuña creations for both sexes, including business suits, fine knits and weekendwear. Don't miss the coat selection, the basis for the store's enduring reputation and made to last a lifetime.
www.aquascutum.co.uk

020 7675 8200 **tube: Piccadilly Circus**
100 Regent Street Mon-Sat 10-6:30 (Thurs 10-7)
London W1 Sun 12-5

Armand Basi

Born half a century ago in Barcelona as a small knitwear shop, this store has blossomed beyond the loom with a selection that includes women's pants, skirts, dresses and tops, and a smattering of younger, hipper streetwear. For men, there are casual shirts and trousers. Colors tend towards muted earth tones, but—like London skies—there are occasional bursts of brightness. www.armandbasi.com

020 7734 9795 **tube: Bond Street/Oxford Circus**
48 Conduit Street Mon-Sat 10-6 (Thurs 10-7)
London W1

Atticus

When the trendy-shoe mood strikes, carpe diem and head to Atticus where prices are only mildly damaging and the staff are, refreshingly, more than happy to help. Brown suede cowboy boots, light blue leather slip-ons with white stitching and pink kitten heels with flowers at the toes are all perfect for play-time or those moments when style speaks louder than sense.

020 7376 0059 **tube: High Street Kensington**
14 Kensington Church Street Mon-Sat 10-7 (Thurs 10-8)
London W8 Sun 12-6

020 7823 6622 **tube: Sloane Square**
64 King's Road Mon-Sat 10-7 (Wed 10-8)
London SW3 Sun 12-6

Audley

Crafted from the finest leather, Audley shoes are hard to find fault with. The inspiration behind their designs ranges from Carmen Miranda to Balenciaga, with plenty of nods to the catwalk in the form of conical heels, peep toes and

Prada-esque patent lace-ups. The color palette is broad and so is the selection, from casual loafers to wedding slippers. They also offer a bespoke service, for those desperate to design their own, and don't miss their small accessories range: shoes and leather-lined bags in eye-catching chinoiserie designs. www.audley.com

020 7730 2903 **tube: Sloane Square**
72 Duke of York Square Mon-Sat 10-6
London SW3

Austin Reed

More basic than bold, the selection at Austin Reed covers all the bases. Men can find everything for both their workday and weekend wardrobes, with particular emphasis on classic suits and casualwear. The smaller womenswear collection fits the same sensibility. It's a look better for blending in than for getting noticed. www.austinreed.co.uk

020 7734 6789 **tube: Piccadilly Circus**
103-113 Regent Street Mon-Sat 10-7 (Thurs 10-8),
London W1 Sun 12-6

020 7213 9998 **tube: Bank (exit 8 or 9)**
1 Poultry Mon-Fri 9-6:30
London EC2

020 7283 3347 **tube: Monument**
13-23 Fenchurch Street Mon-Fri 9-5:30
London EC3

020 7588 7674 **tube: Liverpool Street**
1-14 Liverpool Street Mon-Fri 8:30-7
London EC2

Avi Rossini

Looking for super-luxe tailoring with an English bent? Maybe you know the Rodeo Drive store and think Rossini is LA native? Nope, he's based right here on London's answer to Fashion Avenue. Duck into the Bond Street store for his sumptuous suits and sportswear, including leather-trimmed jeans. Focusing on feel, fit, finish and finesse, the designer turns out haute-ticketed custom ensembles and off-the-rack items. With Avi's guidance, many fans weave their crest or logo into his top-notch fabrics. www.luxurymenswear.com

020 7409 0879 **tube: Bond Street/Green Park**
46 New Bond Street Mon-Sat 9:30-6:30
London W1

Aware

Women are spoilt for choice when it comes to buying underwear in London, while the guys generally have to make do with M&S. This shop features designer underwear and beach accessories for that rare breed of fashion-following male who cares enough to bother. From boxer-briefs by Boss to D&G flip-flops, the international labels prevail. Other bits include Diesel T-shirts, CK washbags and tank tops by DKNY. It's a nice gesture, but it's all likely to remind you of those bare-chested Italians at the beach, posing in their Speedos.

020 7351 6259 **tube: Sloane Square**
182 King's Road Mon-Sat 10-6, Sun 12-5
London SW3

Ballantyne Cashmere

In a city brimming with cashmere shops Ballantyne knows how to give it a bit of fashion edge. The store, which was remodeled for fall, knits the fine fiber into creations of every color and shape, from pullovers to twinsets. Best of all, the laid-back atmosphere means shopping here is low-impact—apart from on the wallet. It is cashmere, after all.

020 7493 4718 **tube: Bond Street/Green Park**
153a New Bond Street Mon-Sat 10-6
London W1

Bally

Another brand trying to make the leap into the luxury world of Gucci and Louis Vuitton, this Swiss company's has a history of producing fine shoes. Quality has perhaps slipped a little since the early days but many still appreciate the sophisticated selection of muted-tone handbags and shoes. Clothing plows the classic furrow while, for what it's worth, the company's "B" logo'd bags and shoes have been hot commodities among the world's fashion editors. www.bally.com

020 7491 7062 **tube: Bond Street**
116 New Bond Street Mon-Sat 10-6 (Thurs 10-7)
London W1

020 7493 2250 **tube: Green Park**
30 Old Bond Street Mon-Sat 10-6 (Thurs 10-7)
London W1

020 7734 2500 **tube: Oxford Circus**
260 Regent Street Mon-Sat 10-6:30
London W1 (Thurs 10-8), Sun 12-6

020 7589 9084 **tube: Sloane Square**
92 King's Road Mon-Sat 10-6:30
London SW3 (Wed 10-7), Sun 12-5

020 7493 5810 **tube: Marble Arch/Bond Street**
472 Oxford Street Mon-Sat 10-6:30
London W1 (Thurs 10-8), Sun 12-6

Bang Bang

This clothing exchange is the perfect antidote to cookie-cutter shopping, with secondhand designer pieces that will even thrill vintage diehards. The exceptional selection of labels spans the fashion timeline from Yves Saint Laurent and Pucci to Betsey Johnson and Nicole Farhi. There's also a fair amount from Zara, Top Shop and Gap. A plethora of little bits—costume jewelry, beaded handbags, leather gloves—means that those in the market for something small won't be left out. Choose wisely, and you'll get some bang bang for your buck.

020 7631 4191 **tube: Goodge Street**
21 Goodge Street Mon-Fri 10-6:30, Sat 11-6
London W1

Bare

It's the new new thing in chic boutiques, and a testament to the rising coolness quotient of nearby Marylebone High Street. Bare founders Tina Ferguson and Daisy Morrison have culled their mature selection from fashion up-and-comers like Sarah Berman, Gharani Strok, Tracey Boyd and British cashmere label Goat. You'll also find a selection of shoes by Esme Ertekin and colorful sweaters from Pringle. The look is grown-up glamour and a sexy Fifties pin-up painted on the wall reflects the tongue-in-cheek mood of fashion in this post, post-modern moment. They were planning to move as we went to press, but promised to keep the telephone number.

020 7486 7779 **tube: Baker Street**
8 Chiltern Street Mon-Fri 10:30-6:30
London W1

Barker Shoes

Established in a Northamptonshire village in 1880, Barker remains a traditional provider of men's footwear with a small-town devotion to the virtues of craftsmanship and comfort. The selection is basic, led by brown and black leather and suede lace-ups, slip-ons and ankle boots. The store brings a pleasant, unpretentious air to big-city shopping. A small women's range is also available.

www.barker-shoes.co.uk

020 7494 3069 **tube: Oxford Circus**
215 Regent Street Mon-Sat 10-6:30 (Thurs 10-7:30)
London W1 Sun 11-5

Barkers of Kensington

(see House of Fraser)

Base

Specializing in sizes 16-28, Base provides modern staples for the plus-size set. Looks remain simple and flattering, featuring colorful coats, linen dresses, pantsuits and silk tops. There is also a wide assortment of wraps and chunky jewelry. A good starting point for rebuilding a seasonal wardrobe. www.base-fashions.co.uk

020 7240 8914 **tube: Covent Garden/Leicester Square**
55 Monmouth Street Mon-Sat 10-6
London WC2

Bates Gentleman's Hatter

Although essentially an old-school hatters for the huntin', shootin' and fishin' crowd, the vagaries of fashion pull in both stylists and big names from entertainment—David Bowie, Diana Ross and Tom Jones have all bought hats here. The specialty in this tiny store is flat wool tweed

caps, but there are also swankier fedoras, trilbies and panamas. Service is friendly and knowledgeable.

www.Bates-Hats.co.uk

020 7734 2722 **tube: Piccadilly Circus**
21a Jermyn Street Mon-Fri 9-5:15
London SW1 Sat 9:30-4

Beatrice von Tresckow

Taffeta gowns, long velvet jackets and curve-enhancing corsets are shamelessly intermingled in this selection of old-fashioned, made-to-order eveningwear. Fuchsia, purple, turquoise and green are the colors in charge, embroidery and beading are intricate, and decorative details prevail. And we thought no one went to hunt balls anymore.

020 7351 5354 **tube: South Kensington**
273 Fulham Road Mon-Sat 10-6 (Wed 10-7)
London SW10

Beau Monde

Beau Monde has been based on this narrow street on the fringe of Soho for 15 years and has established itself as a stalwart of smart classics for mature shoppers. Off-the-peg or custom-made, the dresses, jackets and suits are created from fine fabrics such as cashmere, organza and tweed. Dark colors dominate the winter spectrum, while lilac and peach blossom in summer. www.beaumonde.uk.com

020 7734 6563 **tube: Piccadilly Circus/Oxford Circus**
43 Lexington Street Mon-Sat 10:30-6:30 (Thurs 10:30-7)
London W1

Belinda Robertson

Colorful cashmere is something of a cliché in London. Still, business couldn't be better for Belinda Robertson where Scottish cashmere on a made-to-order basis comes in a 120-color rainbow. Delivery takes 6-8 weeks and prices start at £200 for a simple camisole. Cuts include basic crewneck, cowel-neck and V-neck, with full sleeves, three-quarter length or none at all. Whether you prefer your cashmere plain, trimmed in ruffle or sprinkled with sequins, Robertson will oblige. But beware, this could become a dangerous habit—one customer ordered the same cut in 15 different shades. www.belindarobertson.com

020 7235 0519 **tube: Knightsbridge**
4 West Halkin Street Mon-Fri 10-6, Sat 10-5
London SW1

Ben de Lisi

After a lingering lunch at Olivo, young ladies with hours to kill and cash to burn sneak across the street for a peek through Ben de Lisi's racks. This chic and dressy shop, on one of London's poshest blocks, offers a hip-meets-refined combination of cashmere sweater sets, paillette-covered tank tops, tweed trousers and some of the sexiest eveningwear in town. Modern cuts and a playful approach to fabrics might remind you of Joseph. De Lisi's future looks similarly bright, though for their menswear you still have to go to Harrods because they don't yet have the space in Elizabeth Street.

020 7730 2994 **tube: Sloane Square/Victoria**
40 Elizabeth Street Mon-Fri 10-6, Sat 12-5
London SW1

Berk

Housed in Mayfair's prestigious Burlington Arcade, these two small English shops are heaped with cashmere cardigans, pullovers and scarves. If you only have time for one cashmere stop, Berk might be the place as it offers a wide selection for both women and men. It is also one of the main stockists of John Smedley fine-gauge wool and cotton knitwear, again for both sexes.

Directory

020 7493 0028 **tube: Green Park/Piccadilly Circus**
46-49 Burlington Arcade Mon-Fri 9-5:30, Sat 9:30-5:30
London W1

020 7493 1430 **tube: Green Park/Piccadilly Circus**
6 Burlington Arcade (opening times as above)
London W1

Berluti

Italian in name but of French provenance, Berluti is best known for its innovative, design-led ready-to-wear shoes, though it does also offer a bespoke service. For the man with no need for specially tailored shoes this means getting bespoke looks and quality for about half the price and in a fraction of the time. The staff have been known to take a selection of shoes out to hotels for clients in a hurry, and will even open the store by appointment if need be. Ready-to-wear starts at £390, and the bespoke service at £1,850.

020 7437 1740 **tube: Oxford Circus**
43 Conduit Street Mon-Sat 10-6:30
London W1

Bernini

The traditional haunts of the well-dressed gentleman are Savile Row and Jermyn Street but Bond Street also has a few offerings. At the elegantly reserved Bernini, gents will find tuxedos, three-piece suits, blazers and sports jackets with typical Italian flair. www.bernini.com

020 7491 7865 **tube: Bond Street**
95-96 New Bond Street Mon-Sat 10-7
London W1 (Thurs 10-8), Sun 12-6

Bertie

Trendy shoe fanatics flock here for designer spin-offs at prices so modest you can afford to indulge. Styles range from baby-pink leather slip-on sneakers to stilettos with diamanté straps, and the stock seems to vary slightly according to location: the South Molton branch attracts a

more mature twentysomething fashion flock, while the Covent Garden crowd is young and club-cool. Always worth a look. www.theshoestudio.com

020 7493 5033 **tube: Bond Street**
36 South Molton Street Mon-Sat 10-7
London W1 (Thurs 10-8), Sun 12-6

020 7836 7223 **tube: Covent Garden**
25 Long Acre (opening times as above)
London WC2

Bertie Golightly

Label rats who love low prices will go mad for Roberta Gibbs's immaculate secondhand selection. Christian Dior, Chanel, Valentino and Prada—they've all been here, secondhand or still with the tags on. It's the sort of place for women who would sooner go naked than admit that they're wearing used goods. Gibbs is therefore vigilant about banishing that straight-from-the-attic secondhand state of disrepair, and condition is great. The space is packed with handbags, beaded gowns, suits and shoes, which doesn't make for the most dignified shopping experience. But for a pair of last season's Ferragamos even the most proper of ladies will drop to her knees and dig. www.bertiego.co.uk

020 7584 7270 **tube: Knightsbridge**
48 Beauchamp Place Mon-Sat 10-6 (Wed 10-7)
London SW3 Sun 12-5

Bertie Wooster

The old hunting prints hanging on the wall and the racks of thick tweed jackets give this secondhand gentleman's clothier a very horse-and-hound feel. The selection, a combination of vintage and contemporary suits, shirts, jackets and hats, offers London's Everyman the chance to dress like an English country gent—and at a fraction of Savile Row prices. You'll also find antique leather cigar cases, silver cufflink boxes and gold tiepins, as well as shoes and a selection of boxer shorts.

020 7352 5662 **tube: Fulham Broadway**
284 Fulham Road Mon, Wed, Fri-Sat 10-6
London SW10 Tues, Thurs 10-7

Betsey Johnson

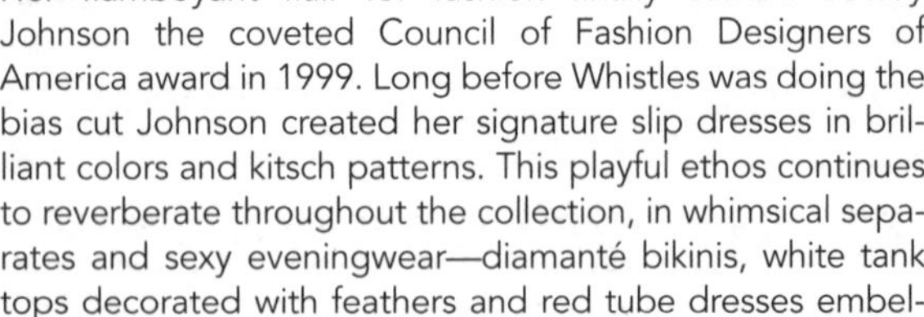

Her flamboyant flair for fashion finally earned Betsey Johnson the coveted Council of Fashion Designers of America award in 1999. Long before Whistles was doing the bias cut Johnson created her signature slip dresses in brilliant colors and kitsch patterns. This playful ethos continues to reverberate throughout the collection, in whimsical separates and sexy eveningwear—diamanté bikinis, white tank tops decorated with feathers and red tube dresses embellished with pistols. Johnson's quirky-meets-sex-bomb effect means you'll never be able to guess what's coming next.

020 7591 0005
106 Draycott Avenue
London SW3

tube: South Kensington
Mon-Sat 10:30-6 (Wed 10:30-7)
Sun 12-5

Betty Jackson

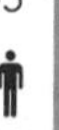

British designer Betty Jackson provides classic style for women who don't want to work too hard at it. From the selection of simple basics you can create a chic, fundamental wardrobe that won't need to be scrapped after a single season. For fall, expect the usual suspects—suede, sheepskin jackets and soft knitwear—as well as a few surprises, like pretty Chinese tops.

020 7589 7884
311 Brompton Road
London SW3

tube: South Kensington
Mon-Fri 10:30-6:30
Sat 10:30-6, Sun 12-5

Directory

Bianchi

This menswear store near Savile Row (from which it could not be more different) sells Italian labels. The stock seems aimed at southern European playboys or salesmen whose dress sense is firmly rooted in the Eighties. Leather blousons are a specialty and there is an extensive selection of suits, pants, shirts and accessories from such names as Fendi, Valentino and Jaguar Clothing.

020 7494 3898
10 Vigo Street
London W1

tube: Piccadilly Circus
Mon-Sat 10-6:30
(Thurs 10-7), Sun 11-5:30

Bill Amberg

Here's an Englishman who's seriously into leather. Imagine anything for the home—table tops, doors, couches, bags, wallets, even wine racks—and Amberg has probably rendered it in hide. At the more mainstream end of the spectrum, handbags and briefcases come in a wide variety of colors and styles from woven to wood-finish. His fur-lined papoose has been a hit with cool mummies like Kate Winslet and Cindy Crawford. www.billamberg.com

020 7727 3560
10 Chepstow Road
London W2

tube: Notting Hill Gate/Bayswater
Mon-Sat 10-6 (Thurs 10-7)

Birkenstock

If you've never gone through a hippy phase you might not have come across these exceptionally comfortable sandals, which feature a footbed specially designed to conform to your feet. The large selection of leather and suede sandals, clogs and slip-ons comes in a variety of colors, patterns and styles. Even grown-up professionals, well past their Grateful Dead days, are bound to find something that will please. There is also a great selection of colorful sandals for kids.
www.birkenstock.co.uk

020 7240 2783
37 Neal Street
London WC2

tube: Covent Garden
Mon-Tues 10-6, Wed-Fri 10-7
Sat 10-6:30, Sun 12-5:30

Blackout II

This is a vintage shop on the outskirts of Covent Garden where you can both buy and sell. Find everything from beaded evening gowns to Seventies plaid pantsuits to denim, as well as a greatest-hits assortment of accessories. Bring your stylistic vision and your sense of adventure—you may have to dig around some for the perfect find. www.blackout2.com

020 7240 5006 **tube: Covent Garden**
51 Endell Street Mon-Fri 11-7, Sat 11:30-6:30
London WC2

Blooming Marvellous

Fulham's "material" maternal girls will be thrilled to find a clothes store as big as their ballooning bellies. From the smart-dressing businesswoman to the stay-at-home mom, there's something comfy for everyone—even the new babe. Jumpers, blankets, bottles and bibs are just a few of the items to stock up on. But come for the size of the selection, not the style statement, as looks can be a bit, er, mumsy.

020 7371 0500 **tube: Parsons Green**
725 Fulham Road Mon-Sat 9:30-5:30
London SW6 Sun 10:30-4:30

020 7240 1018 **tube: Covent Garden**
69-76 Long Acre Mon-Sat 10-7, Sun 12-6
London WC2

Blue Velvet

More of a wander-in shop than a destination in its own right, Blue Velvet is a solid place for smart work shoes. They don't quite reach the height of fashion but the range is varied and the styles contemporary, from colorful kitten heels to black leather loafers. A good last-minute stop before a job interview.

020 7376 7442 **tube: Sloane Square**
174 King's Road Mon-Sat 10-7, Sun 11-6
London SW3

Blunauta

Cashmere sweater sets, raw silk trouser suits, and simple cotton shift dresses rest comfortably in this bright, breezy shop. Organized by color, the racks are easy to navigate for complementary separates—a concept that seems to drive this collection, which is apparently geared more towards comfort than trend. www.blunauta.it

020 7734 9991 **tube: Piccadilly Circus/Oxford Circus**
171-173 Regent Street Mon-Sat 10-7 (Thurs 10-7:30)
London W1 Sun 12-6

Bodas

Lingerie is too flowery a word for this refreshingly basic bra and underwear shop, with only a handful of styles to choose

from, all in soft supportive cotton or a slightly sexier stretch mesh. For bras there are padded, seamless and strapless variations; and below the belt, everything from low-riding hipster thongs to old-fashioned French knickers. It's Calvin Klein simplicity, without the hype. www.bodas.co.uk

020 7229 4464 **tube: Notting Hill Gate**
38b Ledbury Road Mon-Sat 10-6
London W11

020 7626 3210 **tube: Bank**
29 Lime Street Mon-Fri 10-6:30
London EC3

020 7823 5695 **tube: Sloane Square**
74 Duke of York Square (opening times as above)
London SW3

Directory

Bonpoint

There's something about the French—they dress kids like kids, with just the right dose of cute and not a hint of sickly sweetness: floral dresses and headbands with bows, striped T-shirts and dungarees, baby jumpsuits declaring "jolie comme maman" ("pretty like mommy"). Most children's stores make us go melty, but this one really sent us into gooey fits. www.bonpoint.com

020 7792 2515 **tube: Notting Hill Gate**
197 Westbourne Grove Mon-Sat 10-6
London W11

020 7584 5131 **tube: Gloucester Road**
17 Victoria Grove Mon-Fri 9-1, 2-5, Sat 10-1
London W8

020 7235 1441 **tube: Knightsbridge**
35b Sloane Street Mon-Sat 10-6
London SW1

Bottega Veneta

It's a name synonymous with low-key sophisticated glamour, and at last this luxurious Italian label has opened in London. Acquired by the Gucci group in 2001, the brand is rapidly rising to stardom with its super-soft leather bags, sumptuous silk scarves and square-toed shoes. There'll be plenty of room for it all at the huge Sloane Street store, including the ever-popular intrecciato line of woven leather accessories. You'll also find a small smattering of ready-to-wear for both men and women, mostly simple separates such as cashmere pullovers and leather jackets. Impeccable quality and fine craftsmanship combined with the innovative approach of creative director Thomas Maier ensure Bottega Veneta a serious place on the luxury leather scene. We recommend you pop into the store a.s.a.p.—the waiting lists are long.

020 7838 9394 **tube: Knightsbridge**
33 Sloane Street Mon-Sat 10-6 (Wed 10-7)
London SW1

Boxfresh

A purveyor of hip urban clothes, Boxfresh emphasizes comfort and style in a young, contemporary look tinged with retro. Print T-shirts, tracksuit jackets, patch-pocket shirts, baggy jeans and chinos allude to the preppy club kid. Cool, simple and not overly style-conscious. www.boxfresh.co.uk

020 7240 4742 | **tube: Covent Garden**
2 Shorts Gardens | Mon-Sat 10:30-6:30
London WC2 | (Thurs 10:30-7:30), Sun 12-5

Boyd

She's a rising star shooting straight to the top, with her first shop now well established on super-smart Elizabeth Street...not bad digs for a relative newcomer. Tracey Boyd's roughed-up style will add a daring edge to the posh gentility of the neighborhood, giving a naughty twist to lace blouses and pleated skirts. The rock glam spirit of her collections brings to mind Stella McCartney or Luella Bartley, but we've heard that Boyd (who lays claim to the same "lumps and bumps" as everyone else) tailors for a particularly forgiving fit. Amen.

020 7730 3939 | **tube: Sloane Square/Victoria**
42 Elizabeth Street | Mon-Fri 10-6, Sat 12-5
London SW1

Bradleys

A top lingerie spot with celebrities and members of the royal family, Bradleys has a history of fine service and quality—and the price tags to prove it. But the atmosphere is surprisingly relaxed and for those mid-winter island jaunts there is also a selection of beach, evening and leisurewear.

020 7235 2902 | **tube: Hyde Park Corner**
57 Knightsbridge | Mon-Fri 9:30-6, Sat 10-6, Sun 11-5
London SW1

The Bridge

Here is soft Italian leather at its best, from wallets and diaries to baggage and boots. The style statement is old-fashioned rather than streamlined—think Florence, not Milan. Loafers look like they've been dipped in dark chocolate and zip-up boots seduce, but modestly. If you're logo-averse, look out—most things are branded with "The Bridge". www.thebridge.it

020 7589 8055 | **tube: Knightsbridge**
25 Beauchamp Place | Mon-Sat 10-6 (Wed 10-7)
London SW3

☆ Brioni (at Beale & Inman)

One of the great names of Italian tailoring, with suits understated yet fashionable enough even for Pierce Brosnan's James Bond. The fabrics are, as to be expected, sumptuous, from the finest cotton shirts to the thickest silk ties. Prices match the quality, with suits starting at £1,600 and going as high as one can bear.

020 7629 4723 **tube: Bond Street**
132 New Bond Street Mon-Sat 9-6 (Thurs 9-7)
London W1

The British Hatter

Pick your occasion, and Pamela Bromley will design a suitable lid, be it bright and wide-brimmed for Ascot or a tiny pillbox for lunching. Millinery may be fashion's most traditional medium but Bromley favors an unconventional approach. She's not a fan of wearing one color head-to-toe, and many of her designs are more madcap than minimalist.

020 7361 0000 **tube: High Street Kensington**
36b Kensington Church Street Mon-Sat 10:30-6
London W8 (Thurs 11:30-6:30)

Broadway

This is not necessarily the type of shop you come to north London for—the clothing is as basic and inoffensive as you will find on any shopping street. Shoes by Unisa, Great Plains turtlenecks and cotton separates from Jackpot make for some snoozy countrywear, but there are some highlights such as Kenzo shoes and clothing by B.Young. A bit bland for a neighborhood moving steadily upmarket, but a reliable source for the locals. (There are also more restaurants per yard on Upper Street (from pricey posh to cheap eaterie) than on any other street in London.)

020 7359 5655 **tube: Highbury & Islington**
152 Upper Street Mon-Sat 9:30-6 (Thurs-Fri 9:30-7)
London N1 Sun 11-5

Brora

Brora has been London's secret cashmere source for years, gaining particular renown for its Scottish two-ply variety. The collection is more modern than classic, with peasant tops, halternecks, ballet wraps, tanks and cardigans in a mouth-watering color palette, from basic black to lime to strawberry. Equally fine accessories are on offer, such as picnic baskets, scarves, blankets and socks. Don't miss it. www.brora.co.uk

020 7352 3697 **tube: Sloane Square**
344 King's Road Mon-Sat 10-6
London SW3

020 7224 5040 **tube: Baker Street**
81 Marylebone High Street Mon-Sat 10-6 (Thurs 10-7)
London W1

☆ Browns

This elite emporium has nurtured design talent, from Giorgio Armani to John Galliano, for more than 25 years, maintaining South Molton Street's reputation as a fashion-lover's destination. Spread among five Mayfair townhouses (four for womenswear, one for men's), the store now features such labels as Jil Sander, Marni, Issey Miyake and Helmut Lang. The below-ground floor offers an assortment of housewares, including cushions, candles and throws. Impeccably dressed staff can be snooty and the selection is glamorously grown-up—in styles and prices. Still, it's a perennial favorite with those in the know, and a good place for picking up fashion industry gossip. www.brownsfashion.com

020 7491 7833 — **tube: Bond Street**
23-27 South Molton Street — Mon-Sat 10-6:30
London W1 — (Thurs 10-7)

020 7514 0040 — **tube: Knightsbridge**
6c Sloane Street — Mon-Sat 10-6 (Wed 10-7)
London SW1

Browns Focus

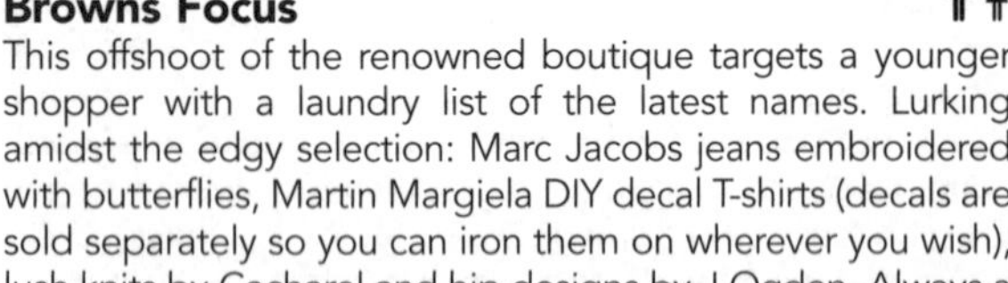

This offshoot of the renowned boutique targets a younger shopper with a laundry list of the latest names. Lurking amidst the edgy selection: Marc Jacobs jeans embroidered with butterflies, Martin Margiela DIY decal T-shirts (decals are sold separately so you can iron them on wherever you wish), lush knits by Cacharel and hip designs by J.Ogden. Always a step ahead of the mainstream. www.brownsfashion.com

020 7514 0063 — **tube: Bond Street**
38-39 South Molton Street — Mon-Sat 10-6:30
London W1 — (Thurs 10-7)

Browns Labels For Less

Across the street from the Browns conglomerate, this small shop is efficiently packed with a mixed bag of last season's leftovers. Some of the same names offered at its full-price counterpart are available here at up to 80% off (Chloé, Marc Jacobs, Sonia Rykiel and Matthew Williamson), though you may have to dig deep to find them. Compared to the mother-shop, the atmosphere here is low on sophistication, but you'll be too dazzled by the prices to notice. www.brownsfashion.com

020 7514 0052 — **tube: Bond Street**
50 South Molton Street — Mon-Sat 10-6:30
London W1 — (Thurs 10-7)

Bruce Oldfield

Renowned for sophisticated couture, Oldfield has found his niche in Knightsbridge. The sales staff can be a bit reticent but the dresses, in such fabrics as silk, crepe and chiffon, are styled to please ladies of a certain sort. Antique lace and hand-printed patterns give some gowns a precious quality—suitable for fancy cocktail parties but hardly serious fashion. Other styles, including the wedding dresses, are attracting a younger, fashion-conscious following. A famous window display featured a mannequin wearing a studded collar and a strapless white dress with a pink poodle parading on a red leash.

020 7584 1363 — **tube: Knightsbridge**
27 Beauchamp Place — Mon-Fri 9:30-5:30, Sat 11:30-4
London SW3

Buffalo Boots 

Taking traditional trainers to new heights, Buffalo features splashy colors and the sort of gravity-defying chunky soles that elevated Mel B at her Spice Girl peak. If you have no desire to add inches to your stature, there's also a selection of standard-soled pink, purple, orange, yellow and red shoes. High or low, these sneakers make a statement. www.buffalo-boots.com

020 7379 1051 **tube: Covent Garden**
65-67 Neal Street Mon-Sat 10:30-7, Sun 12-5
London WC2

020 7424 9014 **tube: Camden Town**
190 Camden High Street Tues-Sat 10:30-6:30
London NW1 Sun 11-6

Directory

Burberry 

Burberry is a British icon that has metamorphosed from stodgy institution to chic power-brand, with giant shop expansions underway at Brompton Road and Regent Street. At the sprawling Bond Street store, Burberry's ubiquitous black, red and camel plaid thrives on, plastered on everything in sight, from umbrellas and scarves to skirts, shirts, pants, berets and knitwear. The ready-to-wear collections also feature plenty of plaid-free choice, from sleekly tailored jackets and pants to sparkly eveningwear.

020 7839 5222 **tube: Bond Street**
21-23 New Bond Street Mon-Sat 10-7, Sun 12-6
London W1

020 7581 0160 **tube: Knightsbridge**
2 Brompton Road (opening times as above)
London SW1

020 7734 4060 **tube: Piccadilly Circus**
165 Regent Street (opening times as above)
London W1

Burro 

A subdued atmosphere complements Burro's collection of colorful men's streetwear. Patterns can veer to the abstract (a cotton sweater with a giant eye) and excessively brightly colored stripes and polka dots prevail, but there is a cool, vintage flavour to the collection that keeps it from being as cheesy as it may sound.

020 7240 5120 **tube: Covent Garden**
29 Floral Street Mon 11-7, Tues-Sat 10:30-7
London WC2 Sun 12-5

☆ **Butler & Wilson** 

The ground floor of their Fulham Road location features a large, lovely selection of vintage and costume accessories, from butterfly hairpins and topaz chokers to diamanté-studded bracelets and beaded slippers. Upstairs, the pearl evening bags and flapper dresses make us want to raise our glasses to the past, while modern gypsy shirts and crocheted belts are straight off the fashion pages. The South Molton Street branch has more quirky miscellanea and a dose of oriental kitsch, from pretty photo albums and kitty-cat puzzles to sparkling tiaras and bucket bags printed with geishas. Both stores demonstrate the playful and distinctly English approach to fashion, making Butler & Wilson a big hit with American shoppers. www.butlerandwilson.co.uk

020 7409 2955 **tube: Bond Street**
20 South Molton Street Mon-Sat 10-6 (Thurs 10-7)
London W1 Sun 12-6

020 7352 3045 **tube: South Kensington**
189 Fulham Road Mon-Sat 10-6 (Wed 10-7)
London SW3 Sun 12-6

Butterscotch

The front of this cozy shop is filled with goodies for the bedroom: antique quilts and eiderdowns, linen pillowcases, lavender sachets and soft cotton nightdresses for women. In the back there are racks of colorful kids' clothing, from such names as Petit Bateau, Damask and Coup de Coeur. If you're in the area, pop in.

020 7581 8551 **tube: South Kensington**
172 Walton Street Mon-Sat 10-5:30
London SW3

Calvin Klein

Where would we be without our Calvins? Klein reinvented American casual and continues to set the trends with slickly minimal pieces that strike a perfect balance between City polish and Knightsbridge poise. With his precise cuts and monochromatic palettes (you want black, you got it) Klein is the effortless master of cool—the best destination for sleek-chic suits, clingy knits, shirts, dresses, skirts, relaxed sweaters and beautifully basic eveningwear. Not to mention the shoes, accessories, jeans and underwear.

020 7491 9696 **tube: Bond Street/Oxford Circus**
53-55 New Bond Street Mon-Sat 10-6 (Thurs 10-7)
London W1

020 7495 2916 **tube: Bond Street**
(underwear and sleepwear only) Mon-Sat 10-6:30
65 New Bond Street (Thurs 10-7)
London W1

020 7495 3437 **tube: Bond Street**
(underwear and sleepwear only) (opening times as above)
67 South Molton Street
London W1

020 7838 0647 **tube: Sloane Square**
(underwear and sleepwear only) Mon-Sat 10-6:30
68 King's Road Sun 12-6
London SW3

Camden Market

Club-style sneaker and sportswear stalls dominate the southern end of the market on Camden High Street. It's a

bit of a streetwear strip mall—more mainstream than underground and all the vendors sell much the same stuff. You're better off crossing the canal, where Camden Lock offers the first signs of promise. Several levels packed to the rafters with eclectic wood furniture, bohemian jewelry, ethnic homeware and used books make this a hippy's paradise. If it's dope vinyl you're after, head to Stables Yard where the record stalls reign.

(no phone) **tube: Camden Town**
Camden High Street Thurs-Sun 9-5:30
London NW1

(no phone) **tube: Camden Town**
Camden Lock Tues-Sun 10-6
London NW1 (outdoor stalls Sat-Sun 10-6)

Camilla Ridley

This Brit's selection of suits, coats and eveningwear is feminine, floral and Fifties-inspired, and there's not a trouser in sight. Digitally rendered watercolor prints splashed over A-line dresses and floaty skirts are the pride of the current collection. Featuring a soft palette and plenty of matching accessories, this is a great place to drop by before a summer wedding. Off-season, candy-colored cashmere cardigans will keep you from feeling a chill. www.camillaridley.fs.net

020 7351 7259 **tube: South Kensington**
339 Fulham Road Mon-Sat 10-6
London SW10

Camper

You have to admire Camper for the ingenuity of their store layout, if not for their trademark suede bowling shoes with comfy rubber soles. At the Covent Garden branch the entire collection is displayed on a giant rectangular table which customers circle in search of their perfect choice. Though the shop can be packed on a Saturday afternoon, this is an efficient way to see the whole lot in one heap. The shoes are hip without being flashy, and hot with the boho Notting Hill set. www.camper.com

020 7584 5439 **tube: Knightsbridge**
35 Brompton Road Mon-Sat 10:30-7, Sun 12-6
London SW3

020 7379 8678 **tube: Covent Garden**
39 Floral Street (opening times as above)
London WC2

020 7629 2722 **tube: Green Park**
8-11 Royal Arcade Mon-Sat 10-6
28 Old Bond Street (Thurs 10-6:30)
London W1

Canali

The menswear in this bright airy shop rests somewhere between fashion-conscious and beyond caring, with each floor devoted to a different department: shoes, coats and suits and sportswear. Canali targets the natty dresser with an eye for patterns and tailoring—in their words, "Think Cary Grant in To Catch a Thief." There's also a trendier spin-off label, Canali Proposta. www.canali.it

020 7499 5605 **tube: Bond Street**
122 New Bond Street Mon-Sat 9:30-6:30
London W1 (Thurs 9:30-7)

Caramel Baby & Child

Their small sweaters, tiny pants and darling dresses will make your heart melt like hot butter and brown sugar. Featuring embroidered patterns and pastels, Caramel's adorable designs are only enhanced by the intimate space, where scented candles keep everything smelling sweet. Up to age eight.

020 7589 7001 **tube: South Kensington/Knightsbridge**
291 Brompton Road Mon-Sat 10-6:30, Sun 12-5
London SW3

Carhartt

Like an underground nightclub that the right people just know about, this cool American streetwear shop has no exterior sign. Their durable collection features bright, stripy T-shirts, nylon baseball jackets, hooded sweatshirts and, of course, their trademark carpenter pants. For womenswear in a similar spirit, head to the Newburgh Street shop. www.thecarharttstore.co.uk

020 7836 5659 **tube: Covent Garden**
56 Neal Street Mon-Fri 11-6:30 (Thurs 11-7)
London WC2 Sat 11-6:30, Sun 12-5

020 7287 6411 (W) **tube: Oxford Circus**
13 Newburgh Street Mon-Sat 11-6:30, Sun 1-5
London W1

Caroline Charles

Quintessentially elegant clothing featuring classic, couture-quality pieces—this is Ann Taylor for the designer dresser. Those who opt for timeless over trendy will find comfort in the solid-colored selection of linen dresses, full-length skirts, crisp shirts and suits. There is also an assortment of dressy, beaded eveningwear and matching accessories. www.carolinecharles.co.uk

020 7225 3197 **tube: Knightsbridge**
56-57 Beauchamp Place Mon-Sat 10-6
London SW3

Caroline Holmes

Femme fatale, pretty princess or modish modern minimalist...whatever style a bride wants to embody, Caroline Holmes can bring it to life. With three separate couture collections (Glamour, Classic and Contemporary) there's something for everyone, be it strapless bodice and evening gloves or short sleeves and a bias cut. Visits are by appointment only, and service comes with all the bridal salon trimmings—tons of attention and that made-just-for-you feel. As the weather warms, business booms, so you're liable to face a battle of the brides if you don't call well in advance. www.carolineholmes.com

020 7823 7678 **tube: South Kensington**
176 Walton Street Mon-Sat 10-5:30 (by appointment)
London SW3

Cashmere London

There are those who love cashmere and then there are those who are obsessed with it. This shop is definitely for the latter, with a stunning selection of the highest quality Scottish cashmere in a glorious 10-color rainbow. If you're not satisfied with the season's palette special orders can be placed, with 150 shades and multiple styles to choose from. They also do formalwear.

020 7838 1133 **tube: South Kensington/Knightsbridge**
180 Walton Street Mon-Sat 10-6:30
London SW3

Cath Kidston

Nobody does domestic retro better than Cath Kidston. She's best known for roses but she has a rainbow of other kitsch patterns, including bright strawberries (think country kitchen), candy-colored pinstripes and vintage cowboys (imagine a boy's bedroom in the Fifties). Pick your pattern and you can have it in any form you please, from pajamas to linens. If you just can't stop, Kidston also has a small clothing collection, complete with T-shirts, skirts, dresses and cardigans and a selection of antique jewelry to round out the old-time effect. www.cathkidston.co.uk

020 7584 3232 **tube: South Kensington/Sloane Square**
8 Elystan Street Mon-Sat 10-6
London SW3

020 7221 4000 **tube: Holland Park**
8 Clarendon Cross Mon-Fri 10-6, Sat 11-6
London W11

020 7731 6531 **tube: Parsons Green**
668 Fulham Road Mon-Sat 10-6
London SW6

Catherine Buckley

Catherine Buckley is famous for her handmade vintage-style wedding dresses. Worn by Elizabeth Taylor, Patsy Kensit and Joanna Lumley, her designs are for the bride who wants to wear something unusual and flamboyant, rather than simple and classic. (For her wedding, the singer Sinead O'Connor chose a sexy bodice and gathered skirt covered with a pattern of rambling roses.) With names like Titania, Gainsborough and Out of Africa, you can imagine how some of these dresses look—romantic, stylized and from another era. Antique lace veils are also available. www.catherinebuckley.com

020 7229 8786 — **tube: Notting Hill Gate**
302 Westbourne Grove — (by appointment)
London W11

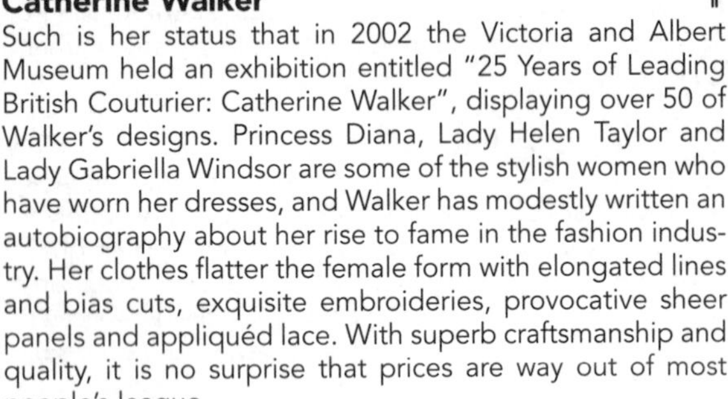

Catherine Walker

Such is her status that in 2002 the Victoria and Albert Museum held an exhibition entitled "25 Years of Leading British Couturier: Catherine Walker", displaying over 50 of Walker's designs. Princess Diana, Lady Helen Taylor and Lady Gabriella Windsor are some of the stylish women who have worn her dresses, and Walker has modestly written an autobiography about her rise to fame in the fashion industry. Her clothes flatter the female form with elongated lines and bias cuts, exquisite embroideries, provocative sheer panels and appliquéd lace. With superb craftsmanship and quality, it is no surprise that prices are way out of most people's league.

020 7581 8811 — **tube: South Kensington**
46 Fulham Road — Mon-Sat 10-6 (by appointment)
London SW3

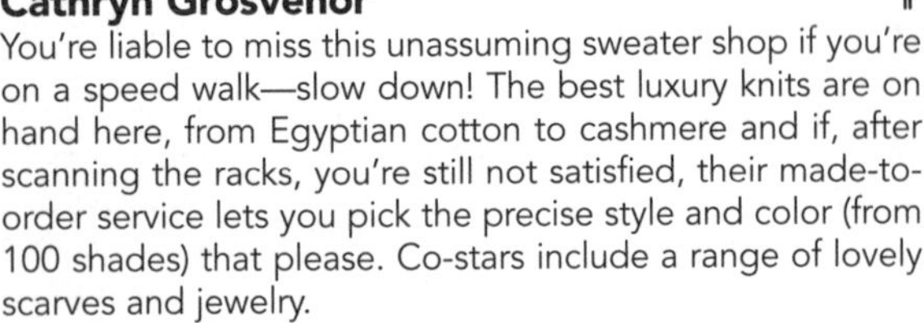

Cathryn Grosvenor

You're liable to miss this unassuming sweater shop if you're on a speed walk—slow down! The best luxury knits are on hand here, from Egyptian cotton to cashmere and if, after scanning the racks, you're still not satisfied, their made-to-order service lets you pick the precise style and color (from 100 shades) that please. Co-stars include a range of lovely scarves and jewelry.

020 7584 2112 — **tube: South Kensington/Sloane Square**
3 Elystan Street — Mon-Fri 10-5:30, Sat 10-4
London SW3

Catimini

Dressing the little ones with flair is a simple task at Catimini. Soft and cosy, the enchanting collection comes in shades of navy, olive, ruby and tangerine, embellished with ethnic patterns and embroidered animals. There's also a small selection of shoes and a colorful assortment of hats, gloves and scarves. For children up to 14.

020 7629 8099 — **tube: Bond Street**
52a South Molton Street — Mon-Sat 10-6 (Thurs 10-7)
London W1

Caz

You've probably learned by now that Londoners can't live without their cashmere. It's an addiction that Caz feeds happily, with bright solid, striped and two-toned cardigan sets, short-sleeved sweaters, tank tops and shawls. Juicy Couture T-shirts and a lightweight Scottish cashmere blend mean that even in the summer months nobody has to abstain.

020 7589 1920 — **tube: South Kensington**
177 Draycott Avenue — Mon-Fri 10-6 (Wed 10-6:30)
London SW3 — Sat 10:30-6, Sun 1-5:30

CCO'

Think Italian Riviera and you'll understand the ethos of this Fulham newcomer. Stocking a sophisticated selection of daywear from Italian designers only, including Amina Rubinacci, Carlo Zini and Grazia Severi, the classic styles are more suited to the glamorous Dolce Vita woman in her 50s than to young hippy chicks. You'll find Kelly bags made in Florence, soft cashmere jumpers and cardigans and slim-lined Portofino pants by Alberto Biani. The chunky jewelry by Daniel Cornaggia is also popular.

020 7376 5542 — **tube: South Kensington**
307 Fulham Road — Mon-Wed 10:30-6
London SW10 — Thurs-Sat 10:30-6:30

020 7751 8344 — **tube: Fulham Broadway**
273 New King's Road — Mon-Sat 10-6
London SW6

Directory

Cecil Gee

Low-key seems to be the sales mantra at this refreshingly relaxed emporium where customers are left to sift in peace through Versace, Burberry, Dolce & Gabbana, Hugo Boss and other high-end designers. The selection is as understated as the ambience and includes suits, shirts, sweaters, pants and accessories.

020 7629 4441 — **tube: Bond Street**
92 New Bond Street — Mon-Sat 10-7
London W1 — Sun 12-6

020 7491 2292 — **tube: Oxford Circus**
287 Oxford Street — Mon-Sat 10-7 (Thurs 10-8)
London W1 — Sun 12-6

020 7436 8752 — **tube: Oxford Circus**
170 Oxford Street — (opening times as above)
London W1

020 7376 1268 — **tube: High Street Kensington**
172 Kensington High Street — Mon-Sat 10-6:30
London W8 — Sun 11-5

020 7626 5011 — **tube: Bank**
153 Fenchurch Street — Mon-Fri 8:30-6
London EC3

020 7240 1020 — **tube: Covent Garden**
47 Long Acre — Mon-Fri 10-7 (Thurs 10-8)
London WC2 — Sat 9:30-6:30, Sun 12-6

Celia Loe

Petite women, step up. The pickings here may be somewhat limited but the smart collection of dresses, suits and eveningwear is pretty and well made. Linen dresses sprinkled with rosebuds and lavender pinafores with white stitching are classic à la Ann Taylor, while striped suits strike a more professional note. A useful place for those who are tired of making trips to the tailor. www.celialoe.com

020 7409 1627 — **tube: Bond Street**
68 South Molton Street — Mon-Sat 10-6:30
London W1 — (Thurs 10-7:30)

Céline

A relative newcomer to Bond Street, this French label fits right in, featuring trends tailored to the high end with prices to match. Designer Michael Kors has made it his mission to capture all the various characters of the runway, from Catholic schoolgirl to army recruit. Traditional pleated skirts and sweaters find contemporary flair in sexy leather trim and plunging necklines, while the vacationwear takes you straight to Palm Beach. Recent seasons have brought Kors a rabid following among female rappers, but the label's luxury fabrics please Park Avenue princesses, too. www.celine.com

020 7297 4999 — **tube: Bond Street/Green Park**
160 New Bond Street — Mon-Sat 10-6 (Thurs 10-6:30)
London W1 — Sun 12-5 (seasonal)

Cenci Rags

This vintage selection really captures fashion's chequered past. A Fifties floral swimming cap, a golfing cardigan from the Sixties, a Seventies wool waistcoat...all the stuff most people threw away ages ago has reappeared here. For a vintage shop the air is surprisingly fresh and un-musty, and the clothing meticulously organized. The staff are friendly aficionados, happy to guide you through the racks of knits or help you find the perfect suitcase, hatbox or handbag.

020 7836 1400 — **tube: Covent Garden**
31 Monmouth Street — Mon-Sat 11-6
London WC2

Chanel

Lagerfeld has remodeled more than his famous figure—the interior of the new Bond Street store is as pared-down as he is, and polished to a high gloss. Its ground floor is devoted to sunglasses and cosmetics while a small selection of clothing awaits upstairs. Coco might be shocked to see Lagerfeld's modern take on the quilted bag, rendered in turquoise terry cloth with a white plastic chain (£370) and a perfect match for the terry cloth hotpants. If you're passing by, this store is certainly worth visiting if only to see fashion's most revered label—and the ubiquitous Chanel tweed suit—still thriving 70 years on. www.chanel.com

020 7493 5040 — **tube: Green Park**
26 Old Bond Street — Mon-Sat 10-6
London W1

020 7235 6631 — **tube: Knightsbridge**
167-170 Sloane Street — Mon-Sat 10-6
London SW1

020 7581 8620 — **tube: South Kensington**
278-280 Brompton Road — Mon-Sat 10-6 (Wed 10-7)
London SW3

The Changing Room

If you're suffocating on bustling Oxford Street, take a breather at this out-of-the-way boutique. Designs range from soft feminine slip dresses to smart business suits, featuring Betsey Johnson, Yoshiki Hishinuna, Issey Miyake and Adolfo Dominguez. The looks rate high on character and low on fuss, creating an effect that is funky and fun. www.the-changingroom.com

020 7408 1596 — **tube: Bond Street**
10a Gees Court — Mon-Sat 10:30-6:30
London W1 — (Thurs 10:30-7:30)

Charles Tyrwhitt

This is one of the less expensive shirt stores on Jermyn Street and the maxim "you get what you pay for" applies. There's nothing wrong with the shirts—definitely superior to most mass-market products—but for a little more you can get a finer shirt nearby. Still, an excellent option for the businessman who needs a stack of shirts in his wardrobe. As for the businesswoman, so rapidly is she rising to the top that Charles Tyrwhitt have started a new line, CT woman, available not only in Jermyn Street but also in the heart of the City at Bow Lane. Described as stylish, sexy and smart, these shirts are obviously for the woman who really means business. Good mail-order service too. www.ctshirts.co.uk

020 7839 6060 — **tube: Piccadilly Circus/Green Park**
92 Jermyn Street — Mon-Sat 9:30-6 (Thurs 9:30-7)
London SW1 — Sun 11-5

020 7329 1779 — **tube: St. Paul's/Mansion House**
43 Bow Lane — Mon-Fri 8:30-7
London EC4

Charlotte Smith

One of London's latest fashion hotspots, this boutique offers limited edition clothing from New Zealand, an increasingly popular and trendy destination since *Lord of the Rings*. Charlotte Smith moved to London five years ago and so many people asked her about the origins of her funky wardrobe that she decided it was time to fly her country's flag. Recent highlights include satin tops embroidered with butterflies by Zambesi, military trousers by Carlson, Fifties Prom-style dresses by DNA and sexy retro T-shirts by Hailwood. If you don't yet recognize these names you soon will—Cate Blanchett and Liv Tyler are both fans.

020 7584 3223 — **tube: South Kensington**
160 Walton Street — Mon-Sat 10-6
London SW3

The Chelsea Collections

Daddies bring their precious daughters here for sweet-sixteen silk gowns or a hat for their first Ascot. True trendsetters would blanch at the hot-pink, chiffon ballet skirts and peacock-blue feathered hats but in posh, social terms this

place sits safely within proper bounds. Garden party guests and mothers of the bride could don a smart ensemble here, topped by a Catherine Goodison hat, with elegant wraps and handbags to complete the effect. If all you're lacking is a suitable hat, there's also a made-to-measure milliner service.

020 7581 5792 **tube: South Kensington**
90 Fulham Road Mon-Sat 10-6
London SW3

☆ Chloé

In the past six years this classic French house has been dramatically reinvented. Renowned as a luxurious, romantic and quintessentially French label, the brand has now been infused with a new rock 'n' roll edge that oozes street cred. Style princess Stella McCartney (creative director from 1997 to 2001) began the transformation by teaming delicately feminine pieces with structured, skinny tailoring, and pairing revealing blouses with low-riding jeans and stiletto heels. This look successfully catapulted to the front lines of fashion and the label is now smoothly sailing into the future with another London girl, Phoebe Philo, at the helm. A less expensive casual line, See By Chloé, has been added, along with a smattering of sexy swimwear, all to be seen in the flagship store on Sloane Street, where you'll also find ready-to-wear, leather goods, accessories and, joy of joys, a lower level devoted entirely to shoes.

020 7823 5348 **tube: Sloane Street**
152-153 Sloane Street Mon-Sat 10-6 (Wed 10-7)
London SW1

Christian Dior

Another legendary label that has modernized apace, the clothes at Dior are sensual and stylish but retain their intrinsic femininity. Designer John Galliano offers couture with cheek, bringing camouflage prints to halter dresses and a denim finish to his cocktail frocks. It-girls have never looked so naughty. All you need is the attitude, and the cash, to pull it off. www.dior.com

020 7235 1357 **tube: Knightsbridge**
31 Sloane Street Mon-Sat 10-6 (Wed 10-7)
London SW1

Christian Louboutin

A name often uttered in the same breath as Manolo Blahnik or Jimmy Choo, Louboutin's legendary red soles are coveted by fashion fanatics everywhere. Find lightly embellished mile-high heels and feminine flats amidst the playful store displays (one month featured papier-mâchéd mannequin legs, covered in pages ripped from magazines and tabloids).

020 7823 2234 **tube: Knightsbridge**
23 Motcomb Street Mon-Fri 10-6, Sat 11-6
London SW1

Christiana Couture 

Christiana Couture is a winner of the "Full Romantic British Bridal Award". Her silk bias-cut dress, with a boat neck and low 'v' back trimmed with pearls and crystals and finished off with a detachable silk chiffon train, is delicate and feminine. Most of her designs incorporate details such as cascading silk flowers, silk-covered buttons or fluted chiffon sleeves. The made-to-measure service starts at £2,300.

020 7976 5252 — **tube: Pimlico**
53 Moreton Street — (by appointment)
London SW1

Church's 

A well-known name for classic men's brogues, Church's is now owned by Prada, which can only mean good things for the venerable English brand. At the very least they'll maintain their hard-earned reputation for fine leather shoes sold in a sophisticated setting where the women's line echoes the men's, but in softer forms. www.churchsshoes.com

020 7493 1474 — **tube: Bond Street**
133 New Bond Street — Mon-Sat 9:30-6 (Thurs 9:30-7)
London W1

020 7493 8307 — **tube: Green Park**
58-59 Burlington Arcade — Mon-Sat 9:30-6
London W1

020 7734 2438 — **tube: Oxford Circus**
201 Regent Street — Mon-Sat 10-6:30 (Thurs 10-7:30)
London W1 — Sun 12-6

020 7930 8210 — **tube: Piccadilly Circus/Green Park**
108-110 Jermyn Street — Mon-Sat 9:30-6
London SW1

020 7589 9136 — **tube: Knightsbridge**
143 Brompton Road — Mon-Tues 10-6
London SW3 — Wed-Sat 10-6:30

Claire's Accessories 

When Britney starts a necklace trend, it's bound to turn up at Claire's. Their target is teens, but don't be surprised to find twenty- and thirtysomethings stocking up on hoop earrings, hair toggles and sparkly belts. The cheap prices justify a brilliant bulk-buy, though it's not nearly as nice as Accessorize and the quality is just this side of junk. Still, it's all glittery and girly, and sometimes that's just what we want. www.claires.co.uk

020 7734 4748 — **tube: Piccadilly Circus**
13 Coventry Street — Mon-Wed 10-11
London W1 — Thurs-Sun 10-midnight

020 7434 2938 — **tube: Piccadilly Circus**
49-63 Regent Street — Mon-Sat 9-9, Sun 12-6
London W1

020 7376 9205 — **tube: High Street Kensington**
169 Kensington High Street — Mon-Sat 9-7, Sun 11-6
London W8

020 7240 4121 **tube: Covent Garden**
120 Long Acre Mon-Sat 10-7:30 (Thurs 10-8)
London WC2 Sun 11-6:30

020 7730 5618 **tube: Sloane Square**
55 King's Road Mon-Sat 9-7, Sun 11-6
London SW3

020 7580 5504 **tube: Oxford Circus**
108 Oxford Street Mon-Sat 9-7, Sun 12-6:30
London W1

Clarks 

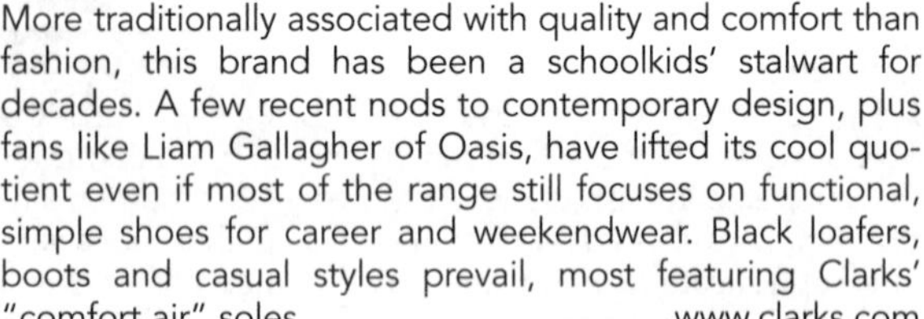

More traditionally associated with quality and comfort than fashion, this brand has been a schoolkids' stalwart for decades. A few recent nods to contemporary design, plus fans like Liam Gallagher of Oasis, have lifted its cool quotient even if most of the range still focuses on functional, simple shoes for career and weekendwear. Black loafers, boots and casual styles prevail, most featuring Clarks' "comfort air" soles. www.clarks.com

020 7734 1339 **tube: Oxford Circus**
203 Regent Street Mon-Fri 10-7 (Thurs 10-8)
London W1 Sat 10-6:30, Sun 12-6

020 7734 5294 **tube: Piccadilly Circus**
101 Regent Street (opening times as above)
London W1

020 7437 2593 **tube: Tottenham Court Road**
15 Oxford Street (opening times as above)
London W1

020 7499 0305 **tube: Oxford Circus**
260 Oxford Street (opening times as above)
London W1

020 7629 9609 **tube: Marble Arch**
476 Oxford Street Mon-Wed 10-7, Thurs-Fri 10-8
London W1 Sat 10-6:30, Sun 12-6

Claudia Sebire

Chelsea ladies have long frequented this smart boutique. The selection is tailored and refined, from tweed suits to cashmere cardigans. Gilets by Karma and Strenesse bags are similarly luxe—no matter if you've never heard of them. Other labels like Marc Cain and Trixi Schober add an extra layer of polish.

020 7835 1327 **tube: South Kensington/Gloucester Road**
136 Fulham Road Mon-Sat 10-6
London SW10

Clementine

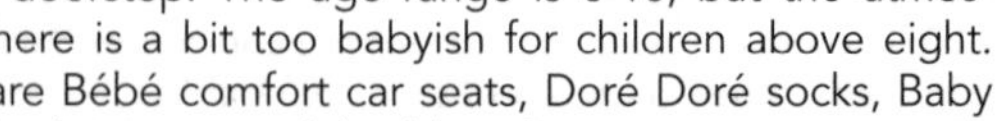

Notting Hill's young boho moms pop in for a fresh pair of pjs or a Petit Bateau T-shirt, their designer prams colliding on the doorstep. The age range is 0-18, but the atmosphere here is a bit too babyish for children above eight. There are Bébé comfort car seats, Doré Doré socks, Baby Graziella knitwear and bedding by Petit Descamps. To parade the playground in style, there's the SUV of strollers, the rugged Emmaljunga all-terrain pram (£300).

020 7243 6331 | **tube: Notting Hill Gate**
73 Ledbury Road | Mon-Sat 10-6
London W11

Cleverley

This little jewel of a store is a relatively recent addition to the ranks of bespoke shoemakers but has a long tradition. Owner-managers George Glasgow and John Carnera worked for years with George Cleverley who, despite a huge weakness for playing the ponies, was universally acknowledged as a footwear magician. Working from the lasts and patterns they inherited, Carnera and Glasgow have recreated Cleverley's unique style and built a bespoke service that is now seen as one of the best in the world by insiders in the shoe trade. Despite this reputation, prices start from around £1,375, a snip compared to what you might pay elsewhere. Ready-to-wear from £280.

020 7493 0443 | **tube: Green Park**
13 Royal Arcade | Mon-Fri 9-5:30
28 Old Bond Street | Sat 10-2
London W1

Clio

More suited to a rich international clientele than to the young and fashion-conscious, this store features bright and jeweled evening shoes in every color of the rainbow. Shapes are dowdy, styles are brazen and prices exceed reason—perfect for the flashy Bond Street brigade.

020 7493 2018 | **tube: Bond Street**
75 New Bond Street | Mon-Sat 10-6:30
London W1

Clusaz

Quietly nestling on a side street with a devoted local clientele, this small shop savors its distance from Islington's main drag. Seek respite in bias-cut silk dresses by Poleci, Chine pants, Nicole Farhi knits and the best from Kate Clarkson.

020 7359 5596 | **tube: Angel**
56 Cross Street | Mon-Sat 10:30-6:30, Sun 12-5
London N1

cm store

This has got to be London's largest purveyor of ripped jeans and tight customized T-shirts. It's typical teen fare: jeans by Miss Sixty, black leather belts with grommets, patched denim skirts and velour sweatsuits in baby pinks and blues. There's fun to be had here, but it'll cost you. You're better off at the Portobello market, where equally trendy streetwear comes at more modest prices.

020 7351 9361 | **tube: Sloane Square**
121 King's Road | Mon-Sat 10-7, Sun 12-6
London SW3

Coach

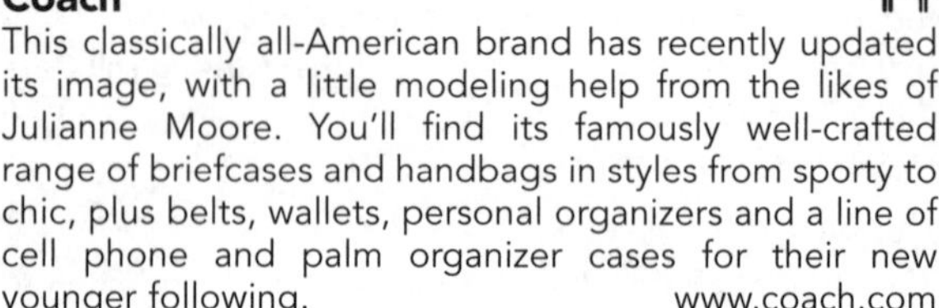

This classically all-American brand has recently updated its image, with a little modeling help from the likes of Julianne Moore. You'll find its famously well-crafted range of briefcases and handbags in styles from sporty to chic, plus belts, wallets, personal organizers and a line of cell phone and palm organizer cases for their new younger following. www.coach.com

020 7235 1507 **tube: Knightsbridge**
8 Sloane Street Mon-Sat 10-6 (Wed 10-7)
London SW1

Coccinelle

The racks at this Italian shop are stacked with handbags of simple, refined design in the latest shapes. The selection is high-end style for the younger set. Colors include rich reds, greens and golds and the Parma leather is especially supple. Bags come with matching wallets and there is also a small collection of shoes, sunglasses, scarves and jewelry. Definitely a name to look out for.

020 7491 7414 **tube: Bond Street**
44 South Molton Street Mon-Sat 10-6:30 (Thurs 10-7)
London W1

020 7730 7657 **tube: Sloane Square**
13 Duke of York Square Mon-Sat 10-7, Sun 11-6
London SW3

Coco Ribbon

Prefer pottering around a stylish friend's boudoir to hardcore shopping? At Coco Ribbon you can do both because everything in this glorious stage set of a boutique is for sale, from the French Empire-style bedside tables to the rose hair-bands strewn on top of the romantic dressing-table. There are Moroccan sequined slippers, lavender heart bags, flower fairy lights and chic scatter cushions. You'll find itsy-bitsy bikinis by Zimmermann, stylish cashmere knitwear by Cameron Taylor and polka-dot knickers by Starlet. It all makes for some seriously girly shopping.

020 7229 4904 **tube: Ladbroke Grove**
21 Kensington Park Road Mon-Sat 10-6, Sun 12:30-6
London W11

Coles the Shirtmakers

Traditional shirtmaker (since 1878) tending towards the more conservative end of this street famed for shirtmakers. Prices are lower than at some of Coles's more illustrious neighbors, and critics argue that the quality is too, but for anyone used to mass-manufactured shirts Coles makes a top-notch product with removable collar-stiffeners, a two-piece yoke, two-fold cotton poplin fabric and pearl buttons. www.coles-shirtmakers.com

020 7930 6448 **tube: Piccadilly Circus/Green Park**
101 Jermyn Street Mon-Sat 9:30-6 (Thurs 9:30-7)
London SW1 Sun 11-5

Collette Dinnigan

She's earned star status in the fashion industry and some of her biggest fans are stars themselves...Elle Macpherson, Cate Blanchett, Nicole Kidman, Cameron Diaz. With a glamorous collection of sheer slip dresses, full floral skirts and sparkly eveningwear this Australian designer has worked her way up from Down Under to top of the heap. Her tricks of the trade include creative, feminine cuts and styles that are just naughty enough. www.collettedinnigan.com.au

020 7589 8897 **tube: South Kensington**
26 Cale Street Mon-Sat 10-6
London SW3

Directory

Collezioni: Giorgio Armani

Resting somewhere between Giorgio Armani's signature label and his street-style Emporio line, Collezioni features all the sleek minimalism we've come to associate with the name—at less damaging prices. Simple monotones resonate throughout this beautifully tailored collection, with suits, shirts and ties for men, lovely knits and silky skirts for women. www.armani.com

020 7491 9888 **tube: Bond Street**
43 New Bond Street Mon-Wed, Fri 10-6 (Thurs 10-7)
London W1 Sat 10-6:30

Comme des Garçons

Just off the heavily-beaten Bond Street trail, this store's minimalist decor provides the perfect background to the overwhelming designs, whose strong colors and striking cuts make for some high-concept fashion. From white, frilly prairie skirts to neon track trousers, this collection expresses its individuality through the unlikely combination of details—a V-neck T-shirt with a peter-pan collar, a classic wool dress with unfinished seams. It's a look best suited to the bold and seriously style-savvy.

020 7493 1258 **tube: Bond Street**
59 Brook Street Mon-Sat 10-6 (Thurs 10-7)
London W1

☆ Connolly

Originally famous for providing leather for the interiors of Rolls-Royce, Jaguar and Aston Martin, Connolly was bought in 1999 by Joseph (of Joseph fame) and Isabel Ettedgui. They have extended its appeal as a logo-free luxury brand for those who prefer to enjoy their wealth with a bit of stealth. The store sells an eclectic mix of chicly understated leather accessories, cashmere knitwear, shoes—including a men's line by Fulham cobbler Tim Little—and other outlandish treats.

020 7439 2510 **tube: Oxford Circus**
41 Conduit Street Mon-Sat 10-6 (Thurs 10-7)
London W1

Cornucopia

On the secondhand spectrum this shop comes off a little shabby. Still, it's an affordable source in a city where vintage comes at a premium. Racks are filled to the rafters and everything has a straight-from-the-attic smell (and the antique shoes are a little sad, with worn-down heels and crushed toes). There are mid-century dresses and tops in abundance, and some truly old goodies hanging up high. Like most vintage stores, you never quite know what you're going to get but if you're in the neighborhood, have a look.

020 7828 5752 **tube: Victoria**
12 Upper Tachbrook Street Mon-Sat 11-6, Sun 12-6
London SW1

The Corridor

A secondhand specialty shop, this is the place to come for last season's affordable (and hardly worn) designer cast-offs. If you can't bear to pay full price and you savor the victory of finding a fantastic deal, stop by and search out your favorite labels—but beware of surly staff.

020 7351 0772 **tube: Sloane Square**
309a King's Road Mon-Sat 10:30-6:30
London SW3

Couverture

Silk nightgowns, cotton kimonos, hand-stitched duvet covers and Indian cotton sheets—the soporific supplies at Couverture will make you want to head straight back to bed. Other covetables include vintage ceramics, cushions printed with little dolls and sequined goatskin slippers. It doesn't get much cozier than this. Zzz...

020 7795 1200 **tube: Sloane Square**
310 King's Road Mon-Sat 10-6
London SW3

Crew Clothing Co

Anyone prone to seasickness might not want to climb aboard...the clothing here has a nautical theme. Fleece jackets, sweatshirts, turtlenecks and polos in navy, light blue and white are perfect for parading the decks. But there are some land-loving brown loafers and simple swimwear.

020 7371 0483 **tube: Parsons Green**
62 New King's Road Mon-Sat 10-6:30, Sun 11-5
London SW6

020 7730 7820 **tube: Sloane Square**
Unit 6, B Block Mon-Sat 10-6 (Wed 10-7) Sun 11-5
Duke of York Square
London SW3

Crichton/Fallan & Harvey

This building is shared by bespoke shirtmakers Crichton and bespoke tailors Fallan & Harvey. Crichton specializes in English stiff-collar shirts but will make anything you like from a vast selection of colorful fabrics. Fallan & Harvey is a classic bespoke tailor of good reputation.

020 7434 3156 (Crichton) **tube: Piccadilly Circus**
020 7437 8573 (Fallan & Harvey)
7 Sackville Street Mon-Fri 8:30-6:30, Sat-Sun 8:30-5:30
London W1

020 7730 7518 (Crichton) **tube: Sloane Square/Victoria**
34 Elizabeth Street Mon-Fri 8:30-6:30, Sat 9-5:30
London SW1

Crockett & Jones

In the premier league of shoemakers, and one of the few survivors from the 1980s when Northampton's brilliant cobblers fell on hard times. With the revival of Savile Row and Jermyn Street, Crockett & Jones is thriving again. C&J do the best English classics—brogues, derbys, oxfords—as well as anyone.

020 7976 2684 **tube: Piccadilly Circus/Green Park**
69 Jermyn Street Mon-Sat 9-6
London SW1

Crombie

This is the flagship store for the venerable coat and suit brand. Crombie's eponymous coat with its distinctive velvet collars is sold in several variations, alongside men's and women's suits in a stunning selection of British fabrics. Classic navys and grays are joined by heathery tweeds and herringbones in this modern, elegant store.

www.crombie.co.uk

020 7839 1375 **tube: Piccadilly Circus/Green Park**
99 Jermyn Street Mon-Sat 10-6:30, Sun 10:30-4:30
London SW1

☆ The Cross

On a tiny residential block in Holland Park, Sam Robinson and Sarah Kean have created a shopper's paradise of dreamy bright colors and girly knick-knacks. Their whitewashed space offers a feast of original fashion and playful, lighthearted gifts, though we think the kids' section is in danger of overtaking the shop. You'll find tub toys and alphabet soaps, linen pants from 120% Linen, glitter candles, beauty products, handmade greeting cards and flower-shaped fairy lights. Downstairs is a den of desirables, from Fake London sequined jumpers to embroidered scarves by Megan Park and slip dresses by Dosa. You'll want it all...until you've seen the price tag.

020 7727 6760 **tube: Holland Park**
141 Portland Road Mon-Sat 10:30-6
London W11

Cyberdog

Cyberdog welcomes its visitors with hard techno music and black walls covered in glowing neon clothing. T-shirts are splashed with video game graphics or feature an electroluminescent plastic panel that flashes a pattern of light to the beat of music—perfect for clubbing. This is true futuristic fashion, Star Wars-style, from cargo pants with padded knees to tank tops with thick black rubber shoulder straps. Perfect clothing for the trilennium. www.cyberdog.net

020 7836 7855 **tube: Covent Garden**
9 Earlham Street Mon-Sat 11-7, Sun 12-6
London WC2

Daisy & Tom

An imperative stop for Chelsea's yummy mummies, this store is a never-never land of children's clothing, furniture and toys. Puppet shows, a train set and a working merry-go-round create a fantastically kid-friendly environment. Clothing includes overalls and colorful jumpers, fairy costumes for girls and Noddy outfits for boys. Classic board games, Barbie dolls and Lego sets are also available, as well as a huge selection of huggable fluffy toys. There's even a hair salon. www.daisyandtom.com

020 7352 5000 **tube: Sloane Square**
181-183 King's Road Mon-Wed, Fri 9:30-6
London SW3 Thurs, Sat 10-7, Sun 11-5

Daks

As London's fashion pack bemoans the overexposure of Burberry's plaid, Daks is attempting to fill the coolness gap with its own more subtle signature check. Bespoke tailor Timothy Everest has created a classically British look in beige check; he also favors romantic floral prints and bright stripes. For women there are elegant narrow trousers, fitted jackets and wrap dresses; for men, cord suits, cotton shirts and preppy knits. None of it is exciting enough to reach the cult status of Burberry, but this label does have its fans. www.daks.com

020 7409 4000 **tube: Green Park**
10 Old Bond Street Mon-Sat 10-6 (Thurs 10-7)
London W1

020 7529 9802 **tube: Piccadilly Circus**
32-34 Jermyn Street Mon-Sat 9-6
London SW1

Davies & Son

Sitting oddly, but not uncomfortably, among the newer shops on the west side of Savile Row, Davies & Son is a thoroughly traditional, all-bespoke tailors which moved into "the Row" from Old Burlington Street at the end of the Nineties. An informal, friendly air is combined with traditionally high standards of service for a largely overseas clientele. Suits, still made round the corner in Old Burlington Street, start from a relatively modest, for Savile Row, £1,760. www.daviesandsonsavilerow.com

020 7434 3016 **tube: Piccadilly Circus/Oxford Circus**
38 Savile Row Mon-Fri 9-5:30, Sat 9:30-1
London W1

Debenhams

Don't be put off by the fact that Debenhams is the archetypal Oxford Street department store, there is real value for money here if you know what to look for. Reasonable prices are the primary pull in the clothing lines, which include exclusive collections by designers John Rocha, Jasper Conran and Ben de Lisi. With a full selection of clothing, accessories, cosmetics, housewares and furniture the airy store is a comfortable if not wildly inspiring place to shop. www.debenhams.com

020 7580 3000 **tube: Bond Street/Oxford Circus**
334-348 Oxford Street Mon-Tues 9:30-8, Wed 10-8
London W1 Thurs 9:30-9, Fri-Sat 9:30-8, Sun 12-6

Debonair Debonair

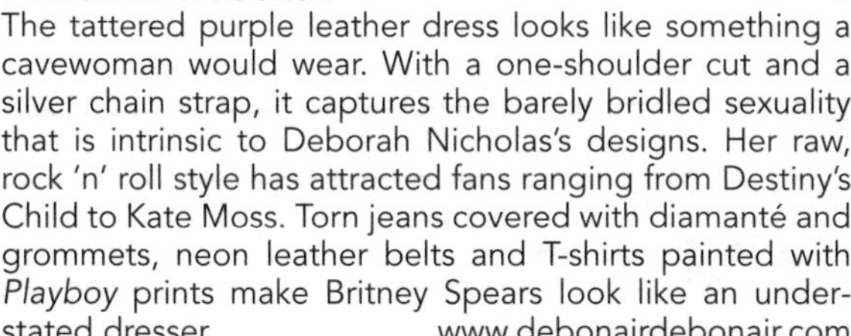

The tattered purple leather dress looks like something a cavewoman would wear. With a one-shoulder cut and a silver chain strap, it captures the barely bridled sexuality that is intrinsic to Deborah Nicholas's designs. Her raw, rock 'n' roll style has attracted fans ranging from Destiny's Child to Kate Moss. Torn jeans covered with diamanté and grommets, neon leather belts and T-shirts painted with *Playboy* prints make Britney Spears look like an understated dresser. www.debonairdebonair.com

020 8960 7679 **nearest tube: Ladbroke Grove**
Portobello Green Arcade Mon 11-6, Tues-Sat 10-6
London W10

Dege & Skinner

The large, well lit and very welcoming premises of Dege & Skinner play host to a firm with a long tradition of military tailoring (the company still makes uniforms for the Queen's cavalry regiments and the Beefeaters at the Tower of London) which has influenced the extremely elegant, high-waisted house style. The suits, coats and (uniquely) shirts are all handmade on the premises, and there is also a wide range of well-chosen gentleman's accessories. www.dege-skinner.co.uk

020 7287 2941 **tube: Piccadilly Circus/Oxford Circus**
10 Savile Row Mon-Fri 9:15-5:15, Sat 9:30-12:30
London W1

Designer Bargains

If you've got the patience, they've got the labels: Prada, Versace, Gucci, DKNY and Chanel are all likely to be lurking in the tightly packed racks at this musty secondhand shop. Handbags by Céline, Voyage cardigans and denim by Anne Klein make up a mix that is mature but occasionally a little stuffy. The shoe selection is the standout, featuring Manolo Blahnik and Jimmy Choo stilettos in exceptionally good shape. And if you're in the market for an Ascot hat, this could be just the place.

020 7795 6777 **tube: High Street Kensington**
29 Kensington Church Street Mon-Sat 10-6
London W8

Designer Club

Even on the dreariest London day these whitewashed walls create a sunny setting for the fine selection of chic, feminine tops, skirts and eveningwear. Sassy designs from Missoni, John Galliano and Roberto Cavalli corner the market in sexy international style.

020 7235 2242 — **tube: Knightsbridge**
9 West Halkin Street — Mon-Fri 10-6, Sat 11-6
London SW1

Dickins & Jones

In an upscale shopping environment surrounded by top labels—Donna Karan, Nicole Farhi, Valentino, Paul Smith and more—one is happily surprised to find almost no sales-staff attitude but just about everything else, from business-wear to bathing-suits. There's also a selection catering to the younger market, including French Connection, Whistles and Morgan, and a Clarins Spa.

020 7734 7070 — **tube: Oxford Circus**
224-244 Regent Street — Mon-Sat 10-7 (Thurs 10-8)
London W1 — Sun 12-6

Diesel

Urban-minded and techno-trendy, this Italian label doesn't pull any punches with its own brand of young, hip street style. One of the first retailers to feature live DJs, Diesel is best known for its wide selection of jeans which come in a variety of colors and cuts. Find T-shirts, baggy pants, button-down shirts and jackets. Bright colors accentuate the collection. www.diesel.com

020 7497 5543 — **tube: Covent Garden**
43 Earlham Street — Mon-Sat 10-7 (Thurs 10-8)
London WC2 — Sun 12-6

020 7434 3113 — **tube: Oxford Circus**
24 Carnaby Street — Mon-Sat 10-7, Sun 12-6
London W1

020 7376 1785 — **tube: High Street Kensington**
38a Kensington High Street — Mon-Sat 10-7 (Thurs 10-8)
London W8 — Sun 12-6

Diesel Style Lab

Striding one step ahead of mainstream streetwear, Diesel Style Lab offers a more innovative (and expensive) fashion alternative to its sibling store. Experimenting with cutting-edge design, engineered fabrics and creative detail, the selection offers a fresh take on the basics. If the fashion leaves you cold, perhaps the work of young artists featured in the gallery space will inspire. www.dieselstylelab.com

020 7836 4970 — **tube: Covent Garden**
12 Floral Street — Mon-Sat 11-7, Sun 12-6
London WC2

The Dispensary

The only thing you'll dispense with is your hard-earned cash. It's all too tempting—bright gingham blouses, ruched jersey dresses, Mavi dark or distressed denim and T-shirts from Antoni*Alison could entice even the most ardent avoiders of trend. Harrison, Duffer, Only Hearts, Fiorucci and Dispensary's own label are also included. Great for logo lovers. www.thedispensary.net

020 7727 8797 **tube: Notting Hill Gate**
200 Kensington Park Road Mon-Sat 10:30-6:30
London W11 Sun 12-5

020 7287 8145 (W) **tube: Oxford Circus**
9 Newburgh Street (opening times as above)
London W1

020 7287 2262 (M) **tube: Oxford Circus**
8 Newburgh Street (opening times as above)
London W1 (renamed JC's Boutique)

020 7221 9290 **tube: Notting Hill Gate**
25 Pembridge Road Mon-Sat 10:30-6:30
London W11

Diverse

It's Islington's equivalent to Matches in Notting Hill but this shop has been going strong for more than a decade. No wonder: selection is Grade A, including Chloé, Clements Ribeiro, Philosophy and Fake London. The style spectrum ranges from reliable Earl Jeans to a gray Matthew Williamson sweatshirt with ripped sleeves and a rainbow of sequins around each shoulder. Don't neglect the equally cool home collection upstairs: Paul Smith cashmere throws, Chinese lanterns, leather coasters by Birdie Num Num and Japanese soup bowls. The menswear selection up the block has a bit more street flavor, with brands like Duffer, Diesel Style Lab, Maharishi and Carhartt.

020 7359 8877 **tube: Angel**
294 Upper Street Mon-Sat 10:30-6:30, Sun 12:30-6
London N1

020 7359 0081 (M) **tube: Angel**
286 Upper Street (opening times as above)
London N1

DKNY

Welcome to Donna Karan's industrial emporium, where a large collection of clothing, from denim to eveningwear to accessories, is more casual and street-styled than her signature line. Gypsy tops, skirts layered with lace ruffles and low-slung leather belts with a single flower at the hip create a distinctly girlish mood. High-heeled Mary Janes and patchwork coats complete the effect. Men will find plenty of choices, too, though styles tend to be simpler. Featuring an in-store café and a pumped-up sound system, the atmosphere recreates the energy of New York City streets—

fashionable, loud, and splashed with color. www.dkny.com

020 7499 6238 **tube: Green Park**
27 Old Bond Street Mon-Sat 10:30-6:30 (Thurs 10:30-7)
London W1 Sun 12-6

Dockers

Dockers made khakis what they are today, so it's no surprise this store is a temple to dress-down-Friday style. But the label has recently injected a bit more hip into its image with techno-fabrics, snowboard styles and cargo pants aimed at a younger crowd. There's also a selection of outerwear, shirts and underwear. www.dockers-uk.co.uk

020 7240 7908 **tube: Covent Garden**
Unit 8, North Piazza Mon-Wed, Fri 10-7; Thurs, Sat 10-8
London WC2 Sun 11-5

Dolce & Gabbana

A trip to Dolce & Gabbana is a walk on fashion's wild side, where Madonna's favorite designing duo turn out one hot creation after another. The mood at the moment is techno-romance featuring tangerine parkas slung over sexy black corset dresses, necklaces made out of bottle-tops and trousers laden with military-style straps and clips. Bright color combinations—acid yellow, royal blue and emerald—make it all pop. The spacious stores, with velvet thrones and large gilded mirrors, diplay the clothes to dramatic effect. www.dolcegabbanaonline.it

020 7659 9000 **tube: Green Park**
6-8 Old Bond Street Mon-Sat 10-6 (Thurs 10-7)
London W1

020 7201 0980 (W) **tube: Knightsbridge**
175 Sloane Street Mon-Sat 10-6 (Wed 10-7)
London SW1

Dolly Diamond

Vintage here dates from the Victorian period, though Diamond (real name, Pauline) has a particular weakness for the Fifties. Evening dresses are her passion, including Pucci, Chanel and the ever-elusive Dior. There are also plenty of leather jackets and everyday accessories in stock. Stroll to the back for a shoe selection, rare not just in its variety but for its exceptional condition (we found suede Thirties peep-toe pumps that looked like they were made yesterday).

020 7792 2479 **tube: Notting Hill Gate**
51 Pembridge Road Mon-Sat 10:30-6:30, Sun 12-6
London W11

Donna Karan

In sharp contrast to the boisterous DKNY down the street, the Donna Karan store is a modern museum of sophisticated designs. Karan's celebrated structured approach has softened a bit, rendering loose tops (off-the-shoulder, in drapey shapes) and suits that are not quite so power-packed. Black is, as always, this New Yorker's color of choice, though bits of burgundy and navy blue highlight the fall collection. Skirts with girlish details, like asymmetric hemlines and layers of ruffles, add a bit of bohemian flavor. Men garner less floor space here, with a department in the basement that houses Karan's classic suits, pants, knitwear, shirts and ties. www.donnakaran.com

020 7495 3100 **tube: Bond Street/Green Park**
19 New Bond Street Mon-Sat 10-6 (Thurs 10-7)
London W1

Dormeuil

One of the most famous suiting fabric manufacturers in the world has its London headquarters and showroom here, selling mainly to tailors but also to customers whose tailor might not have the exact fabric they require. There is a vast selection of cloths in luxury yarns. www.dormeuil.com

020 7437 1144 **tube: Piccadilly Circus**
35 Sackville Street Mon-Fri 9-5:30
London W1

Dorothy Perkins

This massive, multi-level store is a sometime source for affordable basics (stifle that yawn, please). A large assortment of casual, business and eveningwear is on offer, from cotton tops to faux leather skirts to stretchy Lycra cocktail dresses. Underwear, shoes, petites and plus-sizes are all located upstairs. www.dorothyperkins.co.uk

020 7494 3769 **tube: Oxford Circus**
189 Oxford Street Mon-Fri 10-8 (Thurs 10-9)
London W1 Sat 10-8, Sun 12-6

020 7255 2116 **tube: Tottenham Court Road**
118-132 New Oxford Street Mon-Fri 10-8, Sat 10-7
London WC1 Sun 12-6

020 7495 6181 **tube: Bond Street**
West One Shopping Centre Mon-Fri 10-8 (Thurs 10-9)
379 Oxford Street Sat 10-8:30, Sun 12-6
London W1

020 7931 7605 **tube: Victoria**
Victoria Station Mon-Fri 8-8, Sat 10-7, Sun 11-5
London SW1

020 7405 8309 **tube: Holborn**
8-13 High Holborn Mon-Fri 8-6 (Thurs 8-6:30)
London WC1

020 7512 9707 **tube: Canary Wharf**
24 Canada Place Mon-Fri 8:30-7, Sat 10-6, Sun 11-5
London E14

Douglas Hayward

A quirky, verging on eccentric, bespoke tailor who's a favorite with everyone from actor Sir Michael Caine to photographer Terry O'Neill. The interior looks like a slightly dishevelled sitting-room in an English country house and you may be surprised by the teddy bears in the window until you realise just who these teddy bears are. They are made by Steiff, the famous German company which has been the Rolls-Royce of teddy bears (Teddybären!) for 101 years, and they are dressed by Ralph Lauren (retail price $800), so they are the best-dressed and most collectable teddies in the world. Behind them, Dougie Hayward provides his renowned bespoke service, and also offers a broad selection of colorful shirts, sweaters, ties, beachwear, towels and hats. Shirts have soft collars and sweaters are whimsically colored, so this store is aimed at artists as well as, perhaps more than, tycoons.

020 7499 5574 **tube: Bond Street/Green Park**
95 Mount Street Mon-Fri 9-5:30
London W1

Dr. Marten Department Store

Doc Martens have reigned in London since the days of the Sex Pistols, though their range has expanded well beyond the signature combat boots. Featuring fat rubber soles that make you feel you're walking on air, these highly durable, punk-spirited shoes will put a badass kick in your step. Every variation of color and style, from bright yellow clogs to purple lace-ups, comes with Doc Marten's own brand of cool Britannia. www.drmartens.com

020 7497 1460 **tube: Covent Garden**
1-4 King Street Mon-Sat 10-7 (Thurs 10:30-8)
London WC2 Sun 12-6

Due Passi

Due Passi offers a signature shoe collection that doesn't exactly stand out. Designs tend to be more classic and Italian-influenced, which translates into basic black boots and loafers as well as strappy sandals. Reliable and well priced, but we were a bit underwhelmed. www.duepassi.com

020 7224 1921 **tube: Bond Street**
27 James Street Mon-Sat 10-7 (Thurs 10-8), Sun 12-6
London W1

020 7836 7100 **tube: Covent Garden**
15 The Market Mon-Sat 10-7 (Thurs 10-8), Sun 11-6
London WC2

Duffer of St. George

Famous for its in-your-face casual clothing, Duffer made a quietly confident entrance to Savile Row last year. Such is the popularity of the company's playful, funky range that it now sits proudly amongst the older, more formal establishment in the Row. The super-stylish shop offers own-label and designer off-the-peg suits, coats, casual clothes and accessories, ranging from trendy raincoats (Mackintoshes, of course) and lollipop-bright Etro shirts to limited-edition trainers from Adidas and the latest jeans by hip New York label Rogan. Not many brands could be at home in cool Covent Garden and conservative Savile Row.

020 7734 3666 **tube:Piccadilly Circus/Oxford Circus**
31 Savile Row Mon-Sat 10-6
London W1

020 7379 4660 **tube: Covent Garden**
29 & 34 Shorts Gardens Mon-Fri 10:30-7
London WC2 Sat 10:30-6:30, Sun 1-5

Dune

For those drowning in London's vast sea of shoe stores, Dune offers affordable, stylish, simple leather designs. Whether you're working overtime or carousing in clubs, Dune is likely to have something suitable. Selection ranges from sensible loafers to glittering gold boots.
www.dune.co.uk

020 7491 3626 **tube: Bond Street**
18 South Molton Street Mon-Sat 10-7 (Thurs 10-8)
London W1 Sun 12-6

020 7795 6336 **tube: High Street Kensington**
66 Kensington High Street (opening times as above)
London W8

020 7636 8307 **tube: Oxford Circus/Tottenham Court Road**
The Plaza, 120 Oxford Street (opening times as above)
London W1

020 7824 8440 **tube: Sloane Square**
33b King's Road Mon-Sat 10-6:30 (Wed 10-7)
London SW3 Sun 12-6

Dunhill

Like so many other luxury brands, Dunhill has undergone a makeover in order to attract a younger, wealthy clientele. Gone are the stuffy interiors, now replaced with stylish, moody shopfit and lighting. Dunhill's luxurious menswear is sold alongside accessories and cigars. There's casualwear too, as well as the pricey suits and formal shirts. This is a one-stop shop for the jet set. Almost as an afterthought, they have a sideline in games—backgammon, chess, Monopoly, bridge etc—many of them handmade by master-craftsman Max Parker and as fine as anything in Europe.
www.dunhill.com

020 7355 9500 **tube: Green Park**
21 Old Bond Street Mon-Sat 10-6 (Thurs 10-7)
London W1

020 7290 8600 **tube: Piccadilly Circus/Green Park**
48 Jermyn Street Mon-Fri 9:30-6, Sat 10-6
London SW1

East

A gentle, Asian influence infuses the designs at East, where dresses, loose blouses and comfortable trousers are simply cut so the patterns can shine through. Large flower prints and polka dots in colors from bright pink to green make the selection more loud than understated, while the roomy cuts suit mature shoppers. Accessories are also available.

020 7836 6685 **tube: Covent Garden**
16 The Piazza Mon-Sat 10-7 (Thurs 10-8), Sun 11-5
London WC2

020 7351 5070 **tube: South Kensington**
192 Fulham Road Mon-Sat 10-6, Sun 12-5
London SW10

020 7361 1645 **tube: High Street Kensington**
143 Kensington High Street Mon-Sat 10-7
London W8 (Thurs 10-8), Sun 11-6

020 7376 3161 **tube: Sloane Square**
105 King's Road Mon-Sat 10:30-6:30, Sun 12-6
London SW3

Eda Lingerie

Eda takes matching bras and panties to new heights of feminine fancy with fantastical flourish. Stretch net is embroidered with elaborate designs, most of them floral and all intricately detailed. Though not prohibitively priced, the selection seems too special for everyday; there's a separate collection for brides. www.eda-lingerie.com

020 7584 0435 **tube: Sloane Square**
132 King's Road Mon-Sat 10-6:30
London SW3 (Wed 10-7), Sun 12-6

020 7355 1372 **tube: Bond Street**
49 South Molton Street Mon-Sat 10-6:30
London W1 (Thurs 10-7)

020 7361 0077 **tube: High Street Kensington**
173 Kensington High Street Mon-Sat 10-6:30
London W8 (Thurs 10-7), Sun 12-5

Ede & Ravenscroft

London's oldest gentleman's outfitters have been in business since 1689 and have made the coronation robes for the last 11 British monarchs. This store is worth a visit just for its exquisite English country house interior, complete with chandeliers. E&R sell the complete gentleman's wardrobe, off-the-peg and made-to-measure, plus shoes, hats, cufflinks and evening dress.

www.edeandravenscroft.co.uk

020 7734 5450 **tube: Piccadilly Circus**
8 Burlington Gardens Mon-Fri 9-6, Sat 10-6
London W1

020 7405 3906 **tube: Chancery Lane**
93 Chancery Lane Mon-Fri 9-6, Sat 10-3
London WC2

Edward Green

There are plenty of shoe stores in the Burlington Arcade, but those who appreciate real quality and English style head straight for Edward Green. The styles are traditional, and the quality and finish are a byword for excellence amongst the global brotherhood of shoe fanatics. Ready-to-wear gentleman's shoes start at £410 (but they'll still be 60-70% handmade). There is also a fantastic repair service and they will make to order in a style and leather of your choice. www.edwardgreen.com

020 7499 6377 **tube: Green Park**
12-13 Burlington Arcade Mon-Sat 9-5:30
London W1

e.g. Butterfly

If you love all things girly and dainty your heart will go pitter-patter here. Decorated in pale blue, the small shop is laid out like a cluttered boudoir, with one-off skirts spread on a day-bed, tops on hangers dangling from the ceiling, and vintage pieces scattered about. Intricate corset-shirts, beaded bikinis and boxed sets of unmentionables etched with "sinful" will appeal to your naughty side. Embroidered piano shawls make elegant evening cover-ups, while low-slung belts and floral hair accessories chase the trends. A treat for Fulham ladies who no longer have to trek to The Cross.

020 7371 9291 **tube: Parsons Green**
70 New King's Road Mon-Sat 10-6
London SW6

☆ Egg

Tucked away in a whitewashed residential mews in Knightsbridge, Egg orbits in its own soothing universe. Maureen Doherty's fans, who include Donna Karan and Issey Miyake, scour the store for raw, handwoven cotton and silk separates, knitwear by Eskandar, indigo-blue Chinese working clothes, simple plimsolls and panama hats. There are also regular exhibitions of ceramics and photography. Doherty has recently taken her vision into menswear with the opening of a men's store across the street.

020 7235 9315 **tube: Hyde Park Corner/Knightsbridge**
36 & 37 Kinnerton Street Tues-Sat 10-6
London SW1

Egoshego

From trainers by Gola to New Rock platform boots with spring coils in the soles, the selection at Egoshego features an eclectic blend of shoes. The large variety at this cheerful shop also includes brown suede boots, sneakers, and wedges with plastic heels. Other brands include Custom, The Art, un matin d'été and Diesel.
www.egoshegoshoes.com

020 7836 9260 **tube: Covent Garden**
76 Neal Street Mon-Sat 10:30-7 (Thurs 10:30-8)
London WC2 Sun 12-6

Elégance

The name may be naff, but the store is a real asset to shoppers of a certain age who appreciate styles like the double-breasted, piqué coat-dress, durable sweet-pastel suits or blouses and pants in shades of purple, yellow and blue.

020 7409 7210 **tube: Green Park**
14a Grafton Street Mon-Fri 9:30-6
London W1 (Thurs 10-7), Sat 10-6

Eliot Zed

Like it or not, fashion is still seduced by the stiletto, which means chic, flat-heeled shoes are not that easy to come by. Enter Eliot Zed, where the soft leather footwear collection proves that comfort and style don't always contradict each other. If you're after something a bit naughtier, there are higher heels by Arkte, including strappy sandals with a cork wedge and black kitten heels with white stitching and a bow at the toe. Men have their own signature collection, as well as leather loafers and sandals from Hardridge.

020 7589 2155 **tube: South Kensington**
117-119 Walton Street Mon-Sat 10-6 (Wed 10-7)
London SW3 some Sundays 2-5 (call to check)

020 7355 1504 **tube: Bond Street**
4 Avery Row Mon-Sat 10-6
London W1

Ellis Brigham

Whether you're headed to the peaks of Snowdonia or the valleys of the Alps, this is the place to rent or buy equipment for every type of outdoor pursuit. There's also a superior selection of outerwear and footwear brands: Patagonia, The North Face, Columbia, Lowe Alpine, Berghaus and Eider. www.ellis-brigham.com

020 7395 1010 **tube: Covent Garden**
3-11 Southampton Street Mon-Fri 10-7 (Thurs 10-7:30)
London WC2 Sat 9:30-6:30, Sun 11:30-5:30

020 7937 6889 **tube: High Street Kensington**
178 Kensington High Street Mon-Fri 10-7 (Thurs 10-8)
London W8 Sat 9:30-6:30, Sun 11-5

Elspeth Gibson

London's lunching ladies give this tiny boutique the thumbs up. British designer Elspeth Gibson is a favorite with It-girls and Voguettes, who go especially for her critically acclaimed party dresses. It's all fresh, frilly and free-spirited, with a bit of the 19th century thrown in: a lace blouse with eyelets and three-quarter length ruffled sleeves, a scallop-edged layered skirt, a canvas tailored jacket with puffed sleeves. Too bad she's switched to an appointment-only system—mere mortals like us can't simply stoll in. www.fashionatelspethgibson.com

020 235 0601 **tube: Knightsbridge**
7 Pont Street (by appointment)
London SW1

Emanuel Ungaro

This French designer known for colorful prints is making a comeback with his fanciful tailored basics for the jet set. Couture eveningwear is the specialty of the house but there's plenty of everyday fare, from faultless black and brown wool suits to beaded skirts and ruffled blouses. Summer brings an extra dose of feminine flourish, with silk shirts that look like they've been covered in rose petals and slip dresses that couldn't be prettier.

www.emanuelungaro.com

020 7629 0550
150-151 New Bond Street
London W1

tube: Bond Street
Mon-Sat 10-6 (Thurs 10-7)

Ember

More vintage-in-training than the real thing, this is a good spot for students going through their grungy retro phase. The ample selection of Sandra Dee-style Fifties dresses is priced from £10, while the so-lame-they're-cool Hawaiian shirts start even lower. There are also colorful knit purses and T-shirts sprinkled with butterflies and stars. Certainly fun, but not for the experienced aficionado.

(no phone)
206 Portobello Road
London W11

tube: Ladbroke Grove
Daily 12-6

☆ Emma Hope

Her shoes are revered for their beautiful shape and decorative detail. Flats, mules, boots and slingbacks are at once sophisticated and girlish, almost faultless in their design and still colorful enough to seem quintessentially English (visiting Americans often stock up before heading home). Regal deep purples and dark reds are mixed with limey greens and bright yellows. Style-wise, there are extremes—pastel patent slides or gold kitten heels—but most rest pleasingly in the quirky middle. www.emmahope.co.uk

020 7259 9566
53 Sloane Square
London SW1

tube: Sloane Square
Mon-Sat 10-6 (Wed 10-7)

020 7313 7493
207 Westbourne Grove
London W11

tube: Notting Hill Gate
Mon-Sat 10-6 (Thurs 10-7)

020 7833 2367
33 Amwell Street
London EC1

tube: Angel
(opening times as above)

Emma Somerset

Specializing in French luxury clothing, Emma Somerset is a great place if you're looking for a classic dress or suit. Don't be shy about having to ring the bell to gain entrance. Once inside, you'll find a selection with maximum appeal and the bare minimum of embellishment (a subtle stripe or frilled skirt hem). It's a sophisticated look that never risks much and, consequently, rarely looks out of place. www.emmasomerset.co.uk

020 7235 6977 **tube: Knightsbridge/Hyde Park Corner**
69 Knightsbridge Mon-Sat 9:30-6 (Wed 9:30-7)
London SW1

Emma Willis

Bespoke and ready-to-wear men's and women's clothing with an emphasis on special occasions and luxury fabrics: silk, organza and voile for women; Swiss cotton, linen and silk for men. The store adds a feminine, crafty vibe to the otherwise rather masculine ethos of Jermyn Street, with stone floors and lots of lace trimmings. But there is no token feminism here: the grandest of the street's male shirtmakers would admire the quality and craft that permeate Emma Willis. Ideal for fancy weddings in the English countryside.

020 7930 9980 **tube: Piccadilly Circus/Green Park**
66 Jermyn Street Mon-Sat 10-6
London SW1

Emmett Shirts

They fancy themselves something of a cult label among City chaps but this British shirtmaker has a knack for the natty button-down. Their fine fabrics range from poplin to royal twill, and some styles feature contrasting patterns beneath the collars and cuffs to add a bit of personality—even if nobody else can see it. Colors include solid yellow, purple or orange check, with bright ties and cufflinks to match. Thomas Pink, watch your back. www.emmettshirts.com

020 7351 7529 **tube: Sloane Square**
380 King's Road Mon-Sat 10-6:30, Sun 12-5:30
London SW3

020 7247 1563 **tube: Liverpool Street/Moorgate**
4 Eldon Street Mon-Fri 10-6
London EC2

Emporio Armani

The legendary designer's lowest-priced collection makes a stronger color statement than his muted main line. The patterns are all over the map, from polka dots to stripes to flowers. There are ruffled sleeves, sequined jackets, and more standard casual fare for women and men. His jeans are some of the best around in terms of fit and quality. www.emporioarmani.com

020 7491 8080 **tube: Bond Street**
51 New Bond Street Mon-Fri 10-6 (Thurs 10-7)
London W1 Sat 10-6:30, Sun 12-6

020 7823 8818 **tube: Knightsbridge**
191 Brompton Road Mon-Fri 10-6 (Wed 10-7)
London SW3 Sat 10-6:30, Sun 12-6

Episode

Nothing really caught our attention among the racks of colorful suits and separates here—which is not to say that

Episode doesn't serve a useful purpose. There are plenty of variations on the office two-piece, from blue pinstripe to silver, while black ruffled bias-cuts skirts and red leather jackets are a bit more unbuttoned. Easy accessories (with multiple takes on the basic black pump) mix seamlessly with the straight-shooting collection. www.episodegb.com

020 7628 8691 **tube: Liverpool Street**
135 Bishopsgate Mon-Fri 10-6:30
London EC2

020 7355 1410 **tube: Bond Street/Green Park**
69 New Bond Street Mon-Sat 10-6:30 (Thurs 10-7:30)
London W1

☆ Ermenegildo Zegna

Arguably the finest Italian cloth and suit manufacturer takes on traditional English outfitters on their own patch. With over 900 different blends, Zegna's cloth is much finer and softer than English suits generally are. Lightweight wool, linen, mohair, cashmere and silk are used to great effect, and Zegna also has a sports line using the latest fabric technology for weekending thirtysomethings. Luxury menswear doesn't get better than this. Even better news: the new womeswear line Agnonia is now available at Harrods. www.zegnaermenegildo.com

020 7518 2700 **tube: Bond Street/Oxford Circus**
37-38 New Bond Street Mon-Sat 10-6 (Thurs 10-7)
London W1

020 7929 1456 **tube: Bank**
12-13 The Courtyard Mon-Fri 10-6
Royal Exchange
London EC3

Escada

Every Oscar night brings this label back to the fashion headlines when hoards of Escada-clad starlets glide up the red carpet to the flash of a billion bulbs. If you fancy your own paparazzi moment, this is the place to stop for luxurious eveningwear that's a touch naughtier than the basic ballgown. A less formal selection offers suits, dresses, shirts, skirts and pants, as well as denim and soft knitwear from Escada Sport. www.escada.com

020 7629 0934 **tube: Bond Street**
66-67 New Bond Street Mon-Sat 9:30-6:30
London W1 (Thurs 9:30-7)

020 7245 9800 **tube: Knightsbridge**
194-195 Sloane Street Mon-Sat 10-6 (Wed 10-7)
London SW1

Escapade

Given the French predilection for sophisticated style, you might expect this dressy daywear to sparkle a bit more brightly than it does. For the prices, the fabrics (from wrinkled silk blouses to tight shiny pants) don't quite make the

mark. The prime location, amidst some of London's best boutiques in London, makes it even more of a letdown.

020 7376 5767 **tube: Sloane Square**
141 King's Road Mon-Sat 10-7, Sun 12-6
London SW3

Eskandar

The loose shaped clothing is reminiscent of the traditional dress in Eskandar's homeland of Iran, although the designer is also influenced by his travels in China, Japan, India and France. Lovely soft fabrics, mostly linen and cotton, combine with gentle colors like beige, cream and dove blue, in a collection that is comfortable, bohemian and refreshingly non-designer. There are no logos, no metal fixings, no trendy spins. The overall look harks back to simple peasant dress, with boxy baggy sweaters, round-neck linen tops and gathered floor-length skirts. A gorgeous selection of homewares includes antique monogrammed sheets, red striped linen tea towels, old wine goblets and lots of heavy white china.

020 7351 7333 **tube: Fulham Broadway**
134 Lots Road Mon-Fri 10-6, Sat 10:30-5:30
London SW6

Esprit

Last time we heard of Esprit, it was 1986 and their candy-colored clothing was coveted by girls all over suburban America. Fast-forward to the late Nineties, when the ailing German label found new ownership and set out to resuscitate itself. If the Regent Street flagship is anything to go by, the brand is on the upswing. The space houses everything imaginable—trendy street clothes for boys and girls, smart suits for women, activewear for men, loads of accessories and even a toy collection. Well worth a look if you've been wondering where this label has been since Ronnie Reagan was President.

020 7025 7700 **tube: Oxford Circus**
178-182 Regent Street Mon-Sat 10-7 (Thurs 10-8)
London W1 Sun 12-6

Essence

The flavor at Essence is continental and girlish, with Italian, Danish and French designers you've probably never heard of—An-je, Dalhov, Homeless—but will be happy to find. Frilly slip dresses, sheer blouses and bias-cut skirts are vibrantly splashed with sequins, beads or florals. Plain pastel T-shirts and cute woven handbags make the perfect quiet accompaniments. Another independent boutique on the western end of the King's Road, this could be your next stop after MiMi.

020 7349 9988 **tube: Sloane Square**
317 King's Road Mon-Sat 10:30-6:30
London SW3 (Wed-Thurs 10:30-7), Sun 1-6

Etro

A label with a dedicated following for its strong colors, striking patterns and innovative fabrics, Etro is bursting with Italian flair. Women will find bold blouses, wide-legged pants and flouncy dresses; for men there are loud suits and a colorful assortment of ties and shirts. With its combination of eccentric design and beautiful craftsmanship, Etro is a perfect choice for the confident dresser who craves a designer dash of flash.

020 7495 5767 — **tube: Green Park**
14 Old Bond Street — Mon-Sat 10-6
London W1

Euforia

After eight successful years in one Notting Hill location, Annette Olivieri has opened her equally quirky second shop. Her creative collection incorporates kitsch and retro influences: a tapestry bag printed with the slogan "Happiness is Easy", Eighties-style denim hotpants with a rainbow waistband and a white tux shirt with an American flag rendered in ruffles. You'll also find the latest international fashion magazines, as well as a selection of art books.

020 8968 1903 — **tube: Ladbroke Grove**
7 Portobello Green Arcade — Mon-Sat 10:30-6
London W10

020 7243 1808 — **tube: Ladbroke Grove**
61b Lancaster Road — Mon Sat 10:30-6:30
London W11

Expensive!

The explanation mark after the name gives away the joke. This Italian chain is far from expensive, which must be a relief next to the designer labels in Milan but doesn't have the same force in London where cheap fashion is easy to come by. Styles are more eurotrash than streetwise, with string vest tops, silver trainers, chain belts weighed down with metal charms and figure-hugging faded flare jeans. We reckon you would be better off at Zara, Top Shop or Mango.

020 7434 9679 — **Tube: Oxford Circus**
154 Regent Street — Mon-Sat 10-8, Sun 12-6
London W1

020 7851 2747 — **Tube: Oxford Circus**
221-223 Oxford Street — Mon-Sat 10-8 (Thurs 10-9)
London W1 — Sun 12-6

F.Pinet

This old-fashioned shoe store, with its gilded mirrors and velvet chairs, offers genteel service of a sort associated with Bond Street's early days. But the selection itself is surprisingly modern, offering Stuart Weitzman slingbacks, shoes by Zonetti, and a chic children's section with Italian fashion brands Moschino and D&G. The generous men's selection includes such labels as Mauri and Moreschi, with some exotic styles in crocodile, ostrich and snake skins. Pinet's own brand is also here, of course.

020 7629 2174 **tube: Bond Street**
47-48 New Bond Street Mon-Fri 10-6:30 (Thurs 10-7)
London W1 Sat 10:30-6:30

Fabri

Another Italian invader, Fabri sells Italian suits and sportswear amidst the more traditional British names dominating Jermyn Street and its tributary arcades. Smart casual pants and jackets and patterned knitwear are aimed at a 35-plus business clientele looking for a more relaxed option than the stiff collars on the rest of the street. Marble floors and mirrors lend an early Eighties vibe.

020 7839 1155 **tube: Piccadilly Circus/Green Park**
75 Jermyn Street Mon-Sat 10-6
London SW1

Faith

Maintaining its emphasis on affordability and style, Faith recreates the latest trends in footwear from the chunkiest soles to the highest heels. An offbeat selection, displayed on two separate floors, is a breeze to browse—so long as you don't mind the masses of purposeful teens and twentysomethings. Earning the devotion of its young fashion-minded followers, Faith offers a student discount to all those with applicable ID. www.faith.co.uk

020 7580 9561 **tube: Oxford Circus**
192-194 Oxford Street Mon-Sat 10-7
London W1 (Thurs 10-8), Sun 12-6

Fallan & Harvey

(see under Crichton/Fallan & Harvey)

Fat Face

Less offbeat than the name might suggest, this store features a wide J. Crewish selection of men's and women's casualwear inspired by the surf- and snowboarding aesthetic. The polo shirts, fleece jackets, pants and dresses rate high in comfort but ho-hum in style sense. Colors remain solid and simple, so mixing separates is a cinch. www.fatface.com

020 7497 6464 **tube: Covent Garden**
13 Thomas Neals Centre Mon-Sat 10-7, Sun 12-6
London WC2

020 7384 3115 **tube: Parsons Green**
827 Fulham Road Mon-Sat 9:30-7, Sun 11-5
London SW6

Favourbrook

Think Hugh Grant and the various English girls in *Four Weddings and a Funeral* and you'll know Favourbrook's

forte. Velvet cutaways and brocade vests are such specialties that the vests have their own dedicated shop at 19 Piccadilly Arcade, opposite the women's store. There are smoking jackets and cavalry twill pants for men, beaded blouses and side-fastening, embroidered dresses for women. All is opulent, if slightly fussy, at Favourbrook. www.favourbrook.com

020 7493 5060 **tube: Piccadilly Circus/Green Park**
55 Jermyn Street (M) Mon-Wed 9:30-6:30
London SW1 Thurs-Fri 9:30-7, Sat 10-6

020 7491 2331 **tube: Piccadilly Circus/Green Park**
18 Piccadilly Arcade (W) (opening times as above)
London W1

020 7259 5966 **tube: Knightsbridge/Sloane Square**
11 Pont Street Mon-Sat 10-6
London SW1

Feathers

Culling from the collections of various high-end designers, Feathers offers nothing but the finest—and a sales staff that won't let you forget it. Trendy, chic and sophisticated, the colorful (and bountiful) stock of labels includes Roberto Cavalli, Emilio Pucci, Jean Paul Gaultier and Blumarine jeans.

020 7243 8800 **tube: Notting Hill Gate**
176 Westbourne Grove Mon-Sat 10-6
London W11

☆ Fenwick

A favorite with fashionistas and the only department store on Bond Street, Fenwick provides a varied selection that's fun enough for twentysomethings but still stocked with plenty of classics. Take your time on the ground floor as there is much to savor: lingerie, top name cosmetics, hats, hairclips, jewelry (large stone bracelets to floral pins) and bags—Orla Kiely, Osprey, Furla and Coccinelle. Stop for a quick manicure at Nails Inc before heading upstairs. Be on the lookout for new designing talents because Fenwick is particularly good at importing hot names you won't find anywhere else: Wayne Cooper, Anna Sui, Calypso and Alannah Hill. When it comes to the classics, there's Nicole Farhi, Paul Smith, Armani Collezioni, Betsey Johnson and Kenzo, among others. If you need to refuel, head to Joe's café or ride all the way down to the bottom level for a bowl of pasta at Carluccio's. www.fenwick.co.uk

020 7629 9161 **tube: Bond Street**
63 New Bond Street Mon-Sat 10-6:30 (Thurs 10-8)
London W1

Field & Trek

This specialist in outdoor wear and equipment offers high-performance clothing that is equally suitable for the street.

The activewear comes from such top brands as The North Face, Columbia, Lowe Alpine and Patagonia, as well as the store's own label. Selection includes base clothing, polar fleece, waterproof outerwear and footwear, plus maps and navigation equipment. www.fieldandtrek.com

020 7379 3793 **tube: Covent Garden**
42 Maiden Lane Mon-Fri 10-7 (Wed-Thurs 10-8)
London WC2 Sat 9:30-7, Sun 11-5

Fly

The truly heavy (read, cool) come here for urbanwear with garage-music undertones and a skateboarding spin. Hone your street cred on brands like Duffer, Stüssy, Hysteric Glamour, Silas, Nike Probe, Paul Smith Jeans and Gimme Five. Limited edition Maharishi pants painted by graffiti artists Futura and Sharp are badass (translation: precious as gold dust to those in the know).

020 7376 7606 **tube: Sloane Square**
352 King's Road Mon-Sat 10:30-6:30
London SW3 Sun 12:30-5:30

Fogal

The future of the stock market may be uncertain but stockings have never been hotter. On high-designer Sloane Street you'll find the perfect pair to match any color you want, even that particular shade of Prada plum. Socks, bodies and bustiers are also available. After 15 years in the market, these folks really have a leg up. www.fogal.com

020 7235 3115 **tube: Knightsbridge**
3a Sloane Street Mon-Sat 10-6:30
London SW1 (Wed 10-7:30), Sun 12-5

Foot Locker

This most dependable of American sports chains offers a huge variety of athletic clothing, sneakers and accessories. On a weekend afternoon you could wait hours for a salesman to find your size. But the range of choice—every conceivable shoe from Nike, Fila, Adidas, Reebok and New Balance—might make the wait worth while. Bona fide athletes, don't expect knowledgeable sales staff...they're more accustomed to teen patrons looking for the coolest new shoe. www.footlocker.com

020 7491 4030 **tube: Oxford Circus**
363-367 Oxford Street Mon-Wed, Sat 10-7, Thurs-Fri 10-8
London W1 Sun 12-6

020 7379 9398 **tube: Covent Garden**
30-32 Neal Street Mon-Sat 10-7 (Thurs 10-8)
London WC2 Sun 12-6

Formes

Formes is the freshest of the major maternity chains, but the staid selection is more mumsy than yummy-mummy. Designer David Boudon's "Collection Femme Enceinte" features sleeveless tunics, turtlenecks, sweaters, jeans and long skirts, all in the requisite roomy cuts and deliberately cheery colors. The search is never-ending for maternity wear that's truly cool, but in the meantime you might find some suitable bits here. www.formes.com

020 7493 2783 **tube: Bond Street**
33 Brook Street Mon-Wed 10-6, Thurs 10-7
London W1 Fri-Sat 10-6:30

Fortnum & Mason

They're famous for their fine foods, and many visitors may not know that there's clothing here at all. It's easy to be side-tracked by the handmade chocolates, English cheeses, real pumpkin pies for Thanksgiving and foie gras. But climb the plush red-carpeted stairs to the clothing floors and you'll find faultless traditional labels like MaxMara, Betty Jackson and Zegna. It's by no means young and hip, but a perfect place for a taste of the good life. Watch the business pages, though: the billionaire Weston family (who own F&M) are bidding for another of London's favourite up-market department stores, Selfridges. www.fortnumandmason.co.uk

020 7734 8040 **tube: Piccadilly Circus/Green Park**
181 Piccadilly Mon-Sat 10-6:30, Sun 12-6
London W1

Foster & Son

Leather goods specialist selling bespoke and ready-to-wear shoes, boots and luggage for considerable sums. You select in a peaceful, very traditional atmosphere, all leather armchairs and wooden floors, with the goods displayed in glass cabinets. Specialists in riding boots.

020 7930 5385 **tube: Piccadilly Circus/Green Park**
83 Jermyn Street Mon-Fri 10-5:45, Sat 10-3:45
London SW1

Fratelli Rossetti

With a tradition of fine craftsmanship dating back to the Fifties, Fratelli Rossetti is the granddaddy of the brown loafer. The London headquarters are comfortable and refined, with a wide selection that features soft, leather slip-ons and lace-ups for women and men. The store also carries shoes from the casual line Flexa and an assortment of leather accessories. www.rosetti.it

020 7491 7066 **tube: Green Park**
177 New Bond Street Mon-Sat 10-6 (Thurs 10-6:30)
London W1

020 7259 6397 **tube: Knightsbridge**
196 Sloane Street Mon-Sat 10-6 (Wed 10-6:30)
London SW1

Fred Perry

Known for dressing well (and playing even better) on the tennis court, Perry packaged his own brand for the masses

when he became the last Englishman to win the men's singles at Wimbledon in the Thirties. Though he started modestly with polo shirts, today's collection includes retro and contemporary styles of street and sportswear. The polo shirts (now in a multitude of colors) are still the champions of the collection. www.fredperry.com

020 7836 3327 **tube: Covent Garden**
14 The Piazza Mon-Sat 10-7, Sun 11-5
London WC2

French Connection

Catapulted to fashion fame with a cheeky ad campaign and a knack for the trends, French Connection is a star of the British high street. With a 14,000 square foot flagship store at the heart of Oxford Circus, the chain covers all the basics: frilly skirts, button-down blouses, cashmere sweaters, T-shirts, tailored pants and all things denim. Prices are generally above average, but so are the quality and the style. www.frenchconnection.com

020 7493 3124 **tube: Oxford Circus**
249 Regent Street Mon-Sat 10-7 (Thurs 10-8)
London W1 Sun 12-6

020 7589 5560 **tube: Knightsbridge**
44 Brompton Road Mon-Sat 10-7
London SW3 (Thurs 10-8), Sun 12-6

020 7379 6560 **tube: Covent Garden**
99-103 Long Acre Mon-Sat 10-7 (Thurs 10-8)
London WC2 Sun 12-6

020 7629 7766 **tube: Bond Street**
396 Oxford Street Mon-Fri 10-8 (Thurs 10-9)
London W1 Sat 10-7, Sun 12-6

020 7836 0522 **tube: Covent Garden**
11 James Street Mon-Sat 10-7 (Thurs 11-8)
London WC2 Sun 10:30-7

020 7225 3302 **tube: Sloane Square**
140-144 King's Road Mon-Sat 10-7
London SW3 Sun 12-6

020 7937 4665 **tube: High Street Kensington**
168-170 Kensington High Street Mon-Sat 10-7, Sun 12-6
London W8

020 7287 2046 **tube: Oxford Circus**
10 Argyll Street Mon-Sat 10-6:30
London W1 (Thurs 10-8, Fri 10-7)

020 7794 1115 **tube: Hampstead**
29 Hampstead High Street Mon-Sat 10-6, Sun 12-6
London NW3

020 7512 9110 **tube: Canary Wharf**
18 Canada Place Mon-Fri 9-7, Sat 10-6
London E14

French For Less

The name screams naff continental fashion, but it's not as bad as all that. For those who appreciate classic French

designs at decent prices, this might be worth a visit as new styles arrive regularly from Paris. Wool suits, silk shirts and sparkly eveningwear are available, as are scarves, handbags and a surprisingly cool selection of belts. The labels include Terry, Surabaya, Serena Kay and Cara Lotti. www.frenchforless.com

020 7629 9617 **tube: Bond Street**
8 South Molton Street Daily 10-6 (Thurs 10-7)
London W1

French Sole

This shoe store dances to one particular beat, the ballet pump. There are hundreds of them, in snakeskin, gingham and beaded styles, or just basic solid colors. They're more for pirouetting through Harvey Nick's than the Royal Opera House, but Sloaney ladies love them and they're certainly a lot more comfortable than third position.
www.frenchsole.com

020 7730 3771 **tube: Sloane Square**
6 Ellis Street Mon-Sat 10-6
London SW1

Furla

They opened a huge flagship store on Bond Street last year and we're worried—now everyone will know how truly special these handbags are. In classic shapes and lovely, supple leather they're the epitome of Italian style. Colors range from essential black and brown to indulgent tangerine and lemon sorbet, and drawers filled with matching wallets and fine watches will make you feel like you're shopping in a dream closet. www.furla.com

020 7629 9827 **tube: Green Park/Bond Street**
31 New Bond Street Mon-Sat 10-6 (Thurs 10-7)
London W1

020 7823 5110 **tube: Sloane Square**
17 King's Road Mon-Sat 10-6:30
London SW3 (Wed 10-7), Sun 12-5

Galerie Gaultier

It's all fast-forward fashion at Jean Paul Gaultier's London shop, where media, culture and street style collide. Shirts that look like they've been slashed with a knife might startle the traditionalist, but don't be scared off: Gaultier also has a classic side, expressed in the sharply tailored suits and sexy short dresses that pop up season after season. Still, it's his outlandish sensibility—who else has spun spider-web print pants?—that keeps his devotees coming back for more.

020 7584 4648 **tube: South Kensington**
171-175 Draycott Avenue Mon-Sat 10-6 (Wed 10-7)
London SW3

Gamba

If your feet were made for dancing, look no further. In the heart of London's theatre district Gamba is a small shop stocked with everything you could need to pirouette, tango or tap. Clothing starts at age four with adorable mini pink ballet pumps and white tulle tutus. For adults there are leotards, Lycra T-shirts, leggings and all sorts of different dance shoes. Whether you're a professional or a happy amateur, this is an essential stop for anyone seeking a dance wardrobe.

020 7437 0704 — **tube: Leicester Square**
3 Garrick Street — Mon-Sat 10:30-6
London WC2

Gant USA

Linen blazers and drawstring chinos are standard fare at Gant, a store that offers several different spins on classic American style. Gant Madison attracts the 30-plus demographic with V-neck sweaters and tailored pants, while Gant Ivy League aims for the younger preppy crowd with piqué and oxford cloth shirts. While the new flagship store may be bigger and brighter, the clothing is comfortable, practical and as timeless as *Love Story*. www.gant.com

020 7584 8077 — **tube: Knightsbridge**
47-49 Brompton Road — Mon-Sat 10-6:30 (Wed 10-7)
London SW3 — Sun 12-5

Gap

No surprises here...Gap has been providing the same flavor of casualwear for 30 years. There's still no better place to grab wardrobe basics like jeans, khakis and cotton tops. You'll also find a small selection of office-friendly fare: brightly colored sweater sets, leather skirts and black tailored pants are perennial pieces. With a men's selection as varied as the women's, Gap is a consistent, dependable source of comfortable clothing. But beware, prices are about 30% higher here than in the US. Of course, there's always a sales rack, so search it out. www.gap.com

020 7287 3851 — **tube: Oxford Circus**
146 Regent Street — Mon-Sat 10-7
London W1 — (Thurs 10-8), Sun 12-6

020 7323 1152 — **tube: Oxford Circus**
118 Oxford Street — (opening times as above)
London W1

020 7355 1255 — **tube: Marble Arch**
473 Oxford Street — (opening times as above)
London W1

020 7225 1112 — **tube: Knightsbridge**
145-149 Brompton Road — Mon-Tues 9:30-7
London SW3 — Wed-Sat 9:30-8, Sun 12-6

020 7437 0138 — **tube: Piccadilly Circus**
1-7 Shaftesbury Avenue — Mon-Sat 10-8
London W1 — Sun 12-6

020 7734 3312 **tube: Oxford Circus**
223-235 Oxford Street Mon-Fri 10-8, Sat 10-7
London W1 Sun 12-6

020 7836 8148 **tube: Covent Garden**
2-3 James Street Mon-Sat 10-7 (Thurs 10-8), Sun 10-6
London WC2

020 7379 0779 **tube: Covent Garden**
30-31 Long Acre Mon-Sat 10-7 (Thurs 10-9), Sun 12-6
London WC2

020 7493 3316 **tube: Oxford Circus/Bond Street**
315 Oxford Street Mon-Sat 10-7:30 (Thurs 10-8)
London W1 Sun 12-6

020 7408 4500 **tube: Bond Street**
376-384 Oxford Street Mon-Sat 9:30-8 (Fri 9:30-9)
London W1 Sun 11:30-6:30

020 7823 7272 **tube: Sloane Square**
122 King's Road Mon-Sat 9:30-7, Sun 12-6
London SW3

020 7486 9199 **tube: Baker Street/Bond Street**
93-94 Marylebone High Street Mon-Sat 10-6
London W1 (Thurs 10-7), Sun 12-6

020 7489 0214 **tube: Bank**
1 Poultry Mon-Fri 8:30-7
London EC2

020 7221 5828 **tube: Notting Hill Gate**
132-136 Notting Hill Gate Mon-Sat 10-7
London W11 Sun 12-6

Gap Kids (& Baby Gap)

Everything we love about Gap, but shrunk for children and in bright colors and fabrics that will last forever. The baby clothing is also just as it should be—durable, cheap and cute, but never nauseatingly so. From outdoor weekend wear to back-to-school basics, Gap Kids has it all for your junior hipsters and babies-about-town. www.gapkids.com

020 7287 5095 **tube: Oxford Circus**
208 Regent Street Mon-Sat 10-7 (Thurs 10-8)
London W1 Sun 11-5

020 7836 0646 **tube: Covent Garden**
121-123 Long Acre Mon-Sat 10-7 (Thurs 10-8)
London WC2 Sun 12-6

020 7355 1255 **tube: Marble Arch**
473 Oxford Street (opening times as above)
London W1

020 7513 0241 **tube: Canary Wharf**
330-340 Cabot Place East Mon-Fri 9-7, Sat 10-6
London E14 Sun 11-5

020 7437 0138 **tube: Piccadilly Circus**
1-7 Shaftesbury Avenue Mon-Sat 10-8, Sun 12-6
London W1

Directory

020 7493 3316 **tube: Oxford Circus/Bond Street**
315 Oxford Street Mon-Sat 10-7:30 (Thurs 10-8)
London W1 Sun 12-6

020 7368 2900 **tube: High Street Kensington**
99-101 Kensington High Street Mon-Wed 9:30-7
London W8 Thurs-Sat 9:30-8, Sun 12-6

020 7313 9693 **tube: Queensway/Bayswater**
Whiteley's, Queensway Mon-Sat 10-8, Sun 12-6
London W2

020 7586 6123 **tube: St. John's Wood**
47-49 St. John's Wood High Street Mon-Sat 9:30-6
London NW8 Sun 11-5

020 7408 4500 **tube: Bond Street**
376-384 Oxford Street Mon-Sat 9:30-8 (Fri 9:30-9)
London W1 Sun 12-6

020 7225 1112 **tube: Knightsbridge**
147-149 Brompton Road Mon-Tues 9:30-7
London SW3 Wed-Sat 9:30-8, Sun 12-6

020 7823 7272 **tube: Sloane Square**
122 King's Road Mon-Sat 9:30-7, Sun 12-6
London SW3

Gary Anderson

This spacious, modern store specializes in the sale and hire of formal menswear, especially for weddings, in both traditional and contemporary styles. This means that classic cuts mingle with colorful, funky vests and all sorts of cravats and ties. They offer a full bespoke service, with fittings generally by appointment. www.garyanderson.co.uk

020 7287 6662 **tube: Piccadilly Circus/Oxford Circus**
34-35 Savile Row Mon-Sat 10-6
London W1

020 7224 2241 **tube: Baker Street**
36 Chiltern Street Mon-Sat 10-5:30
London W1

Georgina Goodman

As you would expect of a former pupil of Manolo Blahnik, Georgina Goodman is turning out some of the most original designs this town has seen in ages. Joining the ranks of other lady bespoke shoe designers (Jane Brown and Olivia Morris), Goodman's craftsmanship and creativity do not disappoint. Each couture shoe is made from a single piece of vegetable-dyed, hand-painted leather and heels are carved from natural woods. Organic and sculptural, she has slip-ons with the toe cut out, pretty wedge sandals with long woven ankle straps and a small selection of inspiring belts and bags. The part retro, part whacky look will appeal to young boho fashionistas.

020 7499 8599 **tube: Green Park**
12-14 Shepherd Street Mon-Fri 10-6
London W1 Sat by appointment

Georgina von Etzdorf

It's all about print and fabric at this store. Von Etzdorf's popular hand-printed silk scarves truly are works of art (and priced accordingly, at up to £200 and more a piece) and her clothing expresses an equally powerful design sensibility. Many of this English designer's dark-toned designs (in brooding shades of aubergine, black and brown) are splashed, Jackson Pollock style, with streaks of fuchsia or gold. The results are more dramatic than cutting-edge.

020 7409 7789 — **tube: Green Park**
1-2 Burlington Arcade — Mon-Sat 10-6
London W1

Gérard Darel

This French bridge line offers simple, chic businesswear with feminine detail. There are T-shirts edged in ruffles, floral chiffon skirts and silky knits, but the suits and businesswear in subdued colors remain the focus of the line. A classically smart label that the French have grown to depend on.

020 7495 2688 — **tube: Green Park**
31 Old Bond Street — Mon-Sat 10-6 (Thurs 10-7)
London W1

Ghost

If Ophelia, barefoot with flowers in her hair, needed a new dress, this would be her best bet. Ethereal and bias-cut, the drapey viscose/rayon dresses in pale shades like rose, lilac and cream will make you want to wriggle your toes in the grass. The mood for men is more down-to-earth, offering colorful button-down shirts and suits. This simple, comfortable clothing is machine-washable and makes great holidaywear. www.ghost.co.uk

020 7229 1057 — **tube: Notting Hill Gate**
36 Ledbury Road — Mon-Fri 10:30-6:30, Sat 10-6
London W11

020 7486 0239 — **tube: Bond Street**
14 Hinde Street — Mon-Sat 10-6 (Thurs 10-7)
London W1

Gianfranco Ferré

Ferré is an Italian stalwart who seems to be treading younger and more dangerous ground lately, with tight leather pants and tops that dare to bare, low-slung belts and high-riding heels. His older fans needn't fear, though—Ferre's classic sense of style is still present in his collection of cocktail dresses and tailored suits, so well cut they're an enduring reflection of his early training as an architect.

020 7838 9576 — **tube: Knightsbridge**
29 Sloane Street — Mon-Sat 10-6 (Wed 10-7)
London SW1

Gibo

In the past this revered Italian company has manufactured collections for Alexander McQueen, Hussein Chalayan and Helmut Lang among others. Now it has set up its own label, designed by rising star Julie Verhoeven whose background in illustration is evident in her bright, playful and individual creations. Inspired by artists like Matisse and Picasso, her pieces include white shirts with circles of color blobbed on the shoulders, bubblegum-pink combats with ruffled pockets and pleated miniskirts. The shop itself, designed by Cherie Yeo Architecture, is like a conceptual art gallery with clothes hung on square metal bars like exhibits, a bare concrete floor and a changing installation of shoes displayed in holes in the wall.

020 7734 2340 **tube: Oxford Circus/Green Park**
47 Conduit Street Mon-Sat 10-6
London W1

Gieves & Hawkes

Large, impressive premises at this rather special address—No.1 Savile Row—offer a balance of traditional solemnity and metropolitan cool that reflects the vast and excellent range of clothes within. Displays mix numerous royal warrants with beautifully cut casual clothing and a huge selection of shirts, ties, belts, coats and ready-to-wear suits through a dozen different rooms. The company has been undergoing modernization under creative director James Wishaw, who has injected an edgy Sixties feel to many of the separates. For older, more established clients the bespoke service remains, as it always has been, second to none. www.gievesandhawkes.com

020 7434 2001 **tube: Piccadilly Circus/Oxford Circus**
1 Savile Row Mon-Thurs 9:30-6:30
London W1 Fri 9-6, Sat 10-6

020 7730 1777 **tube: Sloane Square**
33 Sloane Square Mon-Sat 9:30-6
London SW1 (Wed 10-7), Sun 11-5

Gigi

Sister-store to Joseph (and named for Joseph Ettedgui's daughter), Gigi is another necessary stop-off for SW's smart set. Labels like Miu Miu, Prada Sport, Plein Sud and Katharine Hamnett embody classic design sense with an edge. Luxurious sweaters, perfect black pants, cute tailored shirts and the odd eccentricity (black mesh tops and glitter underpants) make for a selection that is safe but still fun. Accessories, though limited, couldn't be better.

020 7584 1252 **tube: South Kensington**
124 Draycott Avenue Mon-Sat 10-6:30 (Wed 10-7)
London SW3 Sun 1-6

Gina

Any shoe shopper worth her slingbacks will tell you there are few more tempting places to squander a fortune.

Gina shoes are coveted by London party girls for their striking adornment and sexy styles, from sequin-sprinkled stilettos to gold python mules—most with hazardously high heels. Handbags are also available, for day and evening. www.ginashoes.com

020 7235 2932 **tube: Knightsbridge**
189 Sloane Street Mon-Sat 10-6 (Wed 10-7)
London SW1

020 7409 7090 **tube: Green Park**
9 Old Bond Street Mon-Sat 10-6 (Thurs 10-7)
London W1

Giorgio Armani

Michelle Pfeiffer, Winona Ryder, Ashley Judd...scores of Hollywood goddesses know there's nothing quite so timelessly elegant as a creation from Armani. A quick glance through this store makes it easy to see why, with his beautiful simple suits, pants and blouses in a palette that tends towards monochromes. Men can select from a range of minimalist looks, including the iconic suits. Of all the top designers, Armani is the least likely ever to lead you astray. www.giorgioarmani.com

020 7235 6232 **tube: Knightsbridge**
37 Sloane Street Mon-Sat 10-6 (Wed 10-7)
London SW1

Golden Glow

These tiny gems, one in Mayfair and one in Little Venice, used to be called Amiche (Italian for girlfriends) but now double as boutiques and tanning salons (see Health & Beauty). Afy Naghibi sells the most delightful necklaces, ankle bracelets and other accessories to complement her jewelled shoes, sandals and much coveted Kesslord bags from France. www.goldenglowuk.com

020 7495 7677 **tube: Bond Street**
31 Avery Place Mon-Sat 9:30-6:30
London W1

020 7286 4033 **tube: Warwick Avenue**
1 Lanark Place (opening times as above)
London W9

Gordon Scott

For anyone who was teased as Bigfoot at school this shoe store is a handy place to know. It specializes in wide fittings and extra large sizes for both women and men. The majority of styles are basic, made of leather and business-oriented. Sturdy English staples include Church's and Barkers while Italian labels Stemar, Hugo Boss and Artioli are supple and soft. Sizes go up to an English 13 and there is also a made-to-measure service. www.gordonscott.com

020 7495 3301 **tube: Bond Street**
29 New Bond Street Mon-Sat 10-6:30
London W1 (Thurs 10-7), Sun 12-6

020 7626 3773 | **tube: Cannon Street**
119 Cannon Street | Mon-Fri 9-6:30
London EC4

Gotham Angels

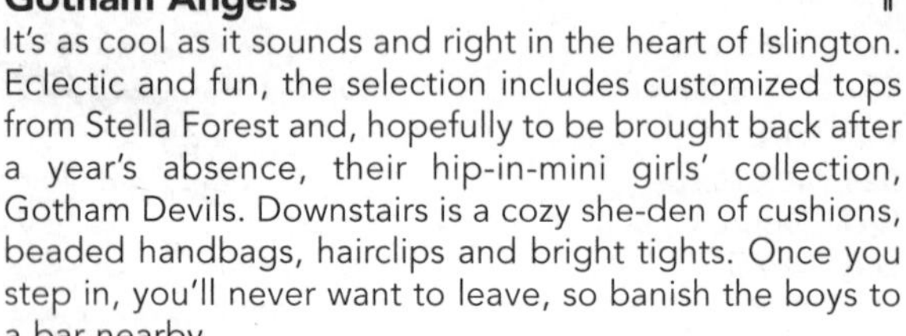

It's as cool as it sounds and right in the heart of Islington. Eclectic and fun, the selection includes customized tops from Stella Forest and, hopefully to be brought back after a year's absence, their hip-in-mini girls' collection, Gotham Devils. Downstairs is a cozy she-den of cushions, beaded handbags, hairclips and bright tights. Once you step in, you'll never want to leave, so banish the boys to a bar nearby.

020 7359 8090 | **tube: Angel**
23 Islington Green | Mon-Fri 10:30-7
London N1 | Sat 10-6, Sun 11-5

Graham & Green

Very pretty but prohibitively priced, the selection here reflects colorful and ethnic inspirations. For the home, there are Venetian mirrors, Moroccan leather beanbags, and Indian bed linens. For your darling self: Orla Kiely bags, pinafores with giant Sixties-style polka dots, cashmere sweaters, skirts and tops to match. An inspired collection of goodies, from such labels as Day, even if you can only afford to browse. www.grahamandgreen.co.uk

020 7352 1919 | **tube: Sloane Square**
340 King's Road | Mon-Sat 10-6
London SW3 | Sun 12-6

020 7727 4594 | **tube: Notting Hill Gate/Ladbroke Grove**
4 & 10 Elgin Crescent | Mon-Sat 10-6
London W11 | Sun 11:30-5:30

020 7586 2960 | **tube: Chalk Farm**
164 Regents Park Road | Mon-Sat 10-6, Sun 12-6
London NW1

Great Expectations

Hidden upstairs from Night Owls is a little shop for the stork watchers. If you're a mother-to-be searching for appealing maternity wear, have a look here. Great Expectations provides a smart selection of pants, dresses, skirts and shirts that are more sympathetic than stylish. Colorful swimwear, maternity bras, cashmere cardigans and business suits with room to breathe will take you all the way to the delivery room.

020 7584 2451 | **tube: South Kensington**
78 Fulham Road | Mon-Sat 10-6 (Wed 10-7)
London SW3

Gucci

Tom Ford gives women's fashion a jolt with every successive Gucci collection. The bold sexuality of his designs and his salacious ad campaigns generate a continuous buzz. The new flagship store on Bond Street is a Gucci temple with the usual selection of striking women's and menswear, super-chic shoes, classic handbags, belts and a new baby line. Go worship. www.gucci.com

020 7629 2716 **tube: Green Park**
34 Old Bond Street Mon-Sat 10-6 (Thurs 10-7)
London W1

020 7235 6707 **tube: Knightsbridge**
17-18 Sloane Street Mon-Sat 10-6 (Wed 10-7)
London SW1

Gymboree

Gymboree offers casual clothing for kids (newborn to seven) in Fisher Price-style primary colors, with flowers, berries and polka dots sprinkled about. A mix-and-match approach, with multiple possible combinations, makes expanding a child's wardrobe easy, expecially when the prices are so reasonable. Bikinis, sunglasses and tiny handbags add a tempting dose of fun for the girls, while boys will look cute in canvas hats and dungarees. www.gymboree.com

020 7494 1110 **tube: Oxford Circus**
198 Regent Street Mon-Sat 10-7 (Thurs 10-8)
London W1 Sun 11:30-5:30

H&M (Hennes & Mauritz)

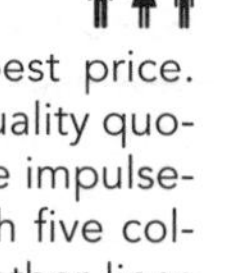

Their formula is fashion and quality at the best price. Some might argue they haven't quite got the quality quotient yet, but this is still a great place to find the impulse-buy that you will wear only once or twice. With five collections for women, four for men and various other lines for teenagers and children, H&M cuts into the trendy cross-section of every market. The emphasis is on merchandise turnaround, so nothing lasts more than a few weeks and they will keep lowering the price, if necessary, until the stock has gone. www.hm.com

020 7493 4004 **tube: Oxford Circus**
261-271 Regent Street Mon-Sat 10-7 (Thurs-Fri 10-8)
London W1 Sun 12-6

020 7493 8557 **tube: Marble Arch**
481 Oxford Street Mon-Sat 10-7 (Thurs 10-8)
London W1 Sun 12-6

020 7612 1820 **tube: Oxford Circus**
174-176 Oxford Street (opening times as above)
London W1

020 7368 3920 **tube: High Street Kensington**
365 Kensington High Street (opening times as above)
London W8

020 7395 1250 **tube: Covent Garden**
27-29 Long Acre Mon-Sat 10-7 (Thurs-Fri 10-8)
London WC2 Sun 12-6

020 7313 7500 **tube: Bayswater/Queensway**
Whiteley's, Queensway Mon-Sat 10-7, Sun 12-6
London W2

Hackett

Many assume this British outfitter has, like many of its neighbors, been around for centuries, but at 20 years old it's a relative newcomer. Nevertheless it has carved a reputation for brilliantly bridging the casual/formal gap. Short-sleeved shirts, merino-wool sweaters, corduroy pants and linen shirts attract both young and old. Hackett's polo shirts are a modern classic. For those looking for a traditional English look with a modern edge, this is the place. www.hackett.co.uk

020 7930 1300 **tube: Piccadilly Circus/Green Park**
87 Jermyn Street Mon-Sat 10-7
London SW1

020 7730 3331 **tube: Sloane Square**
136-138 Sloane Street Mon-Sat 10-7, Sun 11-5
London SW1

020 7494 1855 **tube: Piccadilly Circus**
143-147 Regent Street Mon-Sat 10-7
London W1 Sun 11-5

020 7626 0707 **tube: Monument**
19 Eastcheap Mon-Fri 8:30-6
London EC3

Hardy Amies

Most famous perhaps as a women's couture house making classic, uncluttered designs for the great and good of a certain age (including the Queen), Hardy Amies recently underwent a quiet revolution in its similarly classic bespoke menswear. Indeed, the fusty Savile Row shop played host to the subtle designs of Ian Garlant so successfully that Garlant was poached for a year by Aquascutum. The good news is—he's back and is overseeing both the men's and womenswear. www.hardyamies.com

020 7734 2436 **tube: Piccadilly Circus/Oxford Circus**
14 Savile Row Mon-Fri 9:30-5
London W1

Harley-Davidson

You might think of men with beer guts, beards and tattoos whenever you hear the name, but the Harley-Davidson store gets down to serious business for any kind of bike enthusiast. Genuine motorcycle clothes in all sizes (with or without the gut) are featured in styles tough enough to keep out the wind. Leather accessories are also available and, from the range of collectibles, there are logo'd T-shirts, sweatshirts and jackets. www.warrs.co.uk

020 7376 7084 **tube: Sloane Square**
125 King's Road Mon-Sat 10-6, Sun 1-6
London SW3

Harriet Gubbins

She closed her shop last year, and now focuses on high-end couture from a small studio in Fulham. There's a strong dose of personality and color to everything Gubbins designs. Her made-to-measure suits are tightly tailored and sharp in an Eighties "career gal" sort of way, with an emphasis on flared sleeves and strong, power colors. Mother-of-the-bride suits are less severe, if a bit mumsy. The bridal gowns are the best of the bunch, more understated and infinitely prettier. www.harrietgubbins.co.uk

020 7736 0748 **tube: Parsons Green**
813b Fulham Road
London SW6

☆ Harrods

This Knightsbridge institution is a shopper's paradise. The food halls are legendary and the perfume department will knock you sideways; there are antiques, contemporary furniture, plasma TVs, books, kitchen appliances, bed linens, a wine department, 23 restaurants and a barber shop. It is so huge Harrods has its own in-store map. On the fashion front, you'll find one of the best menswear departments anywhere, with new designers such as Duckie Brown and Cloak keeping company with labels like Etro, Gucci and Paul Smith. Upstairs the women's designer labels range from Fake London, Alice Temperley and Capucci to MaxMara, Nicole Farhi and DKNY. If the kids are tired, the toy department (4th floor) has a karaoke machine where they can flex their vocals. It's more fun than a museum. www.harrods.com

020 7730 1234 **tube: Knightsbridge**
87-135 Brompton Road Mon-Sat 10-7
London SW1

Harvest

Each new season brings a mixed crop to this international designer boutique. The list of featured labels, including Kenzo, Plein Sud and Firenze, seems to promise more than it delivers. The style is confusingly hit-and-miss, from gypsy blouses to bland dresses that might suit a mother of the bride. Flamboyant details (on lacy skirts, ruffled blouses and feathered hats) keep the clothing from being too mainstream, but there's a dowdy flavor to the shop that makes the selection feel flat.

020 7581 9245 **tube: Sloane Square**
136 King's Road Mon-Sat 10-7, Sun 12-5:30
London SW3

☆ Harvey Nichols

The Barneys of Britain, Harvey Nick's (nobody ever says "Nichols") is one of London's leading fashion emporiums. It's hard to know where to start. Behind brilliant window displays the ground floor is devoted to cosmetics and accessories, including an extensive assortment of handbags and a special section for hats. Upstairs, racks are hung with labels of every style, from Pucci, Ralph Lauren and Vivienne Westwood to Helmut Lang, Paul & Joe and Joseph. A new Jimmy Choo concession adds even more pulling power. If you're not up to facing a dressing-room mirror, ride straight up to the fifth floor for a light lunch at the restaurant and a tour of the sprawling food market.

020 7235 5000 **tube: Knightsbridge**
109-125 Knightsbridge Mon-Tues, Sat 10-7
London SW1 Wed-Fri 10-8, Sun 12-6

Harvie & Hudson

Old-school shirt and tie people specializing in the slightly cutaway Kent collar. They also sell mix-and-match suiting so that customers with very different jacket and pants measurements can buy off the peg. Even in the rarefied atmosphere of Jermyn Street Harvie & Hudson are major league, with striped silk shirts and matching ties a well-known specialty. The in-store ambience will seem stuffy to some, but is generally friendly with an air of faded splendor. www.harvieandhudson.com

020 7930 3949 **tube: Piccadilly Circus/Green Park**
77 Jermyn Street Mon-Sat 9-6
London SW1

020 7839 3578 **tube: Piccadilly Circus/Green Park**
97 Jermyn Street Mon-Sat 9-5:30
London SW1

020 7235 2651 **tube: Knightsbridge/Hyde Park Corner**
55 Knightsbridge Mon-Sat 9-5:30
London SW1

Hawes & Curtis

This friendly gentleman's outfitter offers the usual Jermyn Street range of plain, striped and check cotton shirts in a clubby, wood-paneled interior. Downstairs is the formal selection for cutaways and white-tie. Hawes & Curtis made clothes for the Duke of Windsor and bought part of his wardrobe at the famous Sotheby's auction in New York.

020 7287 8111 **tube: Piccadilly Circus**
23 Jermyn Street Mon-Sat 9:30-6:30, Sun 12-5
London SW1

☆ Heidi Klein

Someone's finally done it: beachwear all year long. Sounds like a simple concept, but women are flocking to this new shop, where bikinis and bathing-suits by Melissa Odabash, Dos Mares, Helen Kaminski and Cacharel are all in stock. Find cover-ups by Allegra Hicks for the more modest bunch, as well as a selection of cotton T-shirts, linen trousers and kidswear. Accessories are just as cool, including Chloé sunglasses, washbags and cuff bracelets by Johnny Loves Rosie. Best of all, there's a beauty spa with body brushing, fake tanning, waxing, manicures and pedicures for top-to-toe holiday preparation.

020 7243 5665 **tube: Notting Hill Gate**
174 Westbourne Grove Mon-Sat 10-6
London W11

Hels Bels

This is a Little Venice boudoir with a tented ceiling, art deco lamps, armchairs and objets d'art dotted about, where a mother and daughter team sell designer clothes (and some vintage) at large discounts. They offer, for example, Kyri and Voyage, plus Vive Maria underwear. They have particularly pretty eveningwear, but you will also find customized jeans, party clothes and their own label of inexpensive coordinates. helsbells@amserve.com

020 7286 5573 **tube: Warwick Avenue**
3 Clarendon Terrace Tues-Fri 11-6
London W9 Sat 11-5 (or by appointment)

Henri Lloyd

This company has quite a prestigious history. First, it introduced the revolutionary fabric Bri-Nylon into the marine world and saw a century of oilskin-clad yachtsmen disappear. Then when Sir Francis Chichester undertook his epic single-handed voyage around the world in 1967 he chose Henri Lloyd clothing to protect him from the elements. Today the company remains the choice of yahcting champions and the new flagship shop on Carnaby Street is bursting with top technical boatwear and some fun forays into fashion too. Alongside waterproof, windproof, breathable jackets you'll find striped T-shirts, cotton piqué dresses and cable-knit sweaters. Looking sporty has never been so fashionable.

020 7287 4376 **tube: Oxford Circus/Piccadilly Circus**
48 Carnaby Street Mon-Sat 10-7, Sun 12-6
London W1

Henry Maxwell

These bespoke shoemakers recently relocated from Savile Row to Jermyn Street. Their original specialty was riding boots, but today they will make any shoe or boot you desire at prices from £1,350 upwards. Initial fittings require a wooden last of your foot to be made, and this is kept for all future orders. Good things come to those who wait and patience is definitely a virtue here—it can take up to a year to complete a pair of riding boots and around five months to make a shoe from scratch. www.henrymaxwell.com

020 7930 1839 **tube: Piccadilly Circus/Green Park**
83 Jermyn Street Mon-Fri 10-6, Sat 10-4
London W1

☆ Henry Poole & Co

As you might expect of a company that set the whole Savile Row ball rolling 150 years ago, that clothed the likes of Charles Dickens, Napoleon and Winston Churchill and that invented the tuxedo, Henry Poole & Co is a busy, confident, friendly and firmly traditional business. Eschewing considerations of house style, it offers a popular, purely bespoke suit and shirt service for the high-waisted, slim-fitting look that is classic Savile Row.

020 7734 5985 **tube: Piccadilly Circus/Oxford Circus**
15 Savile Row Mon-Fri 9-5:15
London W1

Herbert Johnson

(see under Swaine Adeney Brigg/Herbert Johnson)

Herbie Frogg

The old Bond Street store has now become Pal Zileri, but the various locations of this traditional British outfitter offer different selections of menswear. Jermyn Street features the Herbie Frogg shirt and suit label, and accessories; and the flagship, in Hans Crescent, offers a selection of leather as well as the Brioni label. Traditional designs are the unifying quality, made-to-measure service is available at all three and Swiss cotton shirts are a specialty. The slightly stuffy but friendly atmosphere is beloved of middle-aged tourists and British alike. www.Herbie-Frogg.co.uk

020 7437 6069 **tube: Piccadilly Circus**
18-19 Jermyn Street Mon-Sat 9:30-6 (Thurs 9:30-7)
London SW1

020 7439 2512 **tube: Piccadilly Circus**
21 Jermyn Street (opening times as above)
London SW1

020 7823 1177 **tube: Knightsbridge**
13 Lowndes Street Mon-Sat 9:30-6 (Wed 9:30-7)
London SW1

020 7629 0446 **Tube: Bond Street/Oxford Circus**
16 Brook Street Mon-Sat 10-6 (Thurs 10-7)
London W1

Hermès

Lovely scarves, uniquely patterned ties and indestructible, elegant leather handbags rank among the most coveted items from the luxury label more luxe than any other. Like its classic Birkin bag, the ready-to-wear for both sexes by Martin Margiela resides in its own sophisticated universe beyond flashy trends. But expect further wonders now that Jean Paul Gaultier has been appointed creative director.

020 7499 8856 **tube: Bond Street**
155 New Bond Street Mon-Sat 10-6
London W1

020 7823 1014 **tube: Knightsbridge**
179 Sloane Street (opening times as above)
London SW1

020 7626 7794 **tube: Bank**
2-3 Royal Exchange Mon-Fri 10-6
London EC3

High & Mighty

If you know a man of NBA or sumo proportions (or if you are one), then you know how hard it can be to shop. Offering business and casual clothing for large and tall men, the selection here features designer suits, shirts, ties, jeans and jackets as well as underwear and accessories. Labels include Louis Féraud, Pierre Cardin and Cartigiani. With sizes maxing out at 40 inches for trouser length, 60 for chest and 56 for waist, big boys have never looked so good. www.highandmighty.co.uk

020 7589 7454 **tube: Knightsbridge**
81-83 Knightsbridge Mon-Fri 10-6:30, Sat 10-6
London SW1

020 7723 8754 **tube: Marble Arch/Edgware Road**
145-147 Edgware Road Mon-Sat 9-6 (Thurs 9-7)
London W2

020 7436 4861 **tube: Oxford Circus**
The Plaza, 120 Oxford Street Mon-Sat 10-7
London W1 (Thurs 10-8), Sun 12-6

High Jinks

This quintessential streetwear shop, thumping with bass, offers a formidable array of the latest in street and skateboard looks. Guys can find cargo pants, Hooch sweatshirts, decal T-shirts and nylon jackets. Girls have slightly fewer choices—distressed cords, ripped cargo skirts and baby tees. Labels include Tribal, The Criminal, Jesus and Mecca, topped off with Kangol visors. www.high-jinks.com

020 7240 5580 **tube: Covent Garden**
25 Thomas Neals Centre Mon-Sat 10-7, Sun 12-6
London WC2

020 7734 6644 **tube: Oxford Circus**
13-14 Carnaby Street (opening times as above)
London W1

☆ Hilditch & Key

According to many observers this is the finest shirtmaker in the world—a survey in *The Times* rated their sea-island shirts highest of seven on Jermyn Street. Mind you, deciding which Jermyn Street shirtmaker is the best is a bit like deciding which angel is most angelic. H&K sell both off-the-peg and bespoke and are one of very few shirtmakers to match the pattern at all the seams, something normally only seen in bespoke shirts. The beautiful, wood-paneled interior is lined with all the shirts you could ever desire. Hilditch have recently added men's trousers and jackets to their repertoire, and there is a selection of shirts for women as well. www.hilditch.co.uk

020 7734 4707 **tube: Piccadilly Circus/Green Park**
37 & 73 Jermyn Street Mon-Sat 9:30-5
London SW1

020 7823 5683 **tube: Sloane Square**
131 Sloane Street Mon-Fri 9:30-5:45, Sat 10-5:45
London SW1

The Hive

This boutique treads the fine line between cool, customized clothing and dubious eurotrash. Jeans with pink lace on the back pockets and diamanté down the thighs made us think of Dolly Parton while T-shirts by Passepartout were trimmed with just the right type of decorative detail and sit among attire from the likes of Studds and Gatano Navaro. If the vibe were cooler (this hive was anything but buzzing) and the sales staff a bit less severe, this would probably be more fun.

020 7467 0799 — **tube: Notting Hill Gate**
3 Lonsdale Road — Mon-Sat 11-6
London W11

Hobbs

Hobbs brings stodgy British style into the 21st century with a soothing atmosphere and a selection of smart women's suits in a palette that borders on business-blah. Faultlessly crafted suits, skirts, dresses and coats come in simple styles. Some shoppers stop by just for the shoes, which are equally unfussy.

020 7629 0750 — **tube: Bond Street**
47-49 South Molton Street — Mon-Sat 10-6:30
London W1 — (Thurs 10-7:30), Sun 12-6

020 7836 9168 — **tube: Covent Garden**
17 The Market — Mon-Fri 10-7 (Thurs 10-7:30)
London WC2 — Sat 10:30-7, Sun 11-5

020 7581 2914 — **tube: Sloane Square**
84-88 King's Road — Mon-Fri 10-7 (Wed 10-7:30)
London SW3 — Sat 10-6:30, Sun 10-6

020 7225 2136 — **tube: Knightsbridge**
37 Brompton Road — Mon-Sat 10-6:30
London SW3 — (Wed, Fri 10-7), Sun 12-6

020 7937 1026 — **tube: High Street Kensington**
63 Kensington High Street — Mon-Wed, Sat 10-6:30
London W8 — Thurs 10-7:30, Fri 10-7, Sun 10-6

020 7836 0625 — **tube: Covent Garden**
124 Long Acre — Mon-Sat 10:30-7 (Thurs 10:30-8)
London WC2 — Sun 12-5

020 7929 4900 — **tube: Monument/Bank**
64-72 Leadenhall Market — Mon-Fri 10-6:30
London EC3

020 7628 6771 — **tube: Liverpool Street**
135 Bishopsgate — Mon-Fri 9-6:30 (Thurs 9-7)
London EC2

Holland & Holland

The legendary rifle company celebrated its 165th anniversary a few years ago with the launch of a luxury clothing line, only to fire the designer a year later and retreat to its shooting roots. The focus is on its heritage as an outdoor brand, with only a small selection of ready-to-wear, so look for plenty of weatherproof and functional clothing perfect for the country house or a ramble in Central (or Hyde) Park.

www.hollandandholland.com

020 7408 7921 — **tube: Green Park**
31-33 Bruton Street — Mon-Fri 9-6, Sat 10-5
London W1

Hope + Glory

This casual, urban clothing store features dressed-down work- and weekendwear for men. Not quite statement-making, but still funky and smart, the clothing's character could be described as one part Ted Baker, one part Hackett. Tweed hats and hound's-tooth trousers are mixed with patterned Seventies-style short-sleeved shirts. Chunky sweaters, rugby shirts and V-neck sweater vests cover the conventional end of the spectrum. A good option for grown-ups who still care about looking cool. www.hopeandglory.com

020 7379 3283 **tube: Covent Garden**
17-19 Thomas Neals Centre Mon-Fri 10-6:30 (Thurs 10-7)
London WC2 Sat 10-7, Sun 12-5

020 7240 3713 **tube: Covent Garden**
Shorts Gardens (opening times as above)
London WC2

020 7628 3328 **tube: Liverpool Street**
Broadgate Link Mon-Fri 7:30-7:30, Sat 8:30-5
Liverpool Street Station
London EC2

House of Cashmere

For years Barbour, makers of the oilskin coat that achieved icon status in the Eighties, was the House of Cashmere's most famous name. Now House of Cashmere has branched out with a line of cozy sweaters, pants and shoes. They might not keep the rain out, but they will deliver excellent quality in just about any color you could want. www.barbour.com

020 7495 7385 **tube: Green Park**
8-9 Burlington Arcade Mon-Sat 9-5:30
London W1

House of Fraser

This department store is perhaps more on a par with Macy's than Saks Fifth Avenue, but if you're passing by you'll find the usual variety of goods from cosmetics to accessories to housewares. Fashionwise, sweet dreams are not made of this. There's a signature clothing collection, Therapy, alongside such designers as Betty Barclay, DKNY, Nicole Farhi, Diesel, French Connection and Austin Reed. Bring low expectations and you may be pleasantly surprised. www.houseoffraser.com

020 7529 4700 **tube: Oxford Circus/Bond Street**
318 Oxford Street Mon-Sat 10-8 (Thurs 10-9)
London W1 Sun 12-6

020 7937 5432 **tube: High Street Kensington**
(Barkers of Kensington) Mon-Fri 10-7 (Thurs 10-8)
63 Kensington High Street Sat 9-7, Sun 12-6
London W8

Hudson

Another shoe shop joins the growing quota on South Molton Street, only Hudson stands out from the rest with its sleek understated look and cool boutique aura. The store is lit with cut-glass contemporary chandeliers and an ultra-modern sofa means you can slip shoes on in comfort. So what's on offer? The choice is not earth-shattering but lovely leather in simple sexy shapes is the answer to everyday tottering. There are soft slip-ons with pointy toes, heels with weaved leather detailing and green slingbacks done up with buttons. Definitely worth a look.

020 7355 0282 **tube: Bond Street**
13 South Molton Street Mon-Sat 10-6:30 (Thurs 10-7)
London W1 Sun 12-6

Hugo Boss

The German juggernaut keeps rolling along. Once a hot menswear label, Boss is now more favored by the wannabe than the truly smart dresser. The collection features suits, sportswear, formalwear and outerwear, all in great quality fabrics. Not a bad place to begin to build your wardrobe. www.hugoboss.com

020 7235 4433 **tube: Knightsbridge**
190 Sloane Street Mon-Sat 9:30-6:30 (Wed 10-7)
London SW1 Sun 12-5

020 7734 7919 **tube: Oxford Circus/Piccadilly Circus**
184-186 Regent Street Mon-Sat 9:30-6:30
London W1 (Thurs 10-8), Sun 12-5

☆ Huntsman

One of Savile Row's most imposing premises is host to one of the street's longest established—and most expensive—tailors. The quality of a Huntsman bespoke suit is undeniable, with 30% more hand work than anyone else. Especially famous and popular for their exclusive Huntsman tweeds, the firm also offers a "special order" tailored service allowing less wealthy customers a choice of fabric and (factory) cut. They don't offer womenswear per se, but some well-known female New York socialites are fans of their blazers and suits and in England the Hon Daphne Guinness (the woman Valentino most likes to dress) happily, and very elegantly, wears Huntsman.

020 7734 7441 **tube: Piccadilly Circus**
11 Savile Row Mon-Fri 9-5:30
London W1

I Love Voyage

I Love Voyage is the diffusion shop of infamous label Voyage (remember their closed door policy?), and although this new store does have a heavy steel door entrance at least it is wide open. Now over its precocious period, Voyage is set to become a major player on the fashion scene. I Love Voyage sells the more accessible lines Passion and Amour, and most of the inventory is colorful, trendy and playful: a rucksack picturing David Beckham playing football, a fitted orange cord jacket covered with a vivid pattern of flowers and fish, and lots of denim customized with sequins and beads. The store itself is a seriously urban space, throbbing with techno music and lit by fluorescent lights. Not for shopping with your mother.

020 7836 5309 **tube: Covent Garden**
33 Monmouth Street Mon-Wed 10-6:30, Thurs-Sat 10-7
London WC2

Iana

They had only been open a week when we dropped by, but the staff at this promising kids' shop seemed optimistic—and no wonder. You can rarely walk this stretch of the King's Road without dodging mummies and their strollers. Now they detour into this shop where cute, practical (and practically-priced) clothing caters to boys and girls aged 0-14. The selection includes all the basics—cargo pants, pinafores and polo shirts—topped off with mini red raincoats, cream leather jackets and cool denim. With 40 shops worldwide and expansion plans for London, this family-owned Italian label might just be the next Petit Bateau.

020 7352 0060 **tube: Sloane Square**
186 King's Road Mon-Fri 10-6 (Wed 10-7)
London SW3 Sat 10-6:30, Sun 11-6

iBlues

Businesswear is never meant to make a fashion statement but there's no question that outdated, ill-cut suits can damage your career. This division of MaxMara will keep you up to speed with smart, stylish suits that are appropriately understated but never frumpy. Pastel dresses, pants and skirts are sold with coordinating jackets, and the few patterns are simple and sweet. A safe investment.

020 7581 0080 **tube: Knightsbridge**
161 Brompton Road Mon-Sat 10-6 (Wed 10-7)
London SW3

020 7824 8000 **tube: Sloane Square**
23 King's Rd Mon-Sat 10-6 (Wed 10-7), Sun 1-6
London SW3

Iceblu

This pricey boutique stocks a range of obscure Italian designers whose names don't roll easily off the tongue, including Gai Mattiolo, Fabrizio Lenzi and Caloma-Clips. If you feel like squeezing yourself into low-waisted, hip-hugging jeans or leather mini-dresses, you could have a field day here. There are also big stone necklaces and diamanté belts for a quick trend-fix.

020 7371 9292 **tube: Parsons Green/Fulham Broadway**
24a New King's Road Tues-Sat 10:30-6
London SW6 (or by appointment)

Il Piacere Donna

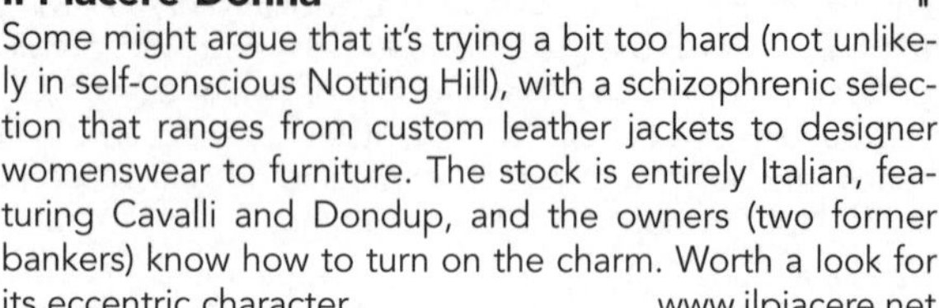

Some might argue that it's trying a bit too hard (not unlikely in self-conscious Notting Hill), with a schizophrenic selection that ranges from custom leather jackets to designer womenswear to furniture. The stock is entirely Italian, featuring Cavalli and Dondup, and the owners (two former bankers) know how to turn on the charm. Worth a look for its eccentric character. www.ilpiacere.net

020 7467 0777 **tube: Notting Hill Gate**
185 Westbourne Grove Mon-Sat 11-7, Sun 12-6
London W11

Isabell Kristensen

Her couture dresses have been featured in countless fashion magazines and worn by numerous luminaries, including Nicole Kidman who donned a very hot and heavy (we mean literally) fuchsia evening gown, with train, for a *Moulin Rouge* cover shoot. Kristensen's bridal creations are structured and glamorous, and a bit bold for the run-of-the-mill bride. Her hefty materials may induce a 19th-century swoon, but you'll undoubtedly be surrounded by amours eager to catch you. www.isabellkristensen.com

020 7589 1798 **tube: Knightsbridge**
33 Beauchamp Place Mon-Fri 10:30-6
London SW3

Issey Miyake

Welcome to high-concept fashion: skirts flare at odd angles, shirts billow awkwardly and colors scream in bright red, yellow or blue. Miyake's patterned men's shirts may look outrageous, the womenswear fabrics a bit too sheer, but this is avant-garde style at its finest, where innovation means having a sense of humor. www.isseymiyake.com

020 7851 4620 **tube: Oxford Circus**
52 Conduit Street Mon-Sat 10-6
London W1

020 7581 3760 **tube: South Kensington**
270 Brompton Road (opening times as above)
London SW3

Ivory

Glitz and pizzazz are the two words that spring to mind at this flashy shoe shop. One imagines a lounge singer finding her perfect show pair here. Most styles are not for blend-in dressers: sandals are covered in gems or beads and sling-backs are rendered in brilliant colors. For those who prefer to stay out of the spotlight, there's a selection of functional black leather lace-ups, pumps and boots.
www.ivoryshoes.com

020 7408 1266 **tube: Bond Street**
104 New Bond Street Mon-Sat 10-6 (Thurs 10-7:30)
London W1 Sun 11-5

J&M Davidson 

More Sloane Square than Notting Hill, this large shop caters to the risk-averse, with pretty womenswear and a home collection that whispers country-chic. Suede bean-bags, zebra pillows and an assortment of lamps reflect a sense of easy living. Inoffensive, if a bit dull, particularly for a neighborhood where quirky is the name of the game.

020 7313 9532 | **tube: Notting Hill Gate**
42 Ledbury Road | Mon-Tues 10-6, Wed-Sat 10-7
London W11 | Sun 12-5

Directory

J.W. Beeton 

Owner Debbie Potts offers an egalitarian mix of trendy streetwear and more wearable, feminine fare. The range features fashion veterans Tracey Boyd and Comme des Garçons, as well as virtual unknowns like Anne-Louise Roswald whose lovely textile-inspired dresses sell like mad. There are also jeans, funky T-shirts and Fake London's recycled cashmere, plus safer linen pieces. A lot less stuffy than the name suggests.

020 7229 8874 | **tube: Notting Hill Gate**
48-50 Ledbury Road | Mon-Fri 10:30-6, Sat 10-6
London W11

020 7602 5757 | **tube: Hammersmith**
121 Shepherd's Bush Road | (opening times as above)
London W6

The Jacksons 

This out-of-the-way shop packs a pleasing punch with colorful accessories from Louise and Joey, the Jackson twins. Summer saw raffia bags, beaded belts and an assortment of their famous flip-flops with interchangeable fake flowers. In fact, flowers bloom throughout the sunny months, on skirts and blouses, hairpins and hats. For winter, there are high-heeled leather boots, sweet embroidered skirts and a range of sheepskin boas—definitely worth a cold-weather detour. www.thejacksons.co.uk

020 7792 8336 | **tube: Ladbroke Grove/Notting Hill Gate**
5 All Saints Road | Mon-Sat 10-6
London W11

Jacqueline Hogan 

This contemporary couture bridal shop is not for the run-of-the-mill princess bride. Dresses are stylishly structured and classic nuptial materials, such as silk and tulle, break with tradition in modern cuts. Swan-like feathers on a fitted bodice add eccentric detail while short trains, full skirts and tiara veils are simple but extravagant. For the unconventional winter wedding there are beautiful jackets to match. The average dress costs £2,000 and takes anywhere from three to six months to finish, well worth it for the head-turning results. www.jacquelinehogan.co.uk

020 7731 0911 | **tube: Parsons Green**
640 Fulham Road | Mon-Fri 10-6 (Thurs 10-7)
London SW6 | Sat 10-5

Jacques Azagury

If you're facing a dressy night out and an uninspiring closet, Jacques Azagury might be your fairy godfather. His sophisticated daytime and evening clothes maintain a following among Knightsbridge ladies who favor classic creations and subtle cuts. To complete the look, head to brother Joseph's exquisite shoe boutique across the street.

020 7245 1216 — **tube: Knightsbridge/Hyde Park Corner**
50 Knightsbridge — Mon-Fri 9:30-5:30, Sat 10-4
London SW1

Jaeger

Jaeger is another British brand that has attempted to undergo a revamp, with the help of hip British designer Bella Freud. There's more room for improvement, though—the styles (sweater sets and tapered trousers) are still staid, while loose cuts make for a dowdy mix. Once favored by older professionals and country ladies, Jaeger hasn't quite left its conservative roots behind.

020 7200 2990 — **tube: Oxford Circus**
200-206 Regent Street — Mon-Sat 10-6:30 (Thurs 10-7:30)
London W1 — Sun 12-5

020 7584 2814 — **tube: Knightsbridge**
16-18 Brompton Road — Mon-Sat 10-7 (Wed 10-8)
London SW1 — Sun 12-6

020 7352 1122 — **tube: Sloane Square**
145 King's Road — Mon-Tues 10-6, Wed-Fri 10-7
London SW3 — Sat 10-6, Sun 12-6

020 8944 7266 — **tube: Wimbledon**
27 High Street — Mon-Fri 9:30-6
Wimbledon Village — Sat 9-6, Sun 12-5
London SW19

James Levett

An experienced Savile Row tailor who set up his own shop about five years ago, James Levett offers traditional bespoke tailoring in everything from business suits to cutaways in his affable, unstuffy basement workshop. Low overhead costs mean that classic Savile Row looks and quality come at surprisingly reasonable prices, with a two-piece bespoke suit starting at £1,400.

020 7287 5995 — **tube: Piccadilly Circus/Oxford Circus**
13 Savile Row — Mon-Fri 9-5:30
London W1

James Purdey & Sons

There's no more famous gunsmith in the world than James Purdey & Sons, and the imposing premises just south of Grosvenor Square and the US Embassy are a treat to visit. Guns remain the core business, but there is a vast range of ultra-high-quality, shooting-orientated clothes and accessories on offer, ranging from clay vests (special vests for skeet shooting, called clay pigeon shooting in Britain) and heavy tweed field coats to padded knitwear, brightly checked shirts, scarves, boots, cufflinks and hi-tech shooting goggles. They have injected a bit more fashion into their menswear recently and have also launched a womenswear collection, including dramatic reversible cloaks in velvet and silk. www.purdey.com

020 7499 1801 **tube: Bond Street**
57-58 South Audley Street Mon-Fri 9:30-5:30
London W1 Sat 10-5

Jane Brown

This Brit designer specializes in heels with the lethal pointy toes that seem to please these days. Some designs have been given playful names by the staff, from the basic three-inch "Man Trap" heel to the "Dominatrix" stiletto made of leather that's been stamped to look like crocodile skin. The pretty bridal collection is, thankfully, more subtle. Prices are on par with Manolo and Jimmy Choo, though Brown doesn't have the same fierce fashion following yet. www.janebrownshoes.co.uk

020 7229 7999 **tube: Notting Hill Gate**
189 Westbourne Grove Mon-Sat 10:30-6:30
London W11

Jane Norman

The old adage "you get what you pay for" applies here. Still, Jane Norman's inexpensive selection reflects the latest in casual fashion trends. Featured pieces include sweaters with giant turtlenecks, stretchy button-down shirts and jeans. The quality leaves something to be desired, but there are times when a throwaway £20 top is what you really want.

020 7225 3098 **tube: Knightsbridge**
59 Brompton Road Mon-Tues 10-7, Wed-Fri 10-7:30
London SW3 Sat 9:30-7, Sun 12-6

Janet Reger

This designer of luxury lingerie has made a lasting sensation with her sensual creations. The selection ranges from basic underwear to bodysuits and tanks, made of the finest fabrics including cashmere and silk. The colors and styles are seductive in that fantastic, seduce-your-husband-all-over-again kind of way. www.janetreger.com

020 7584 9368 **tube: Knightsbridge**
2 Beauchamp Place Mon-Sat 10-6
London SW3

Jauko

Shoppers with a weakness for Asian fashion should stop by. The designs are fresh and modern, with only a handful of each piece in stock. This season, the gypsy influence abounds in ruffled linen skirts, blue T-shirts with puffed sleeves, chiffon dresses sprinkled with flowers and patterned paper fans. If your timing is right you'll leave with a free gift, a Japanese gesture of good fortune.

020 7376 1408 **tube: High Street Kensington**
34c Kensington Church Street Mon-Sat 10-6
London W8

Jeans West

It's self-explanatory: jeans, jeans and more jeans. All types and all brands. Levi's, Pepe, Wrangler, Diesel or Lee; basic blue, stone-washed or dirty denim...Jeans West is an essential source for these essential pants. They may be stacked from floor to ceiling, but don't be daunted. The sales staff know their stuff and can save you hours of digging. With casual shirts, belts, hats, and backpacks Jeans West takes care of your top half, too.

020 7436 0152 **tube: Oxford Circus**
The Plaza, 120 Oxford Street Mon-Sat 10-7 (Thurs 10-8)
London W1 Sun 10-6

020 7491 4839 **tube: Oxford Circus**
5 Harewood Place Mon-Sat 10-7 (Thurs 10-8)
London W1 Sun 12-6

Jenesis

All Jennifer Stuart-Smith's hand-picked pieces are Italian imports, from T-shirts covered with red lips to tiger and flower-print dresses to pink purses tinged with gold. If you could use a dose of detail in your wardrobe, the lily-bloom bracelets and string belts might just be your thing. But when it comes to the fabrics, don't look too closely—quality control sometimes lags.

020 7371 5903 **tube: Parsons Green**
52 New King's Road Mon-Sat 10-6
London SW6

Jesus Lopez

Lime-green snakeskin slip-ons and gold mules fringed in beads are just some of the highlights on the Lopez list. There are other designers, too, including Etro and cobbling king Sergio Rossi. With names like these and a recently launched clothing collection, there is little here to complain about. www.jesuslopez.com

020 7486 7870 **tube: Baker Street/Bond Street**
69 Marylebone High Street Mon-Sat 10-6
London W1

Jigsaw

Ask any London girl and she's likely to tell you that this is a store she holds close to her heart. There's a real flair to the collection, where just about everything strikes the perfect note—not too mainstream, not too offbeat. It's a perfect solution for the last-minute party or the work wardrobe that's gone stale, with a design sensibility that mixes modern edge with vintage romance, from sleek sweaters and boot-leg hipsters to bias-cut skirts and chiffon dresses. Accessories and junior lines (see Jigsaw Junior) are sold at select stores and the company has introduced a restaurant, Jigsaw Kitchen, with a special junior menu—perfect for a mother-daughter shopping day. www.jigsaw-online.com

020 7491 4484 **tube: Bond Street**
126-127 New Bond Street Mon-Sat 10-6:30
London W1 (Thurs 10-7:30), Sun 12-6

020 7437 5750 **tube: Oxford Circus**
9 Argyll Street Mon-Fri 10:30-7 (Thurs 10:30-8)
London W1 Sat 10:30-6:30, Sun 12-6

020 7493 9169 **tube: Oxford Circus**
St. Christopher's Place Mon-Sat 10-6:30
London W1 (Thurs 10:30-8), Sun 12-6

020 7823 7304 **tube: Sloane Square**
126 King's Road Mon-Sat 10:30-7 (Wed 10:30-7:30)
London SW3 Sun 12-6

020 7589 5083 **tube: Sloane Square**
124 King's Road Mon-Fri 10:30-7 (Wed 10:30-7:30)
London SW3 Sat 10-7, Sun 12-6

020 7929 2361 **tube: Monument/Bank**
31 Leadenhall Market Mon-Fri 10-6:30
London EC3

020 7240 3855 **tube: Covent Garden**
21 Long Acre Mon-Fri 10:30-8
London WC2 Sat 10:30-7, Sun 11-6

020 7497 8663 **tube: Charing Cross**
449 The Strand Mon-Fri 10-7 (Thurs 10-8)
London WC2 Sat 10-6:30, Sun 12-6

020 7937 3573 **tube: High Street Kensington**
65 Kensington High Street Mon-Fri 10:30-7
London W8 (Thurs 10:30-7:30), Sat 10-7, Sun 12-6

020 7584 6226 **tube: Knightsbridge**
31 Brompton Road Mon-Fri 10:30-7 (Wed 10:30-7:30)
London SW3 Sat 10-7, Sun 12-6

020 7589 9530 **tube: South Kensington**
91-95 Fulham Road Mon-Sat 10-7 (Wed 10-7:30)
London SW3 Sun 12-6

020 7727 0322 **tube: Notting Hill Gate**
192 Westbourne Grove Mon-Wed 10:30-6:30
London W11 Thurs-Fri 10:30-7, Sat 10:30-6, Sun 12-6

020 7229 7609 **tube: Queensway/Bayswater**
Whiteley's, Queensway Mon-Sat 10-8, Sun 12-6
London W2

020 7794 3014 **tube: Hampstead**
58-62 Heath Street Mon-Sat 10-6, Sun 12-6
London NW3

020 8785 6731 **tube: East Putney/Putney Bridge**
114 High Street Mon-Sat 9:30-6, Sun 12-5
London SW15

020 7329 5752 **tube: Mansion House/St. Paul's**
44 Bow Lane Mon-Wed 10-6:30, Thurs-Fri 10-7
London EC4

Jigsaw Junior

Clothes so cute, you'll wish you could fit into them. This store promises a plethora of pint-size styles for budding young shoppers, with looks that are modern, girlish and perfectly in tune. Find sweet beaded dresses, frilly-trimmed skirts, flowered capri trousers and tiny tees. With sizes that range from a tender age two to a dangerous 13, Jigsaw Junior could be your daughter's undoing.

www.jigsaw-online.com

020 7823 7304 **tube: Sloane Square**
124 King's Road Mon-Fri 10:30-7 (Wed 10:30-7:30)
London SW3 Sat 10-7, Sun 12-6

020 7491 4484 **tube: Bond Street**
126-127 New Bond Street Mon-Sat 10-6:30
London W1 (Thurs 10-7:30), Sun 12-6

020 7823 8915 **tube: South Kensington**
97 Fulham Road Mon-Sat 10-7 (Wed 10-7:30), Sun 12-6
London SW3

020 7229 8654 **tube: Notting Hill Gate**
190 Westbourne Grove Mon, Sat 10:30-6:30
London W11 Tues-Wed 10-6:30, Thurs-Fri 10-7, Sun 12-6

020 7431 0619 **tube: Hampstead**
83 Heath Street Mon-Sat 10-6, Sun 12-6
London NW3

Jil Sander

Housed in what was once an impressive bank, with giant windows and a glass atrium, Sander's London outpost is impressive and flooded with natural light. The more unusual of the designs come with bits of unexpected detail (a shoulder ruffle, a sprinkling of beading) but the majority of Sander's collection is decidedly simple: a suede pin-tucked chemise, a soft beige jumper, clean-cut cotton trousers and crisp white shirts. Even if you can't afford to buy, it's worth popping in just to feel the lovely fabrics.

020 7758 1000 **tube: Green Park/Piccadilly Circus**
7 Burlington Gardens Mon-Sat 10-6 (Thurs 10-7)
London W1

☆ Jimmy Choo

He's been a party staple for years, but it was *Sex and the City* that really put Jimmy Choo on the well-heeled map. Daring heights and dagger-sharp toes make some styles dangerous for walkers, and cumulative cab fares should probably be factored into the price. Still, few shoes come sexier than these and, short of Manolos, there's no quicker way to earn a fashion editor's undying respect.

www.jimmychoo.com

020 7584 6111 **tube: South Kensington/Sloane Square**
169 Draycott Avenue Mon-Sat 10-6 (Wed 10-7), Sun 1-6
London SW3

020 7262 6888 (couture) **tube: Marble Arch**
18 Connaught Street Mon-Fri 10-6 (by appointment)
London W2

Jitrois

Known for its line of stretch leather, Jitrois's collection is predominately black and brown, with a bit of beige suede thrown in for a softer look. From bustiers to halternecks, with trousers that lace up the legs, the effect can be dangerous dominatrix or cool cowgirl. www.jitrois.com

020 7245 6300 **tube: Knightsbridge**
6f Sloane Street Mon-Sat 10-7
London SW1

Directory

Joanna's Tent

Few shops these days can lay claim to a truly unique selection but this is one of them. Decorative designer clothes for women and children could strip the numbers from your credit card, with pants, patterned sweaters and tops from such vivid collections as Betsey Johnson, Jean Paul Gaultier, Marithé et François Girbaud and Ghost. For dressing down, they also offer jeans and mixed separates. The striking hats, like everything else, are hip but still sophisticated.

020 7352 1151 **tube: Sloane Square**
289b King's Road Mon-Sat 10-6 (Wed 10-7)
London SW3 Sun 1-5

Johanna Hehir

A small shop specializing in made-to-measure eveningwear, this store offers a more personalized level of service than most people under 40 are accustomed to. Designs are inspired by the craftsmanship and detail of the Twenties and Thirties, from flapper-style cocktail dresses to bridal gowns with accessories to match. Pinks and purples predominate and prices start at £250. Someone else will have to teach you the Charleston. www.johanna-hehir.com

020 7486 2760 **tube: Baker Street**
10-12 Chiltern Street Mon-Sat 11-7
London W1

John Bray

Mainly known for a vast selection of off-the-peg suits made in Italy from the world's finest cloth manufacturers, including Zegna and Loro Piana. All suits are own-label and made specifically for John Bray. They are particularly good for super-lightweights, and also sell a huge range of ties and shirts. More fashionable than other Jermyn Street stores, so more suitable for the thirtysomething customer who's not too stiff.

020 7839 6375 **tube: Green Park**
78-79 Jermyn Street Mon-Sat 9-6 (Thurs 9-7)
London SW1

John Lewis

Londoners would be lost without their beloved John Lewis. Where else can you buy a stereo, a new pair of shoes, a backgammon board and a box of detergent, all in one go? Poised for some much-needed renovation, this sister department store to Peter Jones in Sloane Square has been around since 1864. Renowned for its good value, the store promises that if you see something you've bought priced for less elsewhere, they'll match it or refund the difference. Chic collections from the likes of Joseph, Betty Barclay and MaxMara are what attract the Sloane Ranger crowd (and some very discerning boys and girls from Vogue House, only a couple of blocks away). www.johnlewis.co.uk

020 7629 7711 **tube: Oxford Circus/Bond Street**
278-306 Oxford Street Mon-Sat 9:30-7 (Thurs 9:30-8)
London W1

☆ John Lobb

Although they have the same name, and John Hunter Lobb himself is on both boards, these are really two different concerns. The airy Jermyn Street store does ready-to-wear and is owned by Hermès of Paris. The more traditional-looking St. James's Street store is independent (dating from 1849) and is the bespoke specialist, often referred to as the world's finest bespoke shoemaker. Some styles might be a bit too dressy, but if you want to be clad in the same quality shoes as royalty and celebrities the world over, John Lobb is the place to go. Remember to go to the bank first, though. A pair of made-to-measure gentleman's shoes (plus their shoe trees) costs £2,023 and a pair of riding boots £3,601...before VAT, of course. www.johnlobb.co.uk

020 7930 8089 **tube: Piccadilly Circus/Green Park**
88 Jermyn Street Mon-Sat 10-6 (Thurs 10-7)
London SW1

020 7930 3664 **tube: Green Park**
9 St. James's Street Mon-Fri 9-5:30, Sat 9-4:30
London SW1

John Smedley

Known for their fine merino wool, this company specializes in sweaters, turtlenecks and twinsets that are beloved by everyone from Madonna to Tom Cruise. They also favor cashmere, woolen silk and sea-island cotton. Classic with the occasional twist, their styles are as universally pleasing as their quality. We would shop here every day if we could afford to. www.johnsmedley.com

020 7495 2222 **tube: Bond Street**
24 Brook Street Mon-Sat 10-6 (Thurs 10-7)
London W1

020 7823 4444 — **tube: Sloane Square**
19 King's Road — Mon-Sat 10-6, Wed 10-7, Sun 12-5
London SW3

Jones

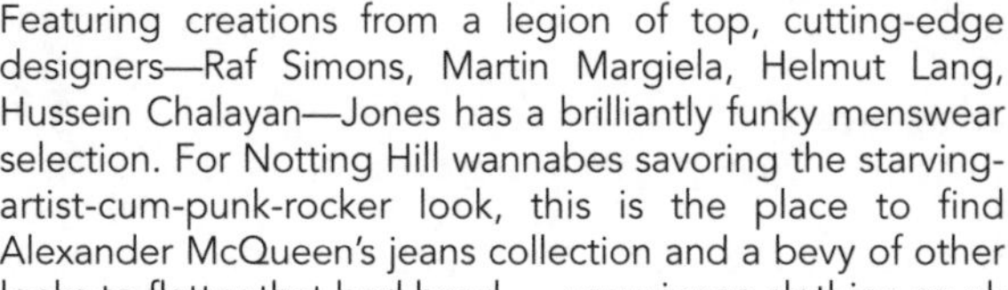

Featuring creations from a legion of top, cutting-edge designers—Raf Simons, Martin Margiela, Helmut Lang, Hussein Chalayan—Jones has a brilliantly funky menswear selection. For Notting Hill wannabes savoring the starving-artist-cum-punk-rocker look, this is the place to find Alexander McQueen's jeans collection and a bevy of other looks to flatter that bed head. www.jones-clothing.co.uk

020 7240 8312 — **tube: Covent Garden**
13 Floral Street — Mon-Sat 10-6:30, Sun 1-5
London WC2

Jones the Bootmaker

Jones pitch themselves at the affordable end of the price scale, so it's best not to expect much in the way of quality or creativity. Trendy styles like Camper lace-ups and rainbow-striped wedge heels blend with classic-standard leather wingtips and loafers. Much of the selection is their own brand and pretty dull at that. www.jonesbootmaker.com

020 7930 8864 — **tube: Piccadilly Circus/Green Park**
112 Jermyn Street — Mon-Sat 9:30-6
London SW1

020 7408 1974 — **tube: Bond Street**
15 South Molton Street — Mon-Sat 10-6:30 (Thurs 10-7)
London W1 — Sun 11-5:30

020 7823 8024 — **tube: Knightsbridge**
187 Brompton Road — Mon-Fri 10-6:30 (Wed 10-7)
London SW3 — Sat 10-6:30, Sun 12-5:30

020 7240 6558 — **tube: Covent Garden**
16 New Row — Mon-Sat 10-6:30 (Thurs 10-7)
London WC2 — Sun 12-5

020 7734 2351 — **tube: Oxford Circus**
15 Foubert's Place — (opening times as above)
London W1

020 7836 5079 (M) — **tube: Covent Garden**
7-8 Langley Court — (opening times as above)
London WC2

020 7937 5440 — **tube: High Street Kensington**
26 Kensington Church Street — (opening times as above)
London W8

020 7730 1545 — **tube: Sloane Square**
57-59 King's Road — Mon-Sat 10-7
London SW3 — Sun 12-6

020 7929 2732 — **tube: Monument**
15 Cullum Street — Mon-Fri 9-5:30
London EC3

020 7248 1828 — **tube: Mansion House**
70-71 Watling Street — Mon-Fri 9-6
London EC4

020 7831 1850 **tube: Chancery Lane**
320 High Holborn Mon-Fri 9-5:30
London WC1

020 7531 1677 **tube: Canary Wharf**
Cabot Place East Mon-Fri 9-7
London E14 Sat 10-6, Sun 11-5

☆ Joseph

Joseph Ettedgui has serious staying power, and in the fashion business that's no easy feat. He was a humble hairdresser on the King's Road in the mid-Seventies, but today he is master of his own style empire with a ubiquitous signature label that feeds London's craving for trends with a twist. The boot-cut, hip-hugging trousers with rear flap pockets are a flattering wardrobe staple. His Brompton Cross flagship carries other designers as well, including Prada, Sergio Rossi, Gucci, Chloé, Marni and Helmut Lang, with a similar selection for men nearby. Limited cash flow need not deter you: the King's Road discount shop offers last season's stock for a lot less.

020 7823 9500 (W) **tube: South Kensington**
77 Fulham Road Mon-Sat 10-6:30
London SW3 (Wed 10-7), Sun 1-6

020 7591 0808 (M) **tube: South Kensington**
74 Sloane Avenue (opening times as above
London SW3 except Sun 12-5)

020 7225 3335 **tube: South Kensington**
315 Brompton Road (opening times as above
London SW3 except Sun 12-5)

020 7235 5470 **tube: Sloane Square**
26 Sloane Street Mon-Sat 10-6:30 (Wed 10-7)
London SW1

020 7629 3713 **tube: Green Park**
23 Old Bond Street Mon-Sat 10-6:30 (Thurs 10-7)
London W1

020 7629 6077 (W) **tube: Bond Street**
28 Brook Street Mon-Sat 10-6:30 (Thurs 10-7)
London W1

020 7730 7562 **tube: Sloane Square**
53 King's Road Mon-Sat 10:30-6:30
London SW3 (Wed 10:30-7), Sun 12-5

020 7243 5915 **tube: Notting Hill Gate**
61 Ledbury Road Mon-Sat 10:30-6:30, Sun 12-5
London W11

020 8946 5880 **tube: Wimbledon**
64 High Street Mon-Sat 10-6, Sun 12:30-5:30
London SW19

020 7722 5883 **tube: St. John's Wood**
21 St. John's Wood High Street Mon-Sat 10-6
London NW8 Sun 12-6

020 7352 6776 **tube: South Kensington**
299 Fulham Road Mon-Fri 11-8
London SW3 Sat 10-6:30, Sun 1-6

020 7730 2395 | **tube: Sloane Square**
Unit E1, Duke of York Square | Mon-Fri 10-7
London SW3 | Sat 10-6:30, Sun 11-5

Joseph Azagury

Across the street from brother Jacques' clothing store, Joseph Azagury offers a refined selection of shoes well worthy of their Knightsbridge address. Strappy sandals and high-heeled boots are favorites, chic but still delicate enough for ladies who lunch.

020 7259 6887 | **tube: Knightsbridge/Hyde Park Corner**
73 Knightsbridge | Mon-Sat 10-6 (Wed 10-7)
London SW1

Joujou Lucy

What is going on? For years British children have delighted in looking like urchins and ragamuffins, and now beauteous boutiques for trendy tots are sprouting everywhere. An Iranian couple recently opened this Little Venice place, stocked with the best international labels: Chipie, Confetti, Petit Bateau, Catimini, Oshkosh, D&G Junior, Jean Bourget and Marfrat from Italy. Up to about age eight.

020 7289 0866 | **tube: Warwick Avenue**
32 Clifton Road | Daily 10-6 (Sun 12-4)
London W9

Jungle

A specialist in army and other government clothing, Jungle is a dense wilderness of camouflage pants, sweaters, rucksacks and shirts. Not a destination for the fashion-conscious per se, but this place offers plenty of sturdy gear at low prices. www.jungleclothing.com

020 7379 5379 | **tube: Covent Garden/Leicester Square**
21 Earlham Street | Mon-Sat 10-6:30, Sun 12-5:30
London WC2

Justin Kara

Last year this husband and wife team upgraded from the Portobello market to a proper shop. Their Australian-designed womenswear is rife with vintage references: Hawaiian florals, girlish gingham, and bikinis made from recycled decal T-shirts. Jewelry and woven belts and bags capture the bohemian-beach flavor of Malibu circa 1976.

020 7792 6920 | **tube: Ladbroke Grove**
253 Portobello Road | Mon-Sat 11-6:30, Sun 12-5
London W11

Karen Millen

One week you might find a hugely desirable selection here and the next, nothing will catch your eye. Such is the unpredictability of Karen Millen. The stores are perfect for confident women looking for feminine fashion at an upper-mid price, but the bold designs aren't for wallflowers. A small selection of footwear is available in all stores, but if you want more the South Molton Street branch carries only bags and shoes. Here you can find the perfect Millen complement, be it a purple snakeskin knee-high boot or a pink gemstone sandal. www.karenmillen.com

020 7495 5297 **tube: Bond Street**
46 South Molton Street Mon-Sat 10-6:30 (Thurs 10-7:30)
London W1 Sun 12-6

020 7287 6158 **tube: Oxford Circus**
262-264 Regent Street Mon-Sat 10-7
London W1 Sun 12-6

020 7938 3758 **tube: High Street Kensington**
4 Barkers Arcade Mon-Sat 10-6:30 (Thurs 10-7:30)
London W8 Sun 12-6

020 7730 7259 **tube: Sloane Square**
33e King's Road Mon-Sat 10-6:30 (Wed 10-7)
London SW3 Sun 12-6

020 7256 6728 **tube: Liverpool Street**
135 Bishopsgate Mon-Fri 10-6:30
London EC2

020 7836 5355 **tube: Covent Garden**
22-23 James Street Mon-Sat 10:30-7:30, Thurs 10:30-8
London WC2 Sun 12-6

020 7225 0174 **tube: Knightsbridge**
33 Brompton Road Mon-Sat 10-7
London SW3 Sun 12-6

020 7629 5539 **tube: Bond Street**
57 South Molton Street Mon-Sat 10-6:30 (Thurs 10-7:30)
London W1 Sun 12-6

Ken Smith Designs

It's possible that the obscure location, on an inconspicuous side street off Goodge Street, has limited the profile of this pleasing little plus-size boutique. There's no reason it should remain a secret, though. Selection is particularly chic for sizes 16-30, from jeans and casual tops to eveningwear. If you're lucky, Ken himself will be there to offer his expert eye.

020 7631 3341 **tube: Goodge Street**
6 Charlotte Place Mon-Fri 10-6, Sat 10-2
London W1 various Sun 11-2

Kenneth Cole

He once sold shoes out of the back of a broken-down trailer. Now Kenneth Cole's ever-expanding $300 million empire has arrived in London with two new locations. Although he is best known for his smart functional shoes—from suede heels to leather loafers—Cole is beginning to translate his hallmark "practicality with a twist" into ready-to-wear lines for men and women. The look is clean-cut and urban—leather jackets, tailored trousers, fitted shirts—smarter than Next but not as interesting as Karen Millen. The shop on Sloane Street sells accessories, luggage, watches and outerwear. www.kennethcole.com

020 7235 0564 **tube: Knightsbridge**
3 Sloane Street Mon-Sat 10-7, Sun 12-6
London SW1

020 7730 4360 **tube: Sloane Square**
33 King's Road Mon-Sat 10-7 (Wed 10-8), Sun 12-6
London SW3

Kenzo 

This is the label beloved by the French for its distinctive modern-meets-classical aesthetic and feminine flourish—expressed in such details as billowing puffed sleeves, high necklines and ruffled trim. Despite the retirement of Kenzo himself in 1999 the collection maintains his penchant for bright colors and florals. Choose from a selection that includes suits, skirts, blouses, tapered pants, coats and knits. Designs can be so avant-garde customers have been known to ask, "How do I wear this?"

020 7235 4021 (W) **tube: Knightsbridge**
15 Sloane Street Mon-Sat 10-6:30 (Wed 10-7)
London SW1

020 7225 1960 (M) **tube: South Kensington**
70 Sloane Avenue Mon-Sat 10-6:30
London SW3 Sun 1-6 (summertime only)

Key Largo

While the name may conjure images of retirees in sun-soaked leisure suits, the store has a bit (but only a bit) more spirit. Among the selection of what is essentially men's casualwear you'll find simple cotton T-shirts, button-downs and khakis. Speedo, Schott and Vanson are here, as well as the store's signature brand. Hassle-free holiday wear. www.key-largo.co.uk

020 7240 7599 **tube: Covent Garden**
19 Shelton Street Mon-Sat 11-6:30 (Thurs 11-7)
London WC2

☆ Kilgour French Stanbury 

Probably the trendiest and savviest of the traditional Savile Row tailors, Kilgour French Stanbury recently revamped a brand that had long been cool enough for the likes of Cary Grant and various James Bonds. Now offering ready-to-wear alongside the traditional bespoke service (and a semi-bespoke service), KFS pulls a wide clientele of celebrities, hip young men about town and more seasoned clients. www.8savilerow.com

020 7734 6905 **tube: Piccadilly Circus/Oxford Circus**
8 Savile Row Mon-Fri 9:15-5:15, Sat 10:30-4:30
London W1

Kim Davis 

She may be new to our shores, but this American designer has cultivated garden-party fashion into a fine and refreshing art form. The small shop is a breeze to browse, with uncluttered racks offering a navy suit with pink pinstripes and pink mother-of-pearl buttons, a Jackie O-style dress with candy-colored polka dots and a bright green chiffon evening gown that drapes dangerously low in the back. Floral day suits come in lovely feather-light silks and bold colors that look more Kensington cool than Boca-Raton brash. We think Davis's future in Chelsea is equally bright.

020 7584 6799 **tube: South Kensington**
84 Fulham Road Mon-Sat 10-6 (Wed 10-7)
London SW3

King's Road Sporting Club

If it's time to update your workout gear, then you might want to jog by this shop...at the very least you'll find ways to look athletic. Season permitting, the range includes bikinis, sports bras, T-shirts, running shorts and jackets. Big brands like Nike, Quiksilver, O'Neill, Nautica and Billabong are stocked alongside the store's reliable signature collection. www.krsc.co.uk

020 7589 5418 **tube: Sloane Square**
38-42 King's Road Mon-Sat 10-6:30 (Wed 10-7)
London SW3 Sun 12-6

Kit Clothing/Twentieth Century Frox

Spring has sprung at this colorful shop where the racks are grouped in pinks, blues and greens with a splash of white thrown in. For women, there are Naf Naf cardigans, lilac linen dresses by Out of Exile and additional wear by Noa Noa and Nougat. Other girly bits include beaded flip-flops and baskets with bows. Kidswear is equally cute, from pedal-pushers to fleece jackets to tiny tees. Got a good babysitter? At the back of the store, you'll find a dress-for-hire service, Twentieth Century Frox, featuring formal eveningwear.

020 7731 3242 **tube: Parsons Green**
614 Fulham Road Mon, Wed-Thurs 10-7
London SW6 Tues, Fri-Sat 10-6

Knickerbox

If you're running low on underwear, and you've already tried Marks & Spencer, Knickerbox is the natural next stop. From sheer to lacy, eye-catching colors and comfortable designs are the key ingredients of this chain's success. Selection includes bras, panties, T-shirts and tanks, featuring a mix of intricate patterns and simpler sporty styles. They also have matching pajama sets.

020 7499 6144 **tube: Oxford Circus**
281a Regent Street Mon-Sat 10-7 (Thurs 10-8)
London W1 Sun 12-6

020 7823 4437 **tube: Sloane Square**
28 Sloane Square Mon-Sat 9-7 (Thurs 9-8), Sun 12-6
London SW1

020 7229 0815 **tube: Queensway/Bayswater**
Whitely's Shopping Centre Mon-Sat 10-8
Queensway Sun 12-6
London W2

020 7937 8887 **tube: High Street Kensington**
Kensington Arcade Mon-Sat 9-7 (Thurs 9-8), Sun 12-5
London W8

☆ Koh Samui

A seriously fashion-savvy boutique, Koh Samui offers some of the season's finest and most eclectic pieces. Clothing tends towards the avant garde and consistently features the hottest British labels. Shoppers can head straight for their favorite colors, as the store is organized by shade: bright and baby pinks in one corner, mossy green and turquoise in another. Only one of each item is displayed, creating the impression that each piece is a one-off. Below the racks of dresses, skirts, and tops rest rows of matching shoes. Designers include Miu Miu, Balenciaga, Collette Dinnigan, Dries Van Noten, and Jimmy Choo. Jewelry and handbags are also available. Paradise for the hardcore shopper.

020 7240 4280 (M) — **tube: Covent Garden**
65-67 Monmouth Street — Mon-Tues, Sat 10-6:30
London WC2 — Wed, Fri 10:30-6:30
Thurs 10:30-7, Sun 11-5:30

020 7838 9292 — **tube: Knightsbridge**
28 Lowndes Street — Mon-Tues, Sat 10-6:30
London SW1 — Thurs-Fri 10:30-6:30
Wed 10:30-7, Sun 11-5:30

Kokon to Zai

This finger-on-the-pulse boutique sells a could-not-be-cooler mix of progressive dance music and fashion. Funky new talents top the rails—Marjan Pejoski, Viktor & Rolf, Bernard Willhelm—and new pieces quickly replace the old. Hip accessories like beaded chokers, diamond gecko pins and extra-wide leather belts are straight out of the fashion pages. Extra points if you can figure out what the name means.

020 7434 1316 — **tube: Piccadilly Circus/ Tottenham Court Road**
57 Greek Street
London W1 — Mon-Sat 11-7:30, Sun 12-6

Kookaï

Trendy Kookaï brings hip disco-style to the masses. Prices are low and colors are all over the spectrum, from a pink baby-doll T-shirt to pants in basic black. Quality, on the other hand, is consistently mediocre. Embellishments like rhinestones and stripes are used liberally, and synthetic skirts, dresses and casual T-shirts are popular pieces. If you're between 14 and 23, Kookaï, Oasis and Warehouse (all cheap and fun) should be on your list.

020 7938 1427 — **tube: High Street Kensington**
123d Kensington High Street — Mon-Sat 10-7 (Thurs 10-8)
London W8 — Sun 12-6

020 7581 9633 — **tube: Knightsbridge**
5-7 Brompton Road — Mon-Fri 10-7 (Wed 10-7:30)
London SW3 — Sat 10:30-7, Sun 12-6

020 7408 2391 — **tube: Oxford Circus**
257-259 Oxford Street — Mon-Wed 10-7, Thurs-Sat 10-8
London W1 — Sun 12-6

020 7730 6903 **tube: Sloane Square**
27a Sloane Square Mon-Sat 10-7 (Wed 10-7:30)
London SW1 Sun 12-6

020 7629 9197 **tube: Oxford Circus**
399 Oxford Street Mon-Wed 10-6, Thurs-Sat 10-7
London W1 Sun 10-6

020 7240 0997 **tube: Covent Garden**
39 Long Acre Mon-Sat 10-7 (Thurs 10-8)
London WC2 Sun 12-6

020 7379 1318 **tube: Covent Garden**
The Market Mon-Sat 10-7, Sun 12-6
London WC2

Krizia

Mariuccia Mandelli, Krizia's creator, so effectively grasps the relationship between fashion and physical form that her designs seem sculpted for the body. From tailored suits to T-shirts the collection is made mostly of cashmere and wool in fall and winter, linen in spring and summer. Her crowning glory is her bright knitwear. Perfectly wearable, although it can be scarily Italian.

020 7491 4987 **tube: Oxford Circus**
24-25 Conduit Street Mon-Sat 10-6
London W1

Kruszynska

You may be Daddy's little princess, but can you persuade him to fork over £15,000 for your wedding dress? If so, a pale pink tulle gown sprinkled with tiny pink stars and finished with a scallop-edged three-metre train could be yours. Since not all blushing brides want to make their guests gasp, the Polish-born Kruszynska sisters also do understated (and more moderately priced) wedding gowns, as well as subtly colored eveningwear elaborately detailed with Swarovski crystals, hand embroidery or trails of chantilly lace.

020 7589 0745 **tube: Knightsbridge**
35 Beauchamp Place Mon-Fri 9:30-7, Sat 10-6
London SW3

Kurt Geiger

The press was hot on Geiger following his recent efforts to create a more fashion-forward line. Has he succeeded? We're not so sure. His latest London location on South Molton Street features a rather basic selection—leather slip-ons, loafers and ankle boots—with only a few more daring styles—sandals with a diamanté union jack and denim kitten heels with buckles. Other brands in stock (Marc Jacobs, Gina) seem to outclass Geiger, but we're still staying tuned for next season.

020 7758 8020 **tube: Bond Street**
65 South Molton Street Mon-Sat 10-7 (Thurs 10-8)
London W1 Sun 12-6

The L Boutique

This is a one-stop shop for cash-rich women seeking an opulent look unique to them. If you're tired of trends or want to transform a simple black dress into something unforgettable, Lucia Silver's boudoir boutique could be the answer. Lucia offers a personal styling service to help customers develop a signature look and her feminine, theatrical clothing makes a strong statement. There are Moroccan Thirties-style organza coats, intricate brocade jackets, pretty bias-cut dresses, silk kimonos and masses of accessories from semiprecious chokers and charm bracelets to ostrich feather headpieces. If you can afford to shop here, rest assured your clothing will help you stand out in a crowd.

020 7243 9190 — **tube: Notting Hill Gate**
28 Chepstow Corner — Tues-Sat 10:30-6
Chepstow Place
London W2

L.K.Bennett

Their shoes exude feminine sophistication in lovely simple silhouettes, often lightly embellished with a tiny bow or a bit of embroidery. Kitten heels are the shape of every season. They also do a line of lovely party clothing—Jackie O-style suits and dinky handbags are on hand for Ascot, and every spring long sheer chiffon dresses breeze in. Some stores also carry other designers, including Ben de Lisi, John Smedley, Kenzo and Sportmax.

020 7491 3005 (footwear & clothing) — **tube: Bond Street**
31 Brook Street — Mon-Sat 10-7 (Thurs 10-8)
London W1 — Sun 11-6

020 7352 8066 (own-label only) — **tube: Sloane Square**
83 King's Road — Mon-Sat 10-7 (Wed 10-8)
London SW3 — Sun 11-6

020 7376 7241 (other labels only) — **tube: Sloane Square**
219 King's Road — Mon-Sat 10-6:30, Sun 11-6
London SW3

020 7379 1710 — **tube: Covent Garden**
130 Long Acre — Mon-Sat 10:30-7:30 (Thurs 10:30-8)
London WC2 — Sun 11-6

La Perla

Delicately exquisite and decadently expensive, La Perla offers what is arguably some of the finest lingerie in the world. From elegant to demure to downright seductive, the whole range of boudoir sensibilities is represented here. Practicality comes into play as well, with multi-functional bras and slimming panties. Don't forget to check out the sleepwear and swimwear. www.laperla.com

020 7245 0527 — **tube: Knightsbridge**
163 Sloane Street — Mon-Sat 10-6 (Wed 10-7)
London SW1

La Scala

This shop joins a smattering of top-end secondhand stores in Chelsea Green featuring nearly-new designer clothing and accessories, from linen dresses by Ralph Lauren to Joseph's perfectly cut pants. Throw in shoes by Prada, Gucci and Jimmy Choo and prospects shine even brighter.

020 7589 2784 **tube: South Kensington**
39 Elystan Street Mon-Sat 10-5:30
London SW3

La Senza

If you're like most women, shopping for underwear is one excursion you're not dying to make. But when it's got to be done, this is a great place to do it. Granny pants or a lace teddy, no matter what your heart (or sweetheart) fancies this store has a wide selection of high-quality, affordably priced lingerie, from matching bra-and-panty sets to provocative silk and satin sleepwear. www.lasenza.com

020 7580 3559 **tube: Oxford Circus**
162 Oxford Street Mon-Sat 10-7 (Thurs 10-8)
London W1 Sun 12-6

020 7630 6948 **tube: Victoria**
8 Kingsgate Parade Mon-Fri 9-6 (Thurs 9-7), Sat 9-5:30
London SW1

Lacoste

The alligator is regaining the status it achieved in the Eighties when the Lacoste polo shirt, collar up, was de rigueur. René Lacoste's knit piqué shirt changed the face of sportswear, so it's nice to know that the legendary symbol of prep is making a comeback, particularly as it softens with every wash. www.lacoste.com

020 7225 2851 **tube: Knightsbridge**
52 Brompton Road Mon-Sat 10-7
London SW1 Sun 12-6

Lanvin

This French label offers classic menswear. The clothing is traditional, simple (though in the most sophisticated sense) and of the highest quality. Known for its fine fabrics and tailored suits, Lanvin takes subtle elegance down to the last stitch.

020 7499 2929 **tube: Bond Street**
108 New Bond Street Mon-Sat 10-6:30 (Thurs 10-7)
London W1

Laundry Industry

It sounds progressive and, in terms of decor, it certainly is, with minimalist space and a stone floor that slopes. The clothing, on the other hand, is quite conventional: cotton tops, linen suits and silk slip dresses in seasonal colors. Three Dutch owner/designers based in Amsterdam have created

an extremely wearable selection of clothing that is practical and generation-free. A useful if not stimulating shop.

020 7792 7967 **tube: Notting Hill Gate**
186 Westbourne Grove Mon-Sat 10-7
London W11 Sun 12-6

Laura Ashley

Typically known for floral fabrics and interior design, Laura Ashley's clothing collection has, in the past, bordered on matronly. These days they're laboring to leave their old-fashioned image behind. The result is light, fresh and simple. Brightly colored T-shirts, cardigans and khaki shorts appear in summer; smart jackets, heavier skirts and thick knits in winter. Of course, the classic tea dress is still available in quaint English floral prints. If you find a pattern you really love, take it home and cover your walls, beds and dressing-table with it. www.lauraashley.com

020 7437 9760 **tube: Oxford Circus**
256-258 Regent Street Mon-Tues 10-6:30, Wed 10-7
London W1 Thurs-Fri 10-8, Sat 9:30-7, Sun 12-6

020 7938 3751 **tube: High Street Kensington**
96b Kensington High Street Mon-Sat 10-6:30, Sun 12-6
London W8

020 7355 1363 **tube: Marble Arch**
449-451 Oxford Street Mon-Tues 10-6:30, Thurs 10-8
London W1 Wed, Fri-Sat 10-7, Sun 12-6

Laura Tom

It's summer all year long at this hidden holidaywear shop in Fulham. You'll find cotton capri pants and long linen trousers, sweet floaty dresses, plenty of T-shirts and a pretty selection of cashmere cardigans for chilly evenings. Other highlights include Thai wraparound trousers made in contrasting shades of shot silk, and clever halterneck tops with built-in bras to be worn with trousers or matching bikini bottoms. Dotted around the store are beach bags embellished with embroidered butterflies, wide-brimmed straw hats and sequined sandals. There are also a few pickings from abroad to get you in the mood—kikoys from Kenya, handmade belts from Guatemala and Chinese floral fans. The perfect stop-off when you're heading for the sun and all the shops are filled with depressing heavy winter stuff.

020 7736 3393 **tube: Fulham Broadway**
The Gasworks Mon-Fri 10-6, Sat 10-4
Redloh House
2 Michael Road
London SW6

Laurèl

Compared to the bold Escada, its sister brand Laurèl is an understated younger sibling. The collection is bright, sexy and vaguely schizophrenic—not quite work, not quite party.

Punched-out leather skirts, shimmering bra tops, pantsuits and sheer dresses abound. Solid colors and lustrous fabrics keep the glitz factor relatively low.

020 7493 1153 **tube: New Bond Street**
105 New Bond Street Mon-Sat 10-6:30
London W1

Laurence Tavernier

Traditional French nightwear comes in materials so soft you'll want to stay in bed all day. From silk nightgowns to striped cotton pajamas, the effect is old-fashioned and homely. Tavernier's bathrobes and cotton dressing-gowns are also perfect for lounging at the weekend, though the prices may not make you feel so relaxed.

020 7823 8737 **tube: South Kensington**
77 Walton Street Mon-Sat 10-6
London SW3

Leather Rat Classics

Head here to satisfy your leather craving. Leather Rat offers a range of colors and models, from biker to blazer to Chanel-style jackets, as well as any cut of pants. It might look like a dump but trust us, it's a treasure-house. Don't be discouraged by the treacherous, winding staircase that leads to the lower floor, where such brands as Redskins and Chevignon await.

020 7491 9753 **tube: Bond Street**
37 South Molton Street Mon-Sat 10:30-6:30
London W1 (Thurs 10:30-7), Sun 12:30-5:30

Levi's

Founded in 1853, this American jeans company has revolutionized its selection beyond the 501, creating innovative "twisted" styles and loose cuts with back pockets turned on a bias and dropped a few inches below the waist. The store is a denim wonderland, with a few T-shirts, jackets and accessories thrown in. And if you can't find that perfect pair off the rack, you can customize your own. www.levi.com

020 7292 2500 **tube: Oxford Circus**
174-176 Regent Street Mon-Wed, Fri 10-7, Thurs-Sat 10-8
London W1 Sun 12-7

020 7409 2692 **tube: Oxford Circus**
269 Regent Street Mon-Sat 10-7 (Thurs 10-8)
London W1 Sun 12-6

020 7497 0566 **tube: Covent Garden**
117a Long Acre Mon-Tues 10-7, Wed-Sat 10-7:30
London WC2 (Thurs 10-8), Sun 12-6

020 7938 4254 **tube: High Street Kensington**
171 Kensington High Street Mon-Sat 10-7
London W8 (Thurs 10-7:30), Sun 12-6

☆ Liberty

Once Arthur Liberty's warehouse for goods shipped from the Orient, this landmark Tudor mansion perfectly placed

between Mayfair and Soho is now a fashion institution. Liberty is recognized for carrying hip names from Alexander McQueen to Ann Demeulemeester as well as its own famous floral prints. There's an astonishing beauty department and separate areas for jewelry, gifts, linens, homewares and Arts and Crafts antiques. The newly refurbished western wing (far too modern for the original structure, if you ask us) offers cosmetics, menswear and accessories. Don't miss this place at sale time. www.liberty.co.uk

020 7734 1234 **tube: Oxford Circus**
210-220 Regent Street Mon-Wed 10-6:30, Thurs 10-8
London W1 Fri-Sat 10-7, Sun 12-6

The Library

Shhh...don't be fooled by the name. The small selection of decorative books on these shelves is only a subplot, the real story being trendsetting menswear. The protagonists are edgy designers like Dirk Schönberger, Martin Margiela and Maharishi and you'll find all styles of casualwear from jeans and cords to funky sweaters. More formal business attire from luminaries like Kilgour French Stanbury can be found downstairs.

020 7589 6569 **tube: South Kensington/Knightsbridge**
268 Brompton Road Mon-Sat 10-6:30 (Wed 10-7)
London SW3 Sun 12:30-5:30

Lilli Diva

An oasis of tempting fashion in an otherwise bleak street on the London shopping trawl, Lilli Diva offers the ever-cheery Orla Kiely, chic Sportmax, Armand Basi and Justin oh. The arrival of ex-Jimmy Choo designer Beatrix Ong has been much heralded and her pair of black heels, one inscribed with "Let's" and the other with "Dance", will put any killjoy in a party mood.

020 7801 9600 **tube: Clapham Common**
32 Lavender Hill Mon-Sat 10-6
London SW11

Lillywhites

Founded in 1863, Lillywhites is England's only sports department store but you won't need another one. Staff members are sports men and women themselves and can help you make precisely the right choice. The equipment (for 35 different pursuits) has evolved quite a bit since the early days—tennis rackets are made of titanium and ladies don't have to play in long skirts, thank god. Whatever comes into sports fashion, you can count on Lillywhites to keep up.

0870 333 9600 **tube: Piccadilly Circus**
24-36 Lower Regent Street Mon-Sat 10-7 (Thurs 10-8)
London SW1 Sun 12-6

Liola

Renowned for featuring comfortable stretch jersey, designs by Liola give the impression of being put together but with room to move. Separates coordinate seamlessly in bold shades and patterns, from blues and greens to a wilder tiger print, with chunky jewelry to complete the effect. In crease-free fabric that's perfect for packing, the collection will strike well-traveled women as both forgiving and chic. Think contemporary earth mother with a sense of style. www.liola.it

020 7581 5677 **tube: South Kensington**
69 Walton Street Mon-Fri 10-5:30, Sat 11-5
London SW3

Liz Claiborne

A fashion mainstay in America, Liz Claiborne remains ever-attuned to dependable comfort with a bit of style. The selection sticks to the basics, using practical wash-and-wear fabrics, solid colors and loose cuts to suit the over-40 crowd. A more casual line features knitwear, dresses, trousers and skirts, and there's a collection just for petites.
www.lizclairborne.com

020 7734 4987 **tube: Oxford Circus**
211-213 Regent Street Mon-Sat 10-7 (Thurs 10-8)
London W1 Sun 12-6

Liza Bruce

Her sexy swimwear, available in every desirable color and cut, is a tour de force but equal airtime should be given to Bruce's holiday clothing. Summer tops, sarongs and slip dresses are set against a bright minimalist interior and modern furniture designed by Bruce's husband, Nicholas Alvis Vega. The atmosphere is enhanced by its location on one of the prettiest little streets in London.

020 7235 8423 **tube: Knightsbridge**
9 Pont Street Mon-Sat 11-6
London SW1

Lock & Co

The most famous hatters in the world have been in business since 1676. They sell a vast selection of styles for men and women—felt hats including homburgs, fedoras, and trilbies; tweeds including flat caps and deerstalkers; waxed fishing hats; panamas and riding hats. There is also a small range of country clothing. The store is so beautiful it's like stepping into a time machine and finding yourself in early 19th-century London. www.lockhatters.co.uk

020 7930 8874 **tube: Green Park**
6 St. James's Street Mon-Fri 9-5:30, Sat 9:30-5:30
London SW1

Loewe

The smell of leather that permeates this store leaves no doubt about Loewe's stock in trade. This Spanish institution has a history of producing fine leather products since 1846. Best known for its luxurious handbags and luggage, the store also carries a sophisticated women's ready-to-wear designed by newcomer Jose Enrique Oña Selfa. Like the accessories, most of the skirts and jackets are created from leather and suede. www.loewe.com

020 7493 3914 **tube: Bond Street**
130 New Bond Street Mon-Sat 10-6
London W1

The Loft

If you prefer to dress designer but your budget won't always cooperate, head here for secondhand (and in some cases unworn) clothing. The space is somewhat cramped and often busy, but don't let that stop you digging through the racks. Womenswear, found downstairs, is organized by color, from evening dresses to Earl jeans. Gucci, Joseph, Nicole Farhi, Paul Smith, Comme des Garçons...and shoes by Prada and Jimmy Choo. It's a label lover's dream. www.the-loft.co.uk

Directory

020 7240 3807 **tube: Covent Garden**
35 Monmouth Street Mon-Sat 11-6, Sun 1-5
London WC2

Long Tall Sally

Women topping the tape measure at five foot nine will find an assortment of casualwear, suits, eveningwear and accessories. Sizes range from 10-20, with a separate maternity collection available if you order it. Cuts are modern, if not quite cool, but traces of denim and diamanté add a spark of style. www.longtallsally.co.uk

020 7487 3370 **tube: Baker Street**
21-25 Chiltern Street Mon-Sat 9:30-5:30 (Thurs 10-7)
London W1

Loro Piana

This is the ultimate in Italian cashmere, with lush sweaters, cozy shirts and shawls in colors from delicate pastels to deep blues and browns. Patterns remain simple, with stripes at the decorative extreme. Pants, shirts and sweater sets are also available in linen, cotton and silk. Buttery soft leather and suede add a true sense of luxury.

020 7235 3203 **tube: Knightsbridge**
47 Sloane Street Mon-Sat 10-6 (Wed 10-7)
London SW1

Louis Féraud

Elegance and desk-to-dinner versatility draw moneyed, sophisticated shoppers to this boutique. French painter-cum-designer Féraud brings bright colors and flattering cuts to tailored suits, blouses, sweaters and skirts, in a collection that stays safely away from trend. Corporate ladies love Féraud's clothes, including scarves inspired by his own paintings.

020 7493 1684 **tube: Bond Street**
73 New Bond Street Mon-Sat 9:30-6:30 (Thurs 9:30-7)
London W1

Louis Vuitton

Marc Jacobs catapulted this legendary French luxury luggage label back into the top tier of fashion must-haves. Waiting lists are long for the latest LV-covered accessories, and style gurus are tripping over themselves to get to his beautifully crafted ready-to-wear. Whatever you find here will send a message, plain as the logo on your bag: impeccable quality at any price. Just be prepared for long lines of Japanese tourists. www.vuitton.com

020 7399 4050 **tube: Green Park**
17-18 New Bond Street Mon-Sat 10-6:30
London W1

020 7399 4050 **tube: Knightsbridge**
198-199 Sloane Street Mon-Sat 10-7, Sun 12-5
London SW1

020 7399 4050 **tube: Bank**
5-6 Royal Exchange Mon-Fri 10-6:30
London EC3

Louise Kennedy

Kennedy's London shop is tiny compared to her Dublin flagship, a grand Georgian house that also functions as her home, but this quiet Belgravia block serves the Irish designer well. She offers beautifully made wool suits, hand-beaded cocktail dresses, cashmere sweaters and coats. Lulu Guinness bags, jewelry by Kenny Mac and rare Indian pashminas mingle with modern Irish crystal. Kennedy's crisp cotton button-down shirts, in purple, blue or camel check, put nearby Pink to shame.

020 7235 0911 **tube: Knightsbridge**
11 West Halkin Street Mon-Sat 10-6
London SW1

Lucy In The Sky

A new addition to the King's Road, this shop stocks a girly mix of jewelry, handbags and accessories. More suited to the younger generation in quality and pricing (nearly everything is under £30), the selection is displayed on chunky white shelves with items grouped together in gentle colors such as pale blue, pink and amber. There are charm bracelets, diamanté cuffs and lots of sparkling paste jewelry, as well as Johnny Loves Rosie flower hairclips and evening bags strewn with pearl drops by Paris label Lollipop. This is the sort of place you might find a present for girls in their teens.

020 7351 1577 **tube: Sloane Square**
178a King's Road Mon-Fri 10:30-6:30, Sun 12-6
London SW3

☆ Lulu Guinness

Lulu's adorable flowerpot bags spread like proverbial wild flowers through the fashion scene. Her designs are so creative they've become collectibles, and some are even on display in the Victoria & Albert Museum. But they're best seen in their element at her shop, where a montage of vintage fashion pages on the floor captures the essence of her kitsch spirit. When it comes to British bag designers, Guinness is neck and neck with Anya Hindmarch. www.luluguinness.com

020 7823 4828 **tube: Sloane Square**
3 Ellis Street Mon-Fri 10-6, Sat 11-6
London SW1

M-A-G Europe

From V-necks to crew necks, baby pink to basic black, this sweater shop offers top-notch cashmere worth seeking out. Simple designs come in seasonal shades with decorative highlights like stripes, beading and specialty stitches. But the general feeling is that the knits border on the too expensive, even if they are cashmere. Pretty belts and bags are also available. www.m-a-g.com

020 7591 0552 **tube: Knightsbridge**
20 Beauchamp Place Mon-Sat 10-6
London SW3

Maharishi

If you know the name, you probably know the cargo pants. Delicately embroidered with fire-breathing dragons, red poppies and other Asian motifs their combination of casual comfort and beautiful decoration has been a hit with fashion followers and hip-hoppers alike. Not a designer per se, the man behind Maharishi, Hardy Blechman, is more of a concept creator. His varying interests in Asian spirituality, technology and the military are all apparent at the Covent Garden store, where Bruce Lee dolls and Samurai action figures sit beside recycled US army fatigues and vacuum-packed T-shirts designed by graffiti artist Futura. Worth a look, even if you're not planning to buy.

020 7836 3860 **tube: Covent Garden**
19a Floral Street Mon-Sat 10-7, Sun 12-5
London WC2

Mandy

Trashy meets trendy at this small shop where glittery T-shirts and studded denim feed a Madonna wannabe crowd. Find skin-baring clubwear, leather pants and colorful vest tops with velvet piping. More than one purchase might send you into trend overdrive—choose carefully.

020 7376 7491 **tube: Sloane Square**
139 King's Road Mon-Sat 10-7, Sun 12-6
London SW3

Mango/MNG

In the same vein as Zara and H&M, this Spanish chain targets young women with knock-offs of the season's catwalk

trends. Selection ranges from weekendwear to suits and businesswear. But don't forget, this is fashion at its most mass, so you might be better off sticking to the casual stuff.

www.mangoshop.com

020 7434 1384 **tube: Piccadilly Circus**
106-112 Regent Street Mon-Sat 10-8
London W1 Sun 12-6

020 7240 6099 **tube: Covent Garden**
8-12 Neal Street Mon-Fri 10-8, Sat 9-6, Sun 11-5
London WC2

020 7434 3694 **tube: Oxford Circus**
225-235 Oxford Street Mon-Sat 10-8 (Thurs 10-9)
London W1 Sun 12-6

Manolo Blahnik

He's the king of the stiletto and shows no signs of abdicating his throne. Fashion fanatics can spot Manolos a mile off—the three-inch heel, the curve of the instep, the point of the toe. From an indispensable black pump to a turquoise stiletto, he anticipates a woman's every step: sometimes practical, sometimes fanciful but, alas, almost always painful. They've been described as better than sex and sample sales drive *Vogue* girls to fisticuffs.

020 7352 3863 **tube: Sloane Square**
49 Old Church Street Mon-Fri 10-5:30, Sat 10:30-5
London SW3

Manucci

Yet another transplanted Italian selling suits, shirts and ties plus a few pieces of smart/casual menswear including the Jaguar Cars line and the Pal Zileri formal and casual collections. In a stark wood-floored interior Manucci offers alterations and free delivery, and rightly advertises its friendly service.

www.ccshirts.com

020 7930 9911 **tube: Piccadilly Circus/Green Park**
108 Jermyn Street Mon-Sat 10-7, Sun 12-5
London SW1

Margaret Howell

Shoppers can quietly accumulate a wardrobe of her well-loved designs without even realizing it, such is the classic appeal of Margaret Howell. Button-down shirts, dresses, pants, jackets and enticing knitwear are all made of the finest fabrics, with prices to match. A recent homeware collection reverberates with the same understated sense of style. Don't be surprised if you're bitten by the Howell bug—many Brits before you have been.

020 7584 2462 **tube: Knightsbridge**
29 Beauchamp Place Mon-Sat 10-6
London SW3

020 7009 9000 **tube: Oxford Circus**
34 Wigmore Street Mon-Sat 10-6 (Thurs 10-7)
London W1

Marilyn Moore

Feminine and fun, Marilyn Moore designs are what every girl needs to cheer up a drab wardrobe. The renowned cashmere-silk knitwear is soft and affordable and comes in summery shades of pale blue, sea-green and pretty pink. Details like ruffled sleeves, appliqué flowers, colorful stripes or ribbons and, on one sweater, an image of a temptingly sweet cupcake, add character and style. You'll also find customized children's T-shirts, handbags decorated with little ladybirds, fitted shirts and skirts and a few well picked pieces by Omnia, Luna Bis and Sheradon Minns.

020 7727 5577 **tube: Ladbroke Grove/NottingHill Gate**
7 Elgin Crescent Mon-Sat 10-6, Sun 12-5
London W11

Marina Rinaldi

This division of MaxMara specializes in understated styles in soft fabrics that don't cling for the bigger woman (sizes 12-26). Suits, pants, knitwear and outerwear are spread throughout this two-floor store, which is typical Italian minimalism. For summer, there's a small selection of sequined sandals and Fendi-style handbags. Marina Sport is their more relaxed casual line.

020 7629 4454 **tube: Green Park**
39 Old Bond Street Mon-Sat 10-6 (Thurs 10-7)
London W1

Marks & Spencer

No shopping street is complete without M&S, a pure slice of English life. Their reputation has wavered in recent years, but lately it's been on the upswing. Their trendy new clothing range, Per Una, has attracted the coveted younger customer and now that they have lured Vittorio Radice—the brilliant retailer who transformed Selfridges from dowdy to magnificent—onto the staff, we are clearly headed for exciting times. Give it a go and you might find a very affordable necessity. It's dual-purpose shopping, as many of the stores also sell top-quality groceries.

020 7935 7954 **tube: Marble Arch**
458 Oxford Street Mon-Fri 9-9, Sat 8:30-8
London W1 Sun 12-6

020 7437 7722 **tube: Oxford Circus**
173 Oxford Street Mon-Sat 9-8 (Thurs 9-9)
London W1 Sun 12-6

020 7376 5634 **tube: Sloane Square**
85 King's Road Mon-Fri 9-8, Sat 8:30-8
London SW3 Sun 12-6

020 7938 3711 **tube: High Street Kensington**
113 Kensington High Street Mon-Sat 8-8, Sun 12-6
London W8

020 8741 8311 **tube: Hammersmith**
27 King Street Mon-Fri 8-9, Sat 8-7, Sun 11-5
London W6

020 7267 6055 **tube: Camden Town**
143 Camden High Street Mon-Fri 8:30-9
London NW1 Sat 8:30-7, Sun 11-5

Marni

Bright blue walls are hung with sweeping silver rails that extend through the middle of the store. All this provides an ethereal backdrop for Marni's lovely fabrics and feminine designs. From soft, chiffon dresses to suede jackets to wide-legged striped pants, the collection and its surrounding environs are so inviting, you might be tempted to linger, post-purchase, downstairs at the in-store café.

020 7235 1991 **tube: Knightsbridge**
16 Sloane Street Mon-Fri 10-6:30 (Wed 10-7)
London SW1 Sat 10-6:30

Mash

Streetwear punters striving to look as if they don't care (even when they care very much) find the latest brands at this wannabe underground boutique. Racks are packed with cool names like Carhartt and Ringspun and G-Star Raw denim jeans that look like they've been rolled in the dirt. Colorful skateboards plastered with extreme sports stickers are perfect for showing off your half pipe, while the huge selection of baseball and ski caps will help you go low-pro.

020 7434 9609 **tube: Oxford Circus**
73 Oxford Street Mon-Sat 10-7 (Thurs 10-8)
London W1 Sun 11-6

☆ Matches

With an A-list clientele and a staff of fashion experts, Matches is having its moment. Dolce & Gabbana, Marc Jacobs, Stella McCartney...the hippest names in fashion hang here, making it one of the best places for strong fresh-from-the-catwalk pieces. Customers can sip chardonnay while they sift through the racks of Helmut Lang trousers, Marni coats and attire from Missoni and Alexander McQueen. Other highlights include a stellar shoe selection, a VIP shopping area with a full bar, and the Marc Jacobs collection at American prices. Hurrah!

020 7221 0255 **tube: Notting Hill Gate**
60-64 Ledbury Road Mon-Sat 10-6, Sun 12-6
London W11

020 8947 8707 (W) **tube: Wimbledon**
34 High Street (opening times as above)
London SW19

020 8946 8218 (M, casual) **tube: Wimbledon**
38 High Street (opening times as above)
London SW19

020 8944 5366 (M) **tube: Wimbledon**
39 High Street (opening times as above)
London SW19

020 8944 5995 (W, casual) **tube: Wimbledon**
56b High Street (opening times as above)
London SW19

Maurice Sedwell

Don't be put-off by the "ring to enter" sign at the door. Despite its instantly apparent and strong sense of tradition, Maurice Sedwell prides itself on being one of the most creative tailors on Savile Row. This urge to stand out from the crowd manifests itself most obviously in its unique bespoke leather suit service as well as a willingness to mix a wide range of traditional fabrics with leather in all sorts of surprising combinations. www.savilerowtailor.com

020 7734 0824 **tube: Piccadilly Circus/Oxford Circus**
19 Savile Row Mon-Fri 9-6, Sat 9-1
London W1

MaxMara

In the relaxed atmosphere of MaxMara all racks lead to simplicity. The understated collection avoids passing fads with a perennial devotion to high quality and style. Soft feminine fabrics in the safe shades of taupe, beige, navy and black are prominent, along with the occasional print. Their beautiful overcoats add the perfect finish.

020 7491 4748 **tube: Bond Street**
153 New Bond Street Mon-Sat 10-6 (Thurs 10-7)
London W1

020 7235 7941 **tube: Knightsbridge**
32 Sloane Street Mon-Sat 10-6 (Wed 10-7)
London SW1

Mexx

Mexx features affordable wardrobe staples with a fashion edge. The selection is dominated by casual mix-and-match separates, with an emphasis on skirts, pants and shirts. From long-sleeved cotton T-shirts to sporty capris, Mexx covers all the bases, including accessories. www.mexx.com

020 7836 9661 **tube: Covent Garden**
112-115 Long Acre Mon-Sat 10:30-7 (Thurs 10:30-8)
London WC2 Sun 12-6

020 7225 2993 **tube: Knightsbridge**
75 Brompton Road Mon-Sat 10:30-7 (Wed 10:30-7:30)
London SW3 Sun 12-6

Mikihouse

You'll feel as if you've climbed into a box of crayons, with red, blue and yellow dripping down the walls. The children's clothing here is Legoland bright and durable enough for rough and tumble. Denim shorts, shoes embroidered with teddy bears, swimsuits with crocheted cherries dangling from the straps and tons of colorful T-shirts will send you off spending, while the assortment of toys and books will keep the kids busy.

020 7838 0006 **tube: South Kensington**
107 Walton Street Mon-Sat 10-6
London SW3

☆ MiMi

Holding court at the western end of the King's Road, MiMi maintains royal status among London's fashion devotees, including Yasmin Le Bon and Madonna. No wonder. The store is popping with color and an energetic mix of designer labels—Marc Jacobs, Gharani Strok, Collette Dinnigan, Boyd and Jimmy Choo. A refreshing reprieve from the usual main street chains, this is a great place to go when you feel like treating yourself.

020 7349 9699 — **tube: Sloane Square**
309 King's Road — Mon-Sat 10:30-6:30, Sun 1-6
London SW3

Miss Selfridge

This very young, trendy shop appeals to teens who spend their idle hours hunting stores in pursuit of the latest looks. The prices are affordable and the selection broad. Find everything from the current cut of jeans to tiny clubwear tops to pink body glitter. Over-21s would do well to skip this stop, as quality is low and the looks tend to be trashy. (Incidentally, Miss Selfridge has no connection with Selfridges department store.) www.zoom.co.uk

020 7927 0188 — **tube: Oxford Circus**
214 Oxford Street — Mon-Sat 9-7 (Thurs 9-9)
London W1 — Sun 11:30-6

020 7938 4182 — **tube: High Street Kensington**
42-44 Kensington High Street — Mon-Wed 10-6:30
London W8 — Thurs-Sat 10-7, Sun 12-6

Miss Sixty

With red leather pants, tiny halter tops, and jeans that lace at the waist this Italian chain has swept young girls off their feet. They come by the gaggle to stock up on the trademark trash-glamour gear: flared, boot-cut and low-waisted denim, micromini skirts, fuchsia hotpants and cowgirl shirts that tie at the waist. This label has lately become a hit with twentysomethings, too, for its low prices and keen trendspotting. Anyone over size 14 should beware, though—Miss Sixty suits tiny sizes best. Also check out the men's line, dubbed Energy. www.misssixty.com

020 7376 1330 — **tube: High Street Kensington**
42 Kensington High Street — Mon-Sat 10-6:30
London W8 — (Thurs 10-7:30), Sun 12-6

020 7434 3060 — **tube: Oxford Circus**
31-32 Great Marlborough Street — Mon-Sat 10-7, Sun 12-5
London W1

020 7836 3789 — **tube: Covent Garden**
39 Neal Street — Mon-Sat 10-6:30
London WC2 — (Thurs 10-7:30), Sun 12-6

Miu Miu

It's billed as the junior line of super-successful Prada, but Miu Miu is hardly a bargain-basement brand. Miu Miu's character tends to be a bit more girlish than Prada, with shift dresses, pleated skirts and sheer, frilly tops. Shoes and handbags are playfully innovative (one recent season introduced a colorful court shoe with a long pointy toe and a bright button). Part headmistress, part schoolgirl, sophistication plus whimsy is the Miu Miu style.

020 7409 0900 **tube: Bond Street**
123 New Bond Street Mon-Sat 10-6 (Thurs 10-7)
London W1

Monogrammed Linen Shop 

If you can't picture your bed linens, kitchen towels and throws without embroidered initials, make your way here, where lovely linen is personalized to order. When it comes to clothes there is a small but very appealing selection of nightwear, and for babies christening dresses and rompers too cute to resist. www.monogrammedlinenshop.co.uk

020 7589 4033 **tube: South Kensington**
168 Walton Street Mon-Sat 10-6
London SW3

Monsoon 

These vibrant, fluttery creations appeal most in the summer, when lightweight silk is all you want to wear. An eastern aesthetic blends with modern tailoring to produce patterned pieces sprinkled with delicate details. The dresses, skirts and sweater sets remain loose and bright, better suited to moms than fashion-conscious teens. Some stores carry a selection for young girls, though much of it is frilly and pink. www.monsoon.com

020 7581 1408 **tube: Knightsbridge**
29 Brompton Road Mon-Sat 9:30-7 (Wed 9:30-8)
London SW3 Sun 12-6

020 7499 2578 **tube: Oxford Circus**
264 Oxford Street Mon-Fri 9:30-7:30 (Thurs 9:30-8)
London W1 Sat 9:30-7:30, Sun 11-5

020 7836 9140 **tube: Covent Garden**
23 The Piazza Mon-Sat 10-8, Sun 11-6
London WC2

020 7379 3623 **tube: Covent Garden**
5-6 James Street (opening times as above)
London WC2

020 7730 7552 **tube: Sloane Square**
33c-33d King's Road Mon-Sat 10-6:30 (Wed 10-7:30)
London SW3 Sun 12-6

020 7376 0366 **tube: High Street Kensington**
5 Barkers Arcade Mon-Sat 10-7 (Thurs 10-8)
Kensington High Street Sun 12-6
London W8

020 7512 9543 **tube: Canary Wharf**
21-22 Canada Square Mon-Fri 8:30-7, Sat 10-6
London E14 Sun 11-5

020 7623 3774 **tube: Monument**
87 Gracechurch Street Mon-Fri 8-6:30
London EC3

020 7435 1726 **tube: Hampstead**
1 Hampstead High Street Mon-Sat 10-6, Sun 11-6
London NW3

020 7486 8466 **tube: Baker Street/Bond Street**
96 Marylebone High Street Mon-Sat 10:30-7
London W1 (Wed 10:30-7:30), Sun 11-5

020 8788 1286 **tube: Putney Bridge**
Unit 25 Putney Exchange Mon-Sat 9-6 (Thurs-Fri 9-7)
High Street Sun 11-5
London SW15

020 8944 8920 **tube: Wimbledon**
220-221 Centre Court Shopping Centre Mon-Fri 9-7
London SW19 (Thurs 9-8), Sat 9-6, Sun 11-5

Morgan

Like many chains, the recent selection here has been inspired by Eighties-style trash-glamour. Slashed tees and tanks with glittery appliqués, black clubbing pants and dark jeans with gold belts slung low across the hips are typical fare. The look is young and sexy, and great for fickle trend-followers. There's no telling what next season will offer, but chances are it will be bright and tight.

www.morgandetoi.com

020 7499 4101 **tube: Bond Street/Marble Arch**
391-393 Oxford Street Mon-Sat 10-7 (Thurs-Fri 10-8)
London W1 Sun 12-6

020 7836 9235 **tube: Covent Garden**
36 Long Acre Mon-Wed 10:30-7:30, Thurs 10-8
London WC2 Fri-Sat 10-7, Sun 11:30-6

020 7376 2108 **tube: High Street Kensington**
88-90 Kensington High Street Mon-Sat 10-7
London W8 (Thurs 10-7:30), Sun 12-6

020 7491 1883 **tube: Oxford Circus**
270 Oxford Street Mon-Wed 10-7:30, Thurs-Fri 10-8
London W1 Sat 10-7:30, Sun 12-6

Moschino

It's high-designer but down to earth, with splashes of bright color and playful details. Stop by for a dose of good fashionable fun: Thirties-style satin evening dresses with batwing sleeves, rough-cut ruffled denim skirts, suits with stand-out stitching and unfinished seams, and "I am Your Baby Doll" T-shirts. If the signature label is out of reach, their bridge line, Cheap & Chic, offers similar flavor at a lower (but not much) price. www.moschino.it

020 7318 0555 **tube: Oxford Circus**
28-29 Conduit Street Mon-Sat 10-6 (Thurs 10-7)
London W1

Moss Bros 

If the invitation arrived months ago but he's only just noticed the words "black tie", tell your date to hotfoot it over here. Moss Bros is the place to rent, or buy, men's formalwear: a complete package—jacket, pants, shirt, cummerbund and bow tie—will set him back £65 a day for a morning suit and £49 for eveningwear. If he's looking to buy, there are several designers for sale: Pierre Cardin, Hugo Boss, Baumler, Dehavilland and the Moss Bros label itself. Periodically, quite often actually, they have serious value-for-money sales...designer shirts in every desirable color reduced to £10-15, for example. (The Strand and Blomfield Street addresses are also the Savoy Tailors Guild, all part of the same group.)

020 7494 0665 **tube: Piccadilly Circus**
88 Regent Street Mon-Fri 9:30-6:30 (Thurs 9-7)
London W1 Sat 9-7, Sun 11-5

020 7632 9700 **tube: Covent Garden**
27 King Street Mon-Sat 9-6 (Thurs 9-7)
London WC2

020 7629 7371 **tube: Oxford Circus**
299 Oxford Street Mon-Sat 10-7 (Thurs 10-8), Sun 12-6
London W1

020 7836 7881 **tube: Charing Cross**
92-93 The Strand Mon-Sat 9-6 (Thurs 9-7)
London WC2 Sun 12-5

020 7588 8038 **tube: Liverpool Street (Eldon Street exit)**
35 Blomfield Street Mon-Fri 8:30-6
London EC2

020 7600 7366 **tube: Bank (exit 9)**
83 Cheapside Mon-Fri 9-6
London EC2

Muji 

Ironically, this Japanese chain has made a name for itself by selling neutral-looking, unbranded products. The highlights of their selection are the no-frills cardboard, plastic, metal and wood homewares but their small collection of clothing is definitely worth a glance. Staying true to the ethos of practical, anonymous style, design remains minimalist, featuring dark monotones and simple patterns. Woolen sweaters, cotton shirts, underwear and linen pants are all reasonably well made and equally well priced. www.muji.co.uk

020 7437 7503 **tube: Oxford Circus**
187 Oxford Street Mon-Wed, Sat 10-7, Thurs 10-8
London W1 Fri 10-7, Sun 12-6

020 7379 0820 **tube: Covent Garden**
135 Long Acre Mon-Sat 10:30-7:30
London WC2 (Thurs 10:30-8), Sun 12-6

020 7436 1779 **tube: Tottenham Court Road**
6 Tottenham Court Road Mon-Sat 10-8
London W1 Sun 12-6

020 7376 2484 **tube: High Street Kensington**
157 Kensington High Street Mon-Fri 10:30-7
London W8 (Thurs 10:30-7:30), Sat 10-7, Sun 12-6

020 7287 7323 **tube: Oxford Circus**
41 Carnaby Street Mon 10:30-7, Tues-Sat 10-7
London W1 Sun 12-6

Mulberry

What began in 1971 with Robert Saul's modest leather goods and jewelry collection has blossomed into an institution for the British country set. The brand was relaunched last year under owner Christina Ong, with an impressive new Bond Street flagship store and clothing collections for women and men. Featuring soft suede trousers, T-shirts with sequin flowers and double-breasted rain jackets, the women's line gives classic tailoring a trendy twist. The cozy Mulberry Home collection includes lovely furniture, crisp linens and floral fabrics, while the leather accessories are still a highlight.

020 7491 3900 **tube: Bond Street**
41-42 New Bond Street Mon-Sat 10-6 (Thurs 10-7)
London W1

020 7838 1411 **tube: Knightsbridge**
171-175 Brompton Road Mon-Fri 10-6 (Wed 10-7)
London SW3 Sat 10-6:30

020 7493 2546 **tube: Bond Street**
11-12 Gees Court Mon-Sat 10-6 (Thurs 10-7)
London W1

Musa

Girly and romantic, this tiny shop features two armoires filled with vintage and one-off pieces. Contemporary selection encourages a mix-don't-match approach, with denim by Sass & Bide, Miss Italy ruffled silk camisoles and dresses by Roland Mouret. Jewelry and homewares are also available, including Fifties Trifari earrings, antique chandeliers and original Venetian mirrors. A lovely little oasis.

020 7937 6282 **tube: High Street Kensington**
31 Holland Street Tues-Sat 11-6
London W8

Myla

Kate Moss and Victoria Beckham are both fans of this 'sex shop with style' that specializes in super-luxe lingerie as well as offering a 'tasteful' collection of sex toys, erotic literature, massage products and 'after dinner mix condoms'. The delicate underwear, in all manner of styles, is made from the finest laces, silks and satins and comes in cup sizes A-E. There are romantic rose tulle camisoles and teasing ruffle-trim thongs, Forties-style French knickers and raunchy hipster thongs. Whatever you desire, the professional fitters in the shop will help you find your perfect fit.

020 7221 9222 **tube: Notting Hill Gate**
77 Lonsdale Road Mon-Sat 10-6
London W11

N.Peal

If it's cashmere you're craving, this label has some of the best. The tiny men's shop, by the entrance to the famous Burlington Arcade, offers a wide variety of styles in colors from navy to bright purple. The women's shop at the other end of the arcade sells equally colorful cardigans embellished with embroidery and sequins, as well as knit halters, scoop-necked twinsets, slippers and shawls. For the cashmere connoisseur, there's a special gentle shampoo to keep your favorite pieces at their finest. www.npeal.com

020 7499 2952 (M) **tube: Green Park**
71-72 Burlington Arcade Mon-Sat 9:30-6
London W1

020 7493 9220 (W) **tube: Green Park**
37 Burlington Arcade Mon-Sat 9:30-6
London W1

Naf Naf

Over the last decade or so this French label has matured. Today, the look is contemporary and colorful—flower-patterned dresses and skirts, bright capris and stretch button-down shirts—though the quality is not exactly built to last. You may not find something you love, but who knows—you might get lucky and it doesn't cost to take a look.

020 7730 7672 **tube: Sloane Square**
13-15 King's Road Mon-Sat 10-6:30
London SW3 (Wed 10-7), Sun 12-5

Nara

Last year two sisters opened this first-floor boutique on Beauchamp Place, giving the sedate block a fresh breath of trendy fashion. Looks are strong if a bit trashy: sequined halternecks, tiny T-shirts and flared jeans covered in diamanté and splashed with bleach. If the clothing is a bit too much, take a smaller dose from the selection of colorful, beaded bags and sparkling jewelry. www.nara-boutique.com

020 7589 6212 **tube: Knightsbridge**
8 Beauchamp Place Mon-Sat 10-6
London SW3

Natural Blue

Staging its own quiet resistance to trend-obsessed men's shops, Natural Blue features simple, functional smart casualwear: T-shirts, ribbed sweaters and cotton trousers come in solid colors from black to lilac. With a subdued atmosphere, this store expresses a relaxed sense of style that would probably put the dedicated follower of fashion to sleep but would delight the shopper looking for better basics. (Fans please note that they've closed their Neal Street and King's Road locations.) www.naturalblue.com

020 7377 8755 **tube: Liverpool Street**
52-54 Artillery Lane Mon-Tues, Fri 10-6:30
London E1 Wed-Thurs 10-7, Sun 11-4

The Natural Shoe Store

They're not the sexiest shoes on the market but they're undeniably easy on your feet. Among the wide variety of well-made brands you'll find Arche, Birkenstock, Trippin and Nature Sko. Basic leather and suede lace-ups from classic brands like Cheaney are the most exhilarating items in a selection short on fashion. But if it's comfort you're after, step right in. www.naturesko.com

020 7836 5254 **tube: Covent Garden**
21 Neal Street Mon-Tues 10-6, Wed-Sat 10-6:30
London WC2 Sun 12-5

020 7351 3721 **tube: Sloane Square**
325 King's Road Mon-Fri 10-6, Sat 10-6:30
London SW3 Sun 12-5:30

020 7727 1122 **tube: Notting Hill Gate**
181 Westbourne Grove (called Issues) Mon-Fri 10-6:30
London W11 Sat 10-6

Neil Cunningham

He has been called a master in the art of female flattery, and with a signature style that combines elegant tailoring with glamorous retro styles Neil Cunningham is one of London's most popular bridal couturiers. A strong Hollywood influence is evident in strapless bias-cut columns, simple sheath dresses and empire and A-lines. Detail is kept to a minimum, perhaps just a twinkle of Swarovski crystal or an eye-catching line of buttons. Classic, sexy and very grown-up. Audrey Hepburn and Jackie O would definitely approve.

020 7437 5793 **Piccadilly Circus**
28 Sackville Street Mon-Sat 10-5:30 (every second Sat)
London W1 (by appointment)

Neisha Crosland

Textile experts will recognize the name Neisha Crosland, a featured designer at Harvey Nichols, Liberty and Harrods. Her magic touch yields many lovely results, from velvet shawls and chiffon scarves to colorful pillows and throws. Whether decorating yourself or decorating your home, Crosland's creations will inspire.

020 7589 4866 **tube: South Kensington**
137 Fulham Road Mon-Sat 10-6, Sun 12-5
London SW3

Net-a-Porter

You won't find this shop on any high street—it's London's best virtual boutique, created by a gang of brilliant alumnae from that stylish and unique magazine *Tatler*. The original concept was to create an online magazine with fashion features just like the glossies, but which visitors could buy from (see Gisele in a stunning Missoni bikini, double-click and it's yours). The idea has since expanded into an online emporium of hot designer names, featuring gypsy tops by Marc Jacobs, Maharishi cargo pants, Jeans by Seven, and Cacharel eveningwear. Shoes by luminaries like Christian Louboutin and Jimmy Choo, and separate sections for beauty, jewelry and music, make this a chic one-stop-shop for those who prefer logging on to trekking about.

www.net-a-porter.com

New & Lingwood

Two stores sit at the Jermyn Street entrance to the charming Piccadilly Arcade. Beautiful, curved windows display a wonderful selection of shirts, shoes, ties and accessories. A Jermyn Street establishment since 1865, New & Lingwood's gorgeous interior must be one of few in the world to feature chandeliers and coats of arms...perhaps it's not surprising that they are traditional outfitters to the boys of Eton College (most famous recent alumni: the late Diana's two sons, Princes William and Harry). Friendly service, plus bespoke shirts in addition to off-the-peg. Great selection of cufflinks, suspenders, socks, dressing-gowns and the rest.

www.newandlingwood.com

020 7493 9621 — **tube: Piccadilly Circus/Green Park**
53 Jermyn Street — Mon-Fri 9-6, Sat 10-6
London SW1

New Look

With prices starting at £5, New Look is a good bet for cheap impulse buys. Teen trends dictate the design direction, in tarty clubbing clothes, decal T-shirts, athletic styles and denim. Stiletto sandals, knee-high boots and tennis shoes are also on hand, but don't look too closely as the quality is unlikely to hold up. The same goes for the self-consciously sexy, synthetic underwear sets. It's worth a spin through, but you've got to have a good eye. www.newlook.co.uk

020 7534 2005 — **tube: Oxford Circus**
175-179 Oxford Street — Mon-Wed 9-8, Thurs 9-9
London W1 — Fri-Sat 9-7, Sun 12-6

020 7802 9768 — **tube: Victoria**
Victoria Station — Mon-Fri 8-8, Sat 9-7, Sun 11-5
London SW1

020 8946 5895 — **tube: Wimbledon**
Centre Court Shopping Centre — Mon-Fri 9:30-7
London SW19 — (Thurs 9:30-8), Sat 9-7, Sun 11-5

Next

This store has less style and spunk than chains like Oasis and Zara, but it can provide an adequate supply of trendy essentials. The selection ranges from business blouses in pretty patterns to colorful athleticwear. Designs remain

generally unremarkable but you might find some stylish staples—raincoats, shoes and maternitywear, for example.
www.next.co.uk

020 7409 2746 **tube: Bond Street**
325-329 Oxford Street Mon-Fri 10:30-8 (Thurs 10:30-9)
London W1 Sat 9:30-8, Sun 12-6

020 7434 2515 **tube: Oxford Circus**
160 Regent Street Mon-Sat 10:30-7
London W1 (Thurs 10:30-8), Sun 12-6

020 7715 9410 **tube: Canary Wharf**
11-12 Canada Place Mon-Fri 8:30-7, Sat 9-6
London E14 Sun 11-5

020 7420 8280 **tube: Covent Garden**
15-17 Long Acre Mon-Fri 10-8 (Thurs 10-9)
London WC2 Sat 10-8, Sun 12-6

020 7938 4211 **tube: High Street Kensington**
54-56 Kensington High Street Mon-Fri 10-7 (Thurs 10-8)
London W8 Sat 10-7, Sun 12-6

020 7659 9730 **tube: Marble Arch**
508-520 Oxford Street Mon 10:30-8, Tues-Sat 10-8
London W1 (Thurs 10-9), Sun 12-6

020 7434 0477 **tube: Oxford Circus**
201-205 Oxford Street Mon-Fri 10-8, (Thurs 10-9)
London W1 Sat 9:30-8, Sun 12-6

Nick Ashley

Tired of searching for functional but stylish clothing during more than 25 years of motorcycle racing and touring, Nick Ashley—of the Laura Ashley clan—decided to design his own line. His vaguely retro leather jackets, pants, T-shirts, helmets and goggles have sold well to the Notting Hill set from a smallish shop in one of London's hottest streets. Recently, the collection has evolved away from biker gear towards "workwear"—plumbers' shirts and carpenter and gardeners' pants manufactured by the last surviving British cotton mill. It's hard-wearing clothing for the not-so-hard-working set.
www.nickashley.com

020 7221 1221 **tube: Notting Hill Gate**
57 Ledbury Road Mon-Fri 10-6, Sat 11-6
London W11

Nicole Farhi

This darling of British design has been revered for some time. Her key to lasting fashion success: classic design, beautiful fabrics and creations that are simple but striking. Soft sweater sets, crisp oxford shirts and sleek pants dominate the women's collection, while a similar selection of menswear reinforces the sense of understated style. Farhi's Home collection is increasingly popular and can be seen at the new Fulham Road store where chunky wooden tables are set with heavy wine glasses, simple vases of flowers and lovely white china.

020 7499 8368 **tube: Bond Street**
158 New Bond Street Mon-Fri 10-6 (Thurs 10-7)
London W1 Sat 10-6:30

020 7235 0877
193 Sloane Street
London SW1
tube: Knightsbridge
Mon-Sat 10-6 (Wed 10-7)

020 7838 0937
115 Fulham Road
London SW3
tube: South Kensington
Mon-Sat 10-6 (Wed 10-7)
Sun 12-5

020 7792 6888
202 Westbourne Grove
London W11
tube: Notting Hill Gate
Mon 10-6, Tues-Sat 10-7
Sun 10-5

Nigel Hall

A small menswear boutique in Covent Garden, Nigel Hall offers sleek designs for the slightly fashion-forward. The simple, modern selection features fine knitwear, shirts, pants and jackets. This otherwise unremarkable shop scores high marks for decent prices and nice detail.

020 7836 8223
18 Floral Street
London WC2
tube: Covent Garden
Mon-Wed 10:30-6:30
Thurs-Sat 10:30-7, Sun 12-5

Night Owls

As different from Agent Provocateur as your granny is from Kate Moss, this high-class shop offers lacy lingerie, see-through chemises and linen loungewear. On the suggestive side there are plenty of pretty thongs with matching garter belts and bras. The pink polka-dot panties are cute, though like most of their pieces they are too elaborate in texture or pattern to be concealed by anything but the thickest pants. www.nightowllingerie.co.uk

020 7584 2451
78 Fulham Road
London SW3
tube: South Kensington
Mon-Sat 10-6 (Wed 10-7)

Niketown

Nike-philes should make a dash for this store, a massive, sleek emporium offering every imaginable piece of swish paraphernalia from coordinating water bottles and keychains to the latest and lightest-weight running shoe. Organized by clothing category and sport, the wide selection of activewear is easy to navigate. But beware: these trademarked stay-dry fabrics and high-tech trainers come at a higher-than-average price. www.nike.com

020 7612 0800
236 Oxford Street
London W1
tube: Oxford Circus
Mon-Wed 10-7, Thurs-Sat 10-8
Sun 12-6

Nine West

American import Nine West retains a reputation for affordable, fashionable leather shoes and accessories. Lately the brand has expanded, offering everything from strappy sandals to towering boots to practical flats. The colors on offer have evolved too, reaching brightly beyond basic black and brown. Sunglasses, handbags, jewelry and outerwear are also available.

020 7629 3875 **tube: Bond Street**
9 South Molton Street Mon-Sat 10-7 (Thurs 10-8)
London W1 Sun 12-6

020 7229 8208 **tube: Queensway/Bayswater**
Whiteley's, Queensway Mon-Sat 10-8, Sun 12-6
London W2

020 7836 8485 **tube: Covent Garden**
1 James Street Mon-Sat 10-8 (Thurs 10-9)
London WC2 Sun 12-6

020 7937 1479 **tube: High Street Kensington**
155 Kensington High Street Mon-Sat 10-7
London W8 (Thurs 10-8), Sun 12-6

020 7581 7044 **tube: Sloane Square**
90 King's Road Mon-Sat 10-7 (Wed 10-8), Sun 12-6
London SW3

Ninivah Khomo

It's a jungle in this clothing and houseware den crawling with animal prints. Tiger, leopard, zebra and giraffe—all the decorative big game is here, scattered across pillows, negligees, T-shirts, blazers and throws. For a lighter touch of the wild there are fur hats, zebra headbands and a handbag with leopard print rendered in tiny glass beads. If you're on the hunt for something fun, this might be the place to prowl into.

020 7245 9533 **tube: Knightsbridge**
4a Motcomb Street Mon-Fri 10-6, Sat by appointment
London SW1

Nitya

Offering a comforting alternative to the sleek Bond Street boutiques, the French brand Nitya features Indian-inspired tunics, skirts, loose pants and scarves that express a body-modest sensibility. Flowing, natural fabrics elegantly drape the body in subtle tones of black, cream, burgundy, navy or brown. Styles are dressy and some are intricately stitched with simple floral patterns. Perfect for the non-traditional mother of the bride.

020 7495 6837 **tube: Bond Street**
118 New Bond Street Mon-Sat 10:30-6:30
London W1 (Thurs 10:30-7)

020 7794 3254 **tube: Hampstead**
19 Hampstead High Street Mon-Sat 10-6
London NW3

Noa Noa

This is a real hit-and-miss label. With wool V-neck cardigans, soft felt handbags and wide-leg corduroys, it's hardly clothing you can find fault with—provided it doesn't put you straight to sleep. Colors are rich and bright, and loose cuts offer a forgiving fit. Trend appears (rarely) in the form of ruffled plaid blouses with unfinished hems and lime suede flip-flops.

020 7704 2131 **tube: Highbury & Islington/Angel**
146 Upper Street Mon-Sat 9:30-6, Sun 11-5
London N1

Nothing

With its modern, bare interior and inspired clothing, this is a quintessential Notting Hill boutique. Carla Portman's designs are original and brilliantly basic, from cotton hipsters to asymmetric skirts to geometric-print dresses. These are hip clothes intended for everyday, rather than self-conscious designer posing (significantly, Portman had no formal fashion training). Other brands such as Soochi, Rude and Sessun fit fantastically with her cool, tailored look.
www.nothingshop.co.uk

020 7221 2910 **tube: Ladbroke Grove**
230 Portobello Road Mon-Fri 11-7, Sat 10:30-6:30
London W11 Sun 12-5

Directory

Oasis

Among the leaders of London's catwalk-to-sidewalk interpreters, Oasis offers a wide variety of affordable, fashionable finds. Twentysomethings flock to this store for all types of trendy essentials, be it skimpy top, flashy skirt, or sweet, sophisticated sweater set. The selection of dresses, pants, suits and sparkly tank tops is accompanied by equally of-the-moment accessories. www.oasis-stores.com

020 7323 5978 **tube: Oxford Circus**
292 Regent Street Mon-Sat 10-7 (Thurs 10-8)
London W1 Sun 12-6

020 7240 7445 **tube: Covent Garden**
13 James Street Mon-Sat 10-7 (Thurs 10-8)
London WC2 Sun 12-6

020 7584 5269 **tube: Sloane Square**
76-78 King's Road Mon-Sat 9:30-6:30 (Wed 9:30-7:30)
London SW3 Sun 12-5

020 7512 9715 **tube: Canary Wharf**
19 Canada Square Mon-Fri 9-7, Sat 10-6
London E14 Sun 11-5

020 7938 4019 **tube: High Street Kensington**
28a Kensington Church Street Mon-Sat 9:30-6:30
London W8 (Thurs 9:30-7:30), Sun 12-6

020 7434 1799 **tube: Oxford Circus**
12-14 Argyll Street Mon-Sat 10-7 (Thurs 10-8), Sun 12-6
London W1

020 7580 4763 **tube: Oxford Circus/**
The Plaza, 120 Oxford Street **Tottenham Court Road**
London W1 Mon-Sat 10-7 (Thurs 10-8), Sun 12-6

020 7359 5620 **tube: Angel**
10 Upper Street Mon-Sat 10-7, Sun 11-5
London N1

020 7256 8608 **tube: Liverpool Street**
85-86 Old Broad Street Mon-Fri 8:30-6:30
London EC2 (Thurs 8:30-7)

020 7248 2922 **tube: Bank**
4 Queen Victoria Street Mon-Fri 8:30-6:15
London EC4 (Thurs 8:30-6:45)

020 7243 2795 **tube: Bayswater/Queensway**
Whiteley's, Queensway Mon-Sat 10-8, Sun 12-6
London W2

Office

The name might fool you with its suggestion of corporate blandness but the majority of the shoes here are far too edgy for an average day at the office. Though not outlandish, the selection puts its own eccentric spin on seasonal basics like crocodile boots, stiletto heels and colorful mules. You'll also find trendy sneakers and, in summer, plenty of flip-flops and espadrilles. www.office.co.uk

020 7491 8027 (W) **tube: Bond Street**
55 South Molton Street Mon-Sat 10-7, Sun 12-6
London W1

020 7581 8750 **tube: Sloane Square**
100 King's Road (opening times as above)
London SW3

020 7221 8424 **tube: Notting Hill Gate/Ladbroke Grove**
217 Portobello Road Mon-Fri 9-6, Sat 10-6:30
London W11 Sun 11-5

020 7379 1896 **tube: Covent Garden**
57 Neal Street Mon-Fri 10-7:30 (Thurs 10:30-8)
London WC2 Sat 10:30-7, Sun 12-6

Offspring

This sporty sibling to Office swaps slingbacks for sneakers, offering a selection that's just as hip as that of big sis. Workout enthusiasts and posers alike will flip for the hip styles from Nike, Adidas, New Balance, Camper, Puma and Converse. If you're going to sweat, at least you can look cool. www.offspring.co.uk

020 7497 2463 **tube: Covent Garden**
60 Neal Street Mon-Sat 10-7 (Thurs 10-8)
London WC2 Sun 12-6

020 7267 9873 **tube: Camden Town**
221 Camden High Street Mon-Fri 9:30-6:30
London NW1 (Tues, Fri 10-6:30), Sat-Sun 10-6:30

020 7221 8424 **tube: Ladbroke Grove**
217 Portobello Road Mon-Fri 9-6, Sat 10-6:30
London W11 Sun 11-5

Oilily

This Dutch line offers just what a dreary London day demands: color, and the brighter the better. Orange, red, yellow and blue are combined in patterns of eye-crossing intricacy in knitwear, pants and skirts. The children's line is delightful—dresses, sweaters, pants and shirts splashed with patterns. Be forewarned, though: these aren't Gap prices. www.oilily.nl

020 7823 2505 **tube: Knightsbridge**
9 Sloane Street Mon-Sat 10-6 (Wed 10-7)
London SW1

☆ Olivia Morris 

She's outgrown her tiny shop (and the price point) at the Portobello Market, so Morris has packed up her pumps and moved a few blocks north. Her first collection was high-concept but fun, featuring do-it-yourself "blank canvas" heels which come in white with paint kit included; the "fluoro", fluorescent leather that glows in ultra-violet light; and the "pearly queen" boots, black felt hand-stitched with antique pearl buttons. Morris is definitely a star on the rise.

020 8962 0353 **nearest tube: Ladbroke Grove**
355 Portobello Road Mon-Thurs by appointment,
London W10 Fri-Sat 10-6

Olowu Golding 

Married design duo Elaine Golding and Duro Olowu quietly created a following at their Ledbury Road store before moving to the bustling Portobello Road. The clothing merges Olowu's West African heritage with Golding's classic East Coast influence in a modern mix of sharp tailoring and offbeat detail. Handmade shoes come with stained wooden heels and in fine materials like calf and snakeskin. Heart-stopping prices may put you off (shoes start at £350), but cool creativity comes at a cost.

020 8960 7570 **tube: Ladbroke Grove**
367 Portobello Road Tues-Sat (by appointment)
London W10

One Night Stand 

If you can't buy the designer dress of your dreams, why not hire it? It will cost you a fraction of the price (from £80 to £175) which means you needn't worry about how much wear you'll get out of it. One Night Stand is London's original dress hire agency with a constantly updated collection of over 400 dresses in sizes 6-18. You'll find everything from ballgowns and chiffon floaty dresses, to long satin evening gowns and corsets with skirts. Designers currently in stock include Robinson Valentine, Jenny Packham and David Fielden. If you're not the one-night type and you're heading off for a mini-break, don't panic, your hire lasts up to four days. Next day delivery is available in the UK and jewelry and accessories can also be hired.

020 7352 4848 **tube: Sloane Square**
8 Chelsea Manor Studios (by appointment)
Flood Street
London SW3

One of a Kind 

Sometimes secondhand doesn't come cheap, even in Notting Hill. They may be pre-worn, but the designer

Directory

goods here—from the likes of Pucci, Gucci and Vivienne Westwood—are regarded more like a rare vintage Scotch, to be savored and respected. Surrounding walls are covered in every cornerstone style of shoe, from peep toes to platforms to pumps. It must be good—top designers have been known to pop in for inspiration. www.1kind.com

020 7792 5284 (high designer) **tube: Ladbroke Grove**
253 Portobello Road (by appointment)
London W11

020 7792 5853 **tube: Ladbroke Grove**
259 Portobello Road Mon-Sat 11-6, Sun 12-5
London W11

O'Neill

Straight from the beaches and boardwalks of Southern California, O'Neill brings sun-streaked surf style to London's streets. Bright T-shirts, long shorts, swimsuits and the inevitable wetsuit are all available, as well as a selection of accessories. Stop here for a heavy dose of the West Coast. www.oneilleurope.co.uk

020 7836 7686 **tube: Covent Garden**
9-15 Neal Street Mon-Sat 10-7 (Thurs 10-8)
London WC2 Sun 12-6

020 7734 3778 **tube: Oxford Circus**
527 Carnaby Street Mon-Fri 10-7 (Thurs 10-8), Sun 12-6
London W1

Orvis

This ho-hum American import is dedicated to outdoorsy sportswear of the L.L.Bean or Land's End variety. Women can find knitwear, cotton tops, classic pants and blazers. Menswear includes vests, pants and button-downs. Designed for comfort and durability, these clothes favor function over form. Sporting goods, outerwear and accessories are also available. www.orvis.co.uk

020 7499 7496 **tube: Green Park**
36a Dover Street Mon-Fri 9:30-6, Sat 10-4
London W1

Osprey

Their plethora of purses, pocketbooks and planners at prices within reason should feed your accessories needs. Gentle pink, brown and navy leather keep many pieces looking simple. For the bolder bunch, there's crocodile, lizard and other styles straight from the wild. The range is promising and the quality top-notch.

020 7935 2824 **tube: Bond Street**
11 St. Christopher's Place Tues-Sat 11-6 (Thurs 11-7)
London W1

Ozwald Boateng

The most high-profile of the new breed of Savile Row tailors, Boateng has brought a touch of flash and a high celeb count to the Row. His razor-sharp suits in bright colors, or more somber with bright linings, are instantly identifiable for their long slim lines. In addition to bespoke suits the store sells off-the-peg suits and brightly colored shirts and ties. Perfect for the tall and trim build, but not for the slim wallet.

020 7437 0620 — **tube: Piccadilly Circus**
9 Vigo Street — Mon-Sat 10-6 (Thurs 10-7)
London W1

Paddy Campbell

This elegant collection of chic, understated seasonal pieces will bring to mind fashion clichés like "Jackie O" and "timeless"—there's no helping it once you've seen the classic, no-frills selection of predominantly pastel dresses, skirts and suits. Best for mature audiences.

020 7225 0543 — **tube: Knightsbridge**
17 Beauchamp Place — Mon-Fri 10-6 (Wed 10-7)
London SW3 — Sat 10:30-6

020 7493 5646 — **tube: Bond Street**
8 Gees Court — Mon-Sat 10-6 (Thurs 10-7)
London W1

Pantalon Chameleon

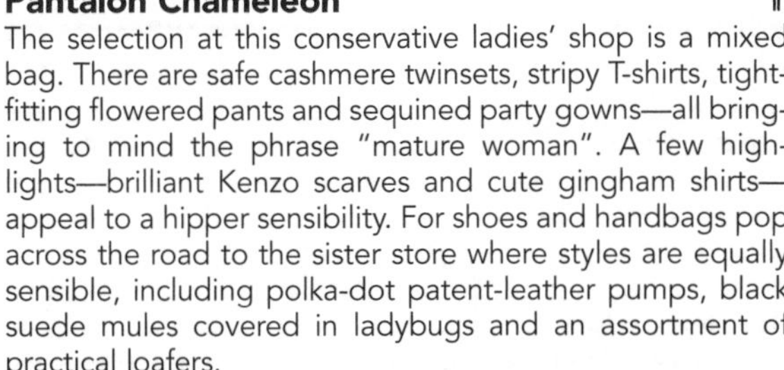

The selection at this conservative ladies' shop is a mixed bag. There are safe cashmere twinsets, stripy T-shirts, tight-fitting flowered pants and sequined party gowns—all bringing to mind the phrase "mature woman". A few highlights—brilliant Kenzo scarves and cute gingham shirts—appeal to a hipper sensibility. For shoes and handbags pop across the road to the sister store where styles are equally sensible, including polka-dot patent-leather pumps, black suede mules covered in ladybugs and an assortment of practical loafers.

020 7384 2909 — **tube: Parsons Green**
28 New King's Road — Mon-Sat 10-6 (Wed, Thurs 10-7)
London SW6

020 7751 9871 — **tube: Parsons Green**
187 New King's Road — (opening times as above)
London SW6

020 7730 0200 — **tube: Sloane Square**
50 Duke of York Square — Mon-Sat 10-6, Sun 12-5
London SW3

Paola Tregemini

If the scores of shoe stores on the King's Road haven't depleted your will to shop, this tiny boutique offers a trendy collection from such designers as Givenchy, Casadei and Plein Sud. Browse through a selection that ranges from high heels with diamanté straps to pink patent-leather ankle boots to more practical leather loafers. Not a place for the fiercest fashion fanatics, but it's an easy source for seasonal styles.

020 7376 3388 — **tube: Sloane Square**
137 King's Road — Mon-Sat 10-7, Sun 12-6
London SW3

Paraboot

This long-established French shoe company opened its first British branch in Savile Row at the end of 1999. Famous for quietly stylish, ultra-durable, hand-stitched men's and women's shoes, Paraboot further specialize in Norwegian and Goodyear waterproof welting. The company's casual, two-hole lace-up leather shoe, known as the Michael, lays claim to being the most copied shoe in the world. Prices range from £125-£250. www.paraboot.com

020 7494 3233 **tube: Piccadilly Circus/Oxford Circus**
37 Savile Row Mon-Fri 10-6, Sat 10-5
London W1

Parallel

Here's another reason to go shoe shopping in London. The ambitious range of styles, from a ruthless high heel to a sympathetic loafer, means you're more than likely to find something worth taking home. European designers include Luc Berjen, Baldinini, Armando D'Allesandro and Braude. Best of all, they've banished the long waits to try on, opting instead for self-service which means you can just grab your size and go.

020 7224 0441 **tube: Baker Street/Bond Street**
22 Marylebone High Street Mon-Sat 10-6:45
London W1 Sun 12-6

020 8785 1441 **tube: Putney Bridge**
23 Putney Exchange Shopping Centre Mon-Sat 10-6
Putney High Street Sun 11-5
London SW15

Parallel Intimo

Just down the block from the shoe shop, Parallel Intimo stocks some top labels to cover your bottom, including Lisa Cuarmel, Argentovivo, Andrea Sarda and Savage. Bra-and-panty sets, bust-boosting lace corsets and men's boxer briefs are all available. Sexy nightgowns that drape to the floor are no more mumsy than a lace teddy, while leaving plenty more to the imagination.

020 7486 7300 **tube: Baker Street/Bond Street**
13 Marylebone High Street Mon-Sat 10-6:45
London W1

Patricia Roberts

International knitting junkies cross the ocean to come to Roberts's 30-year-old shop where bright-colored sweaters for women and kids are displayed amidst yards of yarn. Her 12 published books on the subject are a testament to her cult following, though fans will be hard-pressed to recreate her charming hand-knits. Tiny blue sweaters with angora teddy bears and matching mittens are lovely for little ones.

020 7235 4742 **tube: Knightsbridge**
60 Kinnerton Street Mon-Fri 10-6, Sat 11-3
London SW1

Patrick Cox

His loafer hit the one million mark more than a year ago—impressive sales status for a little-known (outside of fashion circles, anyway) Canadian shoe designer. But Cox has earned his stripes, having worked with such designers as Vivienne Westwood, John Galliano and Anna Sui. The distinctive shapes and noteworthy materials (from patent leather to crocodile) that made his loafer such a mid-Nineties smash have endured, rendering scores of square toes and sexy skins throughout his collection. Cox's designer styles don't come cheap, but the Wannabe diffusion line is just as hip and easier to sneak onto the Visa card without causing domestic strife.

020 7730 8886 — **tube: Sloane Square**
129 Sloane Street — Mon-Sat 10-6 (Wed 10-7)
London SW1 — Sun 11-5

Patrizia Wigan Designs

Kensington's yummy mummies have shopped here for close to 20 years because there's no other kids' store quite like it. Specializing in traditional English clothing, Wigan's smock dresses and boys' breeches look as if they've just stepped out of the Secret Garden. For the best in baby couture, there are Swiss cotton and French lace christening gowns. It's all a brilliant blast to the past. www.patriziawigan.com

020 7823 7080 — **tube: Knightsbridge**
19 Walton Street — Mon-Fri 10:30-6:30, Sat 10:30-6
London SW3

Paul Costelloe

Some designers lose sight of the fact that clothing serves, above all, a practical purpose, but the Irish designer Paul Costelloe is not one of them. Winter brings chic leather pants, tailored wool suits and knee-length dresses with matching jackets. The palette features a career-friendly rainbow, including red, purple, gray and black. Costelloe's styles are quietly classic and can sometimes miss the mark, but you're more than likely to find something satisfying and safe.

020 7590 9902 — **tube: Knightsbridge**
10 Beauchamp Place — Mon-Sat 10-6
London SW3

Paul & Joe

The chilly staff might size you up like you're not quite cool enough, but don't be deterred. French designer Sophie Albon (who named the label after her sons) spins a beautifully cut, eclectic collection of inspired, wearable pieces...crisp cotton button-downs, hip-hugging pants and tattered chiffon skirts sprinkled with dots of gold glitter. It's classic French tailoring with a twist. The funky mood is enhanced by an assortment of colorful gift items, including Acampora perfume, Bloom bath products and cute lacy thongs.

020 7243 5510 **tube: Notting Hill Gate**
39-41 Ledbury Road Mon-Fri 10-6:30, Sat 10-7
London W11

020 7589 2684 **tube: South Kensington**
309 Brompton Road Mon-Fri 10-6:30 (Wed 10-7)
London SW3 Sat 10-7, Sun 1-6

020 7836 3388 (M) **tube: Covent Garden**
33 Floral Street Mon-Fri 10-6:30, Sat 10-7
London WC2 Sun 1-6

☆ Paul Smith

If Alexander McQueen is London fashion's bad boy, Smith is its reigning knight—literally. Sir Paul brings his own quirky spin to classic English tailoring, with madcap collections that offer everything from purple oxfords with red polka dots for men to women's bright turquoise corduroys. Colors are confidently bright and patterns, eye-catching. Smith's personality seems especially present in the details—suits with stand-out stitching, bright green belts with pink undersides and cufflinks shaped like manual typewriter keys. The children's line is especially adorable, featuring football club sweatshirts and pink glittered tees. www.paulsmith.co.uk

020 7379 7133 **tube: Covent Garden**
40-44 Floral Street Mon-Sat 10:30-6:30
London WC2 (Thurs 10:30-7), Sun 1-4

020 7589 9139 **tube: South Kensington**
84-86 Sloane Avenue Mon-Fri 10:30-6:30 (Wed 10:30-7)
London SW3 Sat 10-6:30, Sun 1-5

020 7727 3553 **tube: Notting Hill Gate**
122 Kensington Park Road Mon-Thurs 10:30-6:30
London W11 Fri-Sat 10-6:30

020 7626 4778 **tube: Bank**
7 The Courtyard Mon-Fri 10-6
Royal Exchange
London EC3

Paule Ka

Harking back to the days when ladies wore white gloves on airplanes, this French label maintains an unerring devotion to detail. From a timeless gabardine check suit to a taffeta evening gown, every creation has its own set of accessories (a matching cloche hat or billowing tulle muffs). Designer Serge Cajfinger has reincarnated the total-look approach to dressing once maintained by style icons like Audrey Hepburn and Jackie O. The result is traditional, sophisticated and exceedingly feminine. www.pauleka.com

020 7647 4455 **tube: Green Park**
13a Grafton Street Mon-Sat 10-6 (Thurs 10-7)
London W1

Pegaso

Pegaso is nothing out of the ordinary but still likely to please, with top-end designers like Gucci, Versace and Calvin Klein. There's every cut and color of men's suit, from double-breasted black to more contemporary (and frightening) straight-cut green. The helpful staff might tempt you into finishing the look with collared shirts, cufflinks and shiny leather loafers. www.pegaso.co.uk

020 7602 5225 **tube: High Street Kensington**
275 Kensington High Street Mon-Sun 10-6:30
London W8

Pepe Jeans

Gum-poppers come here for the casual selection of denim jeans, jackets and shirts. The assortment includes jeans with the bum and thighs faded out, cowgirl denim shirts, red cotton pants and simple halternecks. Alas, despite their best efforts, Pepe still doesn't seem to have the status of rivals like Levi's and Diesel. www.pepejeans.com

020 7439 0512 **tube: Oxford Circus**
42 Carnaby Street Mon-Fri 10:30-7:30, Sat 10-7
London W1 Sun 12-6

Directory

Peter Jones

(see John Lewis)

Peter Werth

The best reason to come to this shop are the prices, which hover somewhere between decent and dirt-cheap. The selection suffers from a chronic case of dullness, but if you need the basics you'll find them all here—pants, button-downs, sweaters, T-shirts and loafers. Uninspiring, so best for blokes who prefer blending in to turning heads.
www.peterwerth.co.uk

020 7351 4136 **tube: Sloane Square**
184 King's Road Mon-Sat 10-7, Sun 12-6
London SW3

020 7734 6266 **tube: Oxford Circus**
10 Foubert's Place Mon-Fri 10:30-7 (Thurs 10:30-7:30)
London W1 Sat 10-6:30, Sun 12-5

Petit Bateau

At last, we have own little French boat, direct from the Champs Elysées. For over 100 years Petit Bateau have been France's leading manufacturer of children's undershirts, tees and sleepwear. Their design is comfortingly simple, based on the classic snug, scoop-necked cotton model with long or short sleeves and in softly muted colors. So well loved are they that when they branched out to include tiny women's tees in 1994 it was only a minute before they were in the closets of just about every petite Parisian girl. London girls will surely follow, and London's little darlings can now be as prettily dressed as their Parisian counterparts. www.petit-bateau.com

020 7838 0818 **tube: Sloane Square**
106-108 King's Road Mon-Sat 10-6 (Wed, Thurs 10-7)
London SW3 Sun 12-6

020 7491 4498 **tube: Bond Street**
62 South Molton Street Mon-Sat 10-6:30 (Thurs 10-7)
London W1

Phase Eight

A chain for conservative adults who are loosely tethered to fashion, Patsy Seddon's Phase Eight offers decent, neutral-colored workwear. There's everything you'd expect—suits, pants and sensible shoes. Nothing's liable to leap out at you, save the floor-length silk dresses and practical twin-sets. All better for covering up than showing off.

020 7371 7250 **tube: Parsons Green**
54 New King's Road Mon-Sat 9:30-6
London SW6

020 7352 9025 **tube: South Kensington**
345 Fulham Road (opening times as above, plus Sun 10-5)
London SW10

020 7229 7445 **tube: Notting Hill Gate**
164 Notting Hill Gate (opening times as above)
London W11

020 8947 4140 **tube: Wimbledon**
31 High Street (opening times as above, except Sun 11-5)
London SW19

020 7823 4094 **tube: Sloane Square**
97 Lower Sloane Street Mon-Sat 9:30-6
London SW1

020 7513 0808 **tube: Canary Wharf**
Cabot Place East Mon-Fri 9-7, Sat 10-6, Sun 11-5
London E14

020 7226 1904 **tube: Angel**
211-212 Upper Street Mon-Fri 10-6:30
London N1 Sat 9:30-6, Sun 12-6

020 7730 5921 **tube: Sloane Square**
34 Duke of York Square Mon-Sat 10-7, Sun 11-5
London SW3

Philip Somerville

London is arguably the last cosmopolitan city where women still love to wear hats. Widely considered among the best made-to-order milliners in the world, Somerville's clientele is unsurprisingly A-list. Diana, Princess of Wales was a devotee, and Somerville still holds a royal warrant. The design philosophy combines simple, striking shapes with bold colors and a traditional English feel. Every hat is handmade and every last detail double-checked. For a quick fix, Fortnum & Mason and Selfridges stock some of his ready-to-wear.

020 7224 1517 **tube: Baker Street**
38 Chiltern Street Mon-Fri 9-5:30
London W1

Philip Treacy

If the point of a hat is to be noticed, Philip Treacy's millinery masterpieces top the lot. They're coveted for their bright colors, sharp, quirky shapes and extravagant details (e.g., feathers and veils). No matter how crazy, they're still entirely proper and so distinctive you won't get away with wearing one twice. His couture service will force you into a mortgage but don't lose heart—the ready-to-wear is more reasonable. These hats are special enough for your best friend's wedding—just be careful you don't upstage the bride. www.philiptreacy.co.uk

020 7730 3992 **tube: Sloane Square/Victoria**
69 Elizabeth Street Mon-Fri 10-6, Sat 11-5
London SW1

Phillipa Lepley

Here comes the bride, and if Lepley has designed her dress it's liable to be sprinkled with freshwater pearls, sparkling with Austrian crystals or planted with embroidered peonies. Classic brides can always opt for a gown that's beautifully sculpted but unadorned. All lined in silk, Lepley's simple designs are cut to emphasize assets—A-line skirts and nipped waists give every woman an hourglass. www.phillipalepley.com

020 7386 0927 **tube: Fulham Broadway**
494 Fulham Road Mon-Sat 10-6 (for browsing; otherwise
London SW6 best make an appointment)

Phlip

Don't expect a warm reception at this streetwear store...the attitude is pure Noo Yaawk. With a slogan that boasts "original American clothing" come few surprises: loads of jeans and cargo pants, baseball caps and messenger bags. Labels like Carhartt, Schott, Eastpak and Converse are displayed in their element, among the rough-looking staff and thumping rap music.

020 7352 4332 **tube: Sloane Square**
191 King's Road Mon-Sat 10:30-7, Sun 12-6
London SW3

Pickett

If you tend to relish the finer things in life, this tiny store offers plenty of them. It's full to bursting with heavy-sewn briefcases, exotic hide handbags, leather gloves, stud boxes and wallets. Old-fashioned flavor and a dark wood interior set the perfect tone for this home of lovely luxury gifts, which also offers a custom-made service for everything from desk blotters to luggage sets. Prizes include suede-covered A-Z London guides, trendy Turkish slippers, lovely shawls, and their expanding selection of colorful, chunky jewelry. www.pickett.co.uk

020 7493 8939 **tube: Green Park**
41 Burlington Arcade Mon-Sat 9-6
London W1

020 7493 8939 **tube: Green Park**
32-33 Burlington Arcade Mon-Sat 9-6
London W1

020 7823 5638 (emphasis on W) **tube: Sloane Square**
149 Sloane Street Mon-Sat 9-6 (Wed 9-7)
London SW1

020 7283 7636 (emphasis on M) **tube: Bank**
6 Royal Exchange Mon-Fri 9-6
London EC3

Pied à Terre

This shoe chain owned by Nine West features its own signature collection of well crafted, simple styles, from suede moccasin boots and camel loafers to black stilettos with buckles and grommeted kitten heels. Other names on offer include Angelo Frigus, Passepartout and Alima. www.theshoestudio.com

020 7629 1362 **tube: Bond Street**
19 South Molton Street Mon-Sat 10-7
London W1 (Thurs 10-8), Sun 12-6

The Pineal Eye

One glance in the window and you might mistake it for a gallery—you'd be half right. This ground-floor exhibition space, where contemporary art displays change every month, is part one of The Pineal Eye. Part two is downstairs, where art magazines, Japanese books and designer clothing await. Labels are high-concept, including Dior Homme, Raf Simmons, Bernard Willhelm and Lutz. It's a cool-culture outpost in the middle of the wild west end.

020 7434 2567 **tube: Oxford Circus**
49 Broadwick Street Mon-Fri 11-7, Sat 12-7
London W1

Pineapple

This dancewear shop, established in 1979, has lost little of its Flashdance flavour as it expands its collection to include sporty (and predominately pink) streetwear. Hooded sweatshirts, printed tees and velour sweatpants are mingled with stretchy lace tops and butt-hugging black clubbing pants. We're betting this is best suited to aspiring prima ballerinas and the showgirls who work out in the dance studios nearby.

020 7836 4006 **tube: Covent Garden**
6a Langley Street Mon-Sat 10-7, Sun 11-5:30
London WC2

Please Mum

If your precious son or daughter can't face the first day of pre-school without the latest DKNY, this is the place to come. Featuring such designer labels as Moschino, Replay, Versace and Kenzo, Please Mum dresses budding fashion hounds from birth to teens. The store also specializes in ballgowns for baby's first black-tie. www.please-mum.co.uk

020 7486 1380 **tube: Knightsbridge/Hyde Park Corner**
85 Knightsbridge Mon-Sat 9:45-6:30
London SW1 (Wed 9:45-7), Sun 10-6

Pleats Please: Issey Miyake

It makes perfect sense that a designer sometimes criticized for his unwearable, avant-garde signature collection would create a second line that is comfortable enough to sleep in (and wrinkle-free, so no one will know if you did). Miyake's selection of machine-pleated womenswear is engineered entirely of synthetic fibers and comes in his standard brilliant rainbow colors. These clothes are ideal for traveling and suited to Miyake fans who can't quite afford his main line. www.pleatsplease.com

020 7495 2306 **tube: Bond Street**
20 Brook Street Mon-Sat 10:30-6
London W1

020 7351 0001 **tube: Sloane Square**
313 King's Road Mon-Sat 10:30-6
London SW3

Plein Sud

It's Joseph with more detail, equally well tailored but a bit harder-edged. Subtle shades of beige, pink and green offset the raw character of the clothing: a layered, leather mini skirt with an eyelet pattern and tattered hems, suede pants with criss-crossing waist laces, an asymmetric blouse with ruffled shoulders—everything is left a bit rough. Prices are high and the character is strong, so it's a good place to just dabble.

020 7584 8295 **tube: South Kensington**
151 Draycott Avenue Mon-Fri 10-6:30
London SW3 Wed 10-7, Sun 1-6

Pollyanna

Neighborhood residents and passers-by are the bulk of the traffic at this children's shop. In sizes from newborn to eight years old the clothing is everything you'd expect, from baby grows to denim overalls, with an emphasis on shoes from such brands as Start-Rite. The store is not overrun with toys (a blessing if you're trying to navigate with a pram) but you can find a small selection of traditional playthings.

020 7731 0673 **tube: Parsons Green**
811 Fulham Road Mon-Sat 9:30-5:30
London SW6

Pop Boutique

The moment you step into this shop you're liable to be flooded with flashbacks of junior high and your first Partridge Family lunchbox. Their mantra—"Don't follow fashion, buy something already out of date"—inspires the selection of retro relics that look as fresh as the day they were made. A one-stop disco-era shop for the likes of ex-Spice Girl Geri Halliwell, Pop offers denim jeans, corduroys, flared-collar shirts and leather jackets. Lava lamps and other kitsch housewares are also available.
www.pop-boutique.com

020 7497 5262 **tube: Covent Garden**
6 Monmouth Street Mon-Sat 11-7, Sun 1-6
London WC2

Portobello Market

Friday morning is the best time to visit this stretch of Notting Hill, made famous by Hugh Grant and Julia Roberts. Saturdays are disastrous for claustrophobics, but ambitious visitors might enjoy the spectacle of a tourist stampede. On the southern end of the road you'll find a wide variety of antique shops selling everything from furniture to nautical devices to old prints. Further north, past the produce stalls, the fun begins. Once you've spotted the Westway, an overpass running across Portobello, you're heading into the fashion. Jeans, custom T-shirts, vintage shoes and leather jackets are some of the best trendy bits on hand here. While you're in the area, pop into the Portobello Arcade where some of the street's more established secondhanders hold court. Come with cash, no one takes plastic.

(no phone) **tube: Notting Hill Gate/Ladbroke Grove**
Portobello Road Fri 7-4, Sat 8-5
London W10 Sun 9-4 (clothing stalls)

Poste

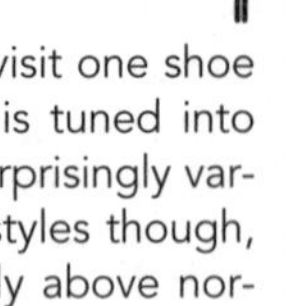

A great place for the man who can stand to visit one shoe shop only, Poste targets the customer who is tuned into trends in footwear. This small store offers a surprisingly varied selection of international designers and styles though, as the proprietor concedes, at a price slightly above normal. Labels include Adidas, Converse, Paul Smith, Camper, Marc Jacobs and Jeffery West, as well as their own in-house brands.

020 7499 8002 **tube: Bond Street**
10 South Molton Street Mon-Sat 10-7, Sun 12-6
London W1

Poste Mistress

As pink and fluffy as a Fifties boudoir, the interior of this store is the perfect backdrop for the quirky selection of shoes. It's a pleasingly unpredictable mix—gingham mules, Eighties patent slingbacks with rainbow stripes, and 19th-century style wingtip boots, plus a few more casual acquaintances (Converse, Adidas, Camper and Birkenstock). All this, and the velvet sofas, gilded mirrors, and old Hollywood head shots (from Audrey Hepburn to Daisy and the Dukes of Hazard), set the tone for old-fashioned glamour with a bit of street cheek and some kitsch sprinkled on top.

020 7379 4040 **tube: Covent Garden**
61-63 Monmouth Street Mon-Sat 10-7, Sun 12-6
London WC2

Prada

A favorite label of the fashion pack, Prada strikes the perfect balance between nostalgic girlishness and sleek sophistication. Though undeniably modern, every collection has its share of vintage references and recent highlights have included knee-length skirts in Willam Morris print fabrics, Sixties-style platform slingbacks and a strong Forties silhouette seen in boxy coats with wide belts cinched at the waist. Displayed against the store's mint-green walls, the selection ranges from tailored suits to casual knitwear to cocktail frocks, with tons of the coveted shoes and handbags on the ground floor (you can't miss the triangle logo—it just keeps getting bigger).

020 7647 5000 | **tube: Green Park**
16-18 Old Bond Street | Mon-Sat 10-6 (Thurs 10-7)
London W1

020 7235 0008 | **tube: Knightsbridge**
43-45 Sloane Street | Mon-Sat 10-6 (Wed 10-7)
London SW1

020 7626 2068 | **tube: Bank**
1 The Courtyard | (opening times as above)
Royal Exchange
London EC3

Preen

The look is Victoriana set askew (à la Vivienne Westwood): puffed sleeves, layered skirts and lots of ragged edges. You might think it OTT at first glance but the handmade character and subtle colors of the collection bring it all firmly down to earth. Notting Hill bohemian boldness at its best.

020 8968 1542 | **tube: Ladbroke Grove**
5 Portobello Green Arcade | Thurs-Sat 10-6
London W10

Press & Bastyan

This big-sister store to Karen Millen has a grown-up collection of womenswear targeted to the shapelier, more decorative dresser. Styles are classic, with pinstripe suits, beaded slip dresses and tailored tweed coats. Feminine designs and sophisticated fabrics put this on a par with iBlues. Our only gripe: patterns can be a bit too distinctive and "outfits" prevail.

020 7491 0597 | **tube: Bond Street**
22 South Molton Street | Mon-Sat 10-6:30
London W1 | (Thurs 10-7:30), Sun 12-6

Pringle

For decades this Scottish sweater brand was associated with geeks, golfers and granddads. Now, under the guidance of Kim Winser (former Marks and Spencers executive), Pringle knitwear has undergone a dramatic rejuvenation

Directory

and emerged with a young, cool image. Madonna, Robbie Williams and David Beckham have all been spotted wearing the traditional diamond-patterned sweaters and curvaceous supermodel Sophie Dahl has been hired to promote the company's sexier image. The new shops on Bond Street and Sloane Street are both light, bright and fun with heaps of the coveted cashmere separates and a few surprises thrown in too—tailored raincoats, Fifties-style pleated skirts and a black sweater with "Pearly Queen" spelt out in mother-of-pearl buttons. The only question is, are you cool enough to get away with wearing it?

020 7297 4580 **tube: Bond Street**
111-112 New Bond Street Mon-Sat 10-6:30
London W1 (Thurs 10-7:30)

020 7881 3061 **tube: Sloane Square**
141-142 Sloane Street Mon-Fri 9:30-6:30 (Wed 9:30-7)
London SW1

Proibito

Designer labels, everywhere you look—Valentino, Moschino, Versace Jeans Couture, Gianfranco Ferré, D&G, Evisu and Cavalli. This big, bright shop houses pants, sweaters and shirts for both genders. The Bond Street location provides next season's collection, while the South Molton Street branch sells last season at a discount.

020 7493 0589 **tube: Bond Street**
94 New Bond Street Mon-Wed 10-6:30
London W1 Thurs 10-8, Fri-Sat 10-7, Sun 12-6

020 7491 3244 **tube: Bond Street**
42 South Molton Street Mon-Wed 10-6:30
London W1 Thurs 10-8, Fri-Sat 10-7, Sun 12-6

Puma

Trendy sports brand Puma has sponsored Pele through World Cup Finals, Boris Becker at Wimbeldon and Linford Christie on the running track. The new concept store on Carnaby Street offers everyone a piece of the action, whatever their game. There's everything from track pants and running shorts to tennis dresses and sports bras. A few more directional pieces, like a limited leather jacket for ladies (only 345 produced worldwide) combine the sporty look with a fashionable modern spin. www.puma.co.uk

020 7439 0221 **tube: Oxford Circus/Piccadilly Circus**
52-55 Carnaby Street Mon-Sat 10-7, Sun 12-6
London W1

Question Air

A bright boutique with a friendly staff and lots of good names such as Issey Miyake, Betsey Johnson, Orla Kiely and Ghost. And if your man needs a wardrobe update, take him to the side-by-side his 'n' hers stores in Wimbledon Village. The menswear selection also has good names—Duffer, Katharine Hamnett, Paul Smith—so you can go your way and he can go his. It's therapy for shopping couples. And now you can also enjoy the therapy at two branches in the pretty leafy urban villages of Barnes and Dulwich.

020 7836 8220 **tube: Covent Garden**
38 Floral Street Mon-Sat 10:30-6:30
London WC2 (Thurs 10:30-7), Sun 12-5:30

020 7221 8163 **tube: Notting Hill Gate**
229 Westbourne Grove Mon-Tues 10:30-6
London W11 Wed-Sat 10:30-6:30, Sun 12-5

020 8879 0366 (M) **tube: Wimbledon**
77 High Street Mon-Sat 10-6, Sun 12-5:30
London SW19

020 8946 6288 (W) **tube: Wimbledon**
78 High Street (opening times as above)
London SW19

020 8748 1772 **Overland train to Barnes**
86 Church Road Mon-Sat 10-5.30, Sun 12-5
London SW13

020 8299 4252 **Overland train to North Dulwich**
85-87 Dulwich Village Mon-Sat 10-6, Sun 11:30-5
London SE21

Quiksilver

If you're a beach bum you already know that the sun always shines at Quiksilver, where board shorts, swimsuits and surfing gear never go out of season. A bright atmosphere is echoed in the brilliantly colored designs. On a rainy day this place will make you long for Santa Monica.

www.quiksilver.com

020 7240 5886 **tube: Covent Garden**
12 North Piazza Mon-Sat 10-7, Sun 11-5
London WC2

020 7836 5371 **tube: Covent Garden**
1 & 23 Thomas Neals Centre Mon-Sat 10-7
London WC2 Sun 12-6

R.M.Williams

The durable selection of khakis, oilskin jackets, thick woolens and moleskin shirts at this Australian outfitter could come in handy on a cold day. For women the pickings are slimmer, being primarily trousers and shirts. Of particular note is their signature leather boot, designed to provide enduring quality, structural support and a particularly rugged style. www.rmwilliams.com.au

020 7629 6222 **tube: Oxford Circus**
223 Regent Street Mon-Sat 10-6:30
London W1 (Thurs 10-7:30), Sun 11-5

R.Soles

Yee-haw! If your shoe closet has been looking a bit too city-slick lately, this is a great place to get some cowboy kicks. The store has a huge, no-holds-barred selection of cowboy

boots in every conceivable style, from basic snakeskin to cow print to lime-green leather. With an assortment of matching accessories, die-hard rodeo fans can rope in the whole kit 'n' caboodle. www.r-soles.com

020 7351 5520 **tube: Sloane Square**
109a King's Road Mon-Sat 10-7, Sun 12-6
London SW3

Rachel Riley

She won an award for her mail-order business, then opened her second London store, and now it seems there's no stopping Rachel Riley. She brings a breath of fresh air to feminine Fifties style in silk dresses with cashmere cardigans, straw hats and handbags to match. The same selection is shrunk-down for the kids' collection, including Liberty print smock dresses with sunhats, sweet embroidered dungarees and Mary Janes by Start-Rite. An enticing stop for a mother-daughter day. www.rachelriley.com

020 7935 7007 **tube: Baker Street/Bond Street**
82 Marylebone High Street Mon-Sat 10-6
London W1

020 7259 5969 **tube: Knightsbridge**
14 Pont Street Mon-Sat 10-6
London SW1

Racing Green

Known for practical clothes in practical cuts, Racing Green offers an extensive selection of J. Crew-style basics. Striped T-shirts, long twill skirts and cotton pants are typical fare from this comfortable collection, which also includes tailored suits, shoes, accessories and outerwear. It all comes in durable fabrics and standard colors. Consider it a British Gap. www.racinggreen.co.uk

020 7437 4300 **tube: Oxford Circus**
195 Regent Street Mon-Sat 10-7 (Thurs 10-8)
London W1 Sun 11-5

Ralph Lauren

From his navy sport jackets to his silk evening gowns, Ralph Lauren's signature collection is as blue-blooded as they come. Even the store on Bond Street, its walls hung with patrician portraits, is liable to evoke fantasies of a life of ease and a weekend house in the country. If you want in to this club, it'll cost you: baby-soft cable-knit cashmere sweaters, crisp shirts and precisely tailored trousers all fetch a high price. The home collection, with silver cocktail shakers, antique French china and black and white vintage photographs (all depressingly expensive) is best admired at the new Fulham Road location. www.polo.com

020 7535 4600 **tube: Green Park**
1 New Bond Street Mon-Sat 10-6 (Thurs 10-7)
London W1 Sun 12-5

020 7590 7990 **tube: South Kensington**
105-109 Fulham Road Mon-Sat 10-6 (Wed, Sat 10-7)
London SW3 Sun 12-5

Ralph Lauren (children)

It's everything you would find at Polo Ralph Lauren, but in miniature. The Polo obsession can be met here from as early as birth and nurtured all the way to girls' size 16 and boys' size 20. There's also a great selection of children's books. www.polo.com

020 7535 4888 | **tube: Bond Street**
143 New Bond Street | Mon-Sat 10-6 (Thurs 10-7)
London W1 | Sun 12-5

Ravel

If you lack the time, interest or resources to seek out designer shoes, this store offers basic styles with no nonsense. Racks are organized by size for self-service, making it an easy, quick hit. Most of the selection reflects the latest trends, but you can also find basic black.

020 7631 4135 | **tube: Oxford Circus**
184-188 Oxford Street | Mon 10:30-7, Tues-Fri 9:30-7
London W1 | (Thurs 9:30-8), Sat 10:30-7, Sun 11:30-6

Reiss

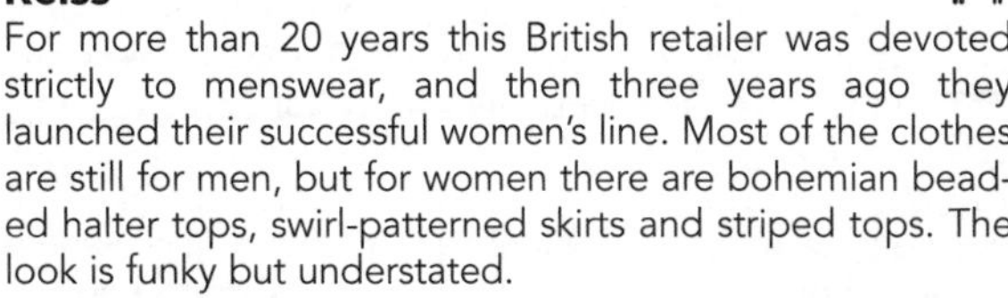

For more than 20 years this British retailer was devoted strictly to menswear, and then three years ago they launched their successful women's line. Most of the clothes are still for men, but for women there are bohemian beaded halter tops, swirl-patterned skirts and striped tops. The look is funky but understated.

020 7637 9112 | **tube: Oxford Circus**
14-17 Market Place | Mon-Sat 10-6:30 (Thurs 10-7:30)
London W1 | Sun 12-6

020 7225 4910 | **tube: Sloane Square**
114 King's Road | Mon-Sat 9:30-6:30 (Wed-Thurs 10-7)
London SW3 | Sun 12-6

020 7493 4866 | **tube: Bond Street**
78-79 New Bond Street | Mon-Sat 10-7 (Thurs 10-8)
London W1 | Sun 12-6

020 7240 7495 | **tube: Covent Garden**
116 Long Acre | (opening times as above)
London WC2

020 7439 4907 | **tube: Oxford Circus**
172 Regent Street | (opening times as above)
London W1

020 7431 5425 | **tube: Hampstead**
52-54 Heath Street | Mon-Fri 10-6 (Thurs 10-7)
London NW3 | Sun 12-6

Rellik

Set at the base of Trellick Tower, Rellik is home to three separate vintage boutiques: Identity, Laissez Faire and Affinity. Each specializes in a different era, so the selection is an eclectic mix, from secondhand Vivienne Westwood to retro to reconstructed designs using antique trimmings. A good stop on the Notting Hill vintage circuit.

020 8962 008 **tube: Westbourne Park**
8 Golborne Road Tues-Sat 10-6
London W10

Ricci Burns

No other London street corner could be better suited to Ricci Burns and his brassy collection of international couture than this pricey section of Belgravia. A Vidal Sassoon protégé in the sixties, Burns has the orange-tanned, heavily maintained look of a man who can't quite accept that his swinging days are over...who better to dress a heavily-pregnant Victoria Beckham in a revealing, diamanté-covered leather dress slit almost to the bump? His over-the-top selection is dripping with names like Givenchy and garish gowns guaranteed to put you on the party pages of *Hello!*

020 7823 1555 **tube: Knightsbridge**
25 Lowndes Street Mon-Sat 10-6 (Thurs 10-7)
London SW1

☆ Richard James

The first shop encountered on entering what everyone still calls "the Row" from the Conduit Street end, Richard James is also the street's most self-consciously fashionable store. This former Menswear Designer of the Year occupies a big-windowed, airy, subtly cool space kitted out with row upon row of vibrant shirts and distinctive long-cut, double-vented ready-to-wear suits mingling with trendy accessories ranging from garish socks to camouflage-print bags. A famously rock 'n' roll bespoke service is also available—just ask Tom Cruise and Elton John. www.richardjames.co.uk

020 7434 0171 **tube: Piccadilly Circus/Oxford Circus**
29 Savile Row Mon-Fri 10-6, Sat 11-6
London W1

Rigby & Peller

A family-run business specializing in made-to-measure lingerie, Rigby & Peller has held a royal warrant from the Queen since 1960. Not surprisingly, then, this is a service-oriented establishment offering bras, panties, corsets, garters, swimwear and nightwear. Labels include Prima Donna, Lise Charmel, Lejaby and Aquasuit, and the color spectrum is standard boudoir: blacks, whites, reds and pastels. A good place for the big-busted to get a perfect fit. www.rigbyandpeller.com

020 7491 2200 **tube: Oxford Circus**
22a Conduit Street Mon-Sat 9:30-6 (Thurs 9:30-7)
London W1 (last fitting half an hour before close)

020 7589 9293 **tube: Knightsbridge**
2 Hans Road Mon-Sat 9:30-6 (Wed 9:30-7)
London SW3

Ritva Westenius

Understated yet original, Ritva Westenius designs fluctuate between classic and trendy, sexy and sophisticated. Using

luxurious fabrics—silk organza, duchesse satin and crepe—her simple, elegant dresses come enhanced with lovely details—beading, bows, crystals and roses. Some styles do look a little bit *Footballers' Wives*, while others save the day with their Martha Stewart wholesomeness. Prices range from £1,700 to £3,500. www.ritvawestenius.com

020 7706 0708 **tube: Marble Arch**
28 Connaught Street Mon-Sat 9-6 (by appointment)
London W2

Directory

River Island

Another store churning out the fleeting trends of teenage fashion. If dressing for effect is your game there are decal "Brit chic" T-shirts, red-flowered sheer blouses, chunky silver bangles and caramel stiletto boots. For a subtler touch, black pants and basic tops hang on the other side of the shop. Men will find khakis and jeans, leather trainers, skate shoes and casual vacationwear. Often underestimated, this shop frequently delivers more than you'd expect. www.riverisland.com

020 7937 0224 **tube: High Street Kensington**
124-126 Kensington High Street Mon-Fri 10-6:30
London W8 (Thurs 10-7), Sat 9-6:30, Sun 11-5

020 7499 3920 **tube: Oxford Circus**
283 Oxford Street Mon-Sat 10-7 (Thurs 10-8)
London W1 Sun 12-6

Robert Clergerie

Everybody knows the French like to step out in style, and they've had more than a little help from Monsieur Clergerie. His Mary Janes, moccasins and mules are perennial classics, and his sandals are lovely down to the last strap (summer 2002 saw a metal-soled thong that could be chilled in the refrigerator for hot-weather wearing). From geometric heels to black ballerina slippers, there's no question that Clergerie has a magic touch.

020 7584 4995 (W) **tube: South Kensington**
122 Draycott Avenue Mon-Fri 10:30-6 (Wed 10:30-7)
London SW3 Sat 10:30-6, Sun 1-5

020 7935 3601 **tube: Bond Street**
67 Wigmore Street Mon-Sat 10:30-6 (Thurs 10:30-7)
London W1

Robina

This is one of those peculiar spots that seem to exist only for rich European tourists "doing" Bond Street. With an emphasis on dressy day looks and sparkly evening wear, Robina offers a variety of designers including Louis Féraud, Bernshaw, Escada and St. John. To the young and trendy this place will seem outdated and expensive.

020 7493 1684 **tube: Bond Street**
68 New Bond Street Mon-Sat 9:30-6:30
London W1 (Thurs 9:30-7)

Robinson Valentine 

Despite an out-of-the-way location down a small side street, Antonia Robinson and Anna Valentine have a loyal following for their chic collection of understated day- and eveningwear. Their background is in couture—ready-to-wear is a relatively new venture—so rest assured that quality from this designing duo is top-end. Their small shop is an oasis for smart Kensington ladies who opt to shop amidst calm surroundings garnished with plenty of personal care.

020 7937 2900 — **tube: Kensington High Street**
4 Hornton Place — Mon-Fri 10-5
London W8

Robot

Their trademark welted lace-ups come with giant black chunky soles in styles ranging from snake-print to purple suede, but it's not all so punk at Robot. The shoe selection also includes safer streetwear standards like Diesel, Firetrap, Gola and Schott. A small clothing section caters to the strictly casual with jeans, sweatshirts and decal T-shirts. It's typical Covent Garden fare. www.robotshoeslondon.co.uk

020 7836 6156 — **tube: Covent Garden**
37 Floral Street — Mon-Sat 10:30-7
London WC2 — Sun 12-5:30

Roderick Charles

A traditional menswear store selling a selection of ready-to-wear and made-to-measure suits, shirts, and ties. Less illustrious than the bespoke shirtmakers nearby but perhaps more in line with the tastes of its core 40-plus businessman customer. www.roderickcharles.co.uk

020 7930 4551 — **tube: Piccadilly Circus/Green Park**
90 Jermyn Street — Mon-Fri 9:30-5:30 (Thurs 9:30-6)
London SW1 — Sat 10-5:30

020 7929 1867 — **tube: Monument**
25 Lime Street — Mon-Fri 9-5
London EC3

020 7242 4554 — **tube: Chancery Lane**
78-80 Chancery Lane — Mon-Fri 9:30-5:30
London WC2 — (Wed, Thurs 9:45-5:30)

020 7248 5303 — **tube: St. Paul's/Mansion House**
52 Bow Lane — Mon-Fri 9:30-5
London EC4

020 7588 2050 — **tube: Liverpool Street**
31 Blomfield Street — Mon-Fri 9:15-5:30
London EC2

Rodier

A well-known name in conservative knitwear, the French-based Rodier's collection remains simple and restrained. Mixed separates, cotton T-shirts and casual suits are the

basis of the selection, which offers high quality and simple cuts suited to mature tastes. You can't get much further from cutting-edge fashion than this. www.rodier.tn.fr

020 8946 6004 **tube: Wimbledon**
4 Church Road Mon-Sat 10-6, Sun 1-5
London SW19

Ronit Zilkha

The softer of Ronit Zilkha's pieces accentuate the female silhouette with tiny ruffles, shimmering sequins and strategically placed slits. But all the suits, dresses, skirts, loose pants and eveningwear are feminine and well made. Highlights include sheer silk cocktail dresses covered in sequins, a chic white suit, a suede jacket with flowers punched out and linen capri pants with a matching tank. Some accessories are also available.

020 7499 3707 **tube: Bond Street**
34 Brook Street Mon-Sat 9:30-6:30 (Thurs 9:30-7)
London W1 Sun 11:30-5:30

020 7431 0253 **tube: Hampstead**
17 Hampstead High Street Mon-Sat 9:30-6:30
London NW3 Sun 11-6

020 7730 2888 **tube: Sloane Square**
21 King's Road Mon-Fri 10-7 (Wed 10-7:30)
London SW3 Sat 9:30-6:30, Sun 12-6

020 7486 6785 **tube: Bond Street/Baker Street**
107 Marylebone High Street Mon-Sat 9:30-6:30
London W1 (Thurs 9:30-7), Sun 11:30-5:30

Ruco Line

The store is brimming with Ruco's signature lace-up leather shoes, all of which feature cartoonishly clumpy rubber soles. The women's line has a bit more flair than the men's, with pink, light blue and gold snakeskin variations, but it still comes down to one style (and not a very appealing one) repeated to exhaustion. www.rucoline.it

020 7629 5702 **tube: Bond Street**
64 South Molton Street Mon-Sat 10-6 (Thurs 10-7)
London W1

Russell & Bromley

Family-owned Russell & Bromley boasts a no-nonsense environment and a large variety of shoes—some with handbags to match. The Jermyn Street branch sells only men's shoes of the classic variety from British manufacturers Church's and Barkers and American brand Sebago, famous for its loafers. Women's selection at other locations includes Stuart Weitzman, Beverly Feldman and Donna Karan. No style strays too far from the mainstream, though some people complain that prices are higher than they should be.
www.russellandbromley.co.uk

020 7629 6903 **tube: Bond Street**
24-25 New Bond Street Mon-Sat 10-6:30
London W1 (Thurs 10-7:30)

Directory

020 7629 4001 **tube: Bond Street**
109-110 New Bond Street Mon-Sat 10-6:30
London W1 Thurs (10-7:30), Sun 11-5

020 7589 8415 **tube: Knightsbridge**
45 Brompton Road Mon-Tues 10-6:30, Wed-Fri 10-7
London SW3 Sat 10-6:30

020 7930 5307 (M) **tube: Piccadilly Circus/Green Park**
95 Jermyn Street Mon-Fri 10-6, Sat 10-5
London SW1

Russell & Haslam

You've probably already seen their designs without even knowing it. Together Gwen Russell and Janette Haslam designed the costumes for, amongst others, Michelle Pfeiffer in *Dangerous Liaisons*, Emma Thompson in *Henry V*, Nicole Kidman in *Eyes Wide Shut* and Elizabeth Spriggs in *The Philosopher's Stone* (Harry Potter). Their couture wedding dresses are equally memorable and, not surprisingly, just as theatrical. Billowing skirts, ornate corsets and sumptuous fabrics will all ensure the Wow factor. Despite their incredible success—two Oscars for costume, two BAFTA awards and numerous other Oscar nominations—the designers remain resolutely down to earth and state: "One of our greatest skills is our ability to interpret the personality and style of each individual; by doing so, her wedding gown becomes a truly personal statement. Having fun is also one of the delights of having a gown designed for you!" www.russelllandhaslam.com

020 8544 1092 **(by appointment**
London SW1 at a private design studio)

Sally Parsons

A haunt for smart Fulham ladies, this small French shop features an appealing array of Philippe Adec button-downs, Lin'n Laundry cropped pants, cardigans by Marion Foale and canvas Superga lace-ups. The classical background music is as soothing as the selection but a few stylish highlights—Gérard Darel T-shirts and cashmere sweaters by M-A-G—turn the volume up a notch.

020 7471 4848 **tube: Parsons Green**
610 Fulham Road Mon-Sat 10-6 (Wed 10-7)
London SW6

020 7584 8866 **tube: South Kensington**
15a Bute Street Mon-Sat 10-6
London SW7

Salvatore Ferragamo

This is one of the great names of Italian style, and if you have the cash flow to shop here you can hardly go wrong. Impeccable quality, superb tailoring and every other clothing superlative you can imagine apply. The Florentine family name has long been celebrated for elegant shoes, still revered by the most discriminating ladies. For men, the ties in particular strike a stylish note. Ready-to-wear is available for women only, though men will find accessories such as shoes and briefcases. www.ferragamo.com

020 7629 5007 **tube: Green Park**
24 Old Bond Street Mon-Sat 10-6
London W1

020 7838 7730 **tube: Knightsbridge**
207 Sloane Street Mon-Sat 10-6 (Wed 10-7)
London SW1

Samsonite

It is best known for its classic, durable luggage, but Samsonite also offers a small, travel-friendly clothing collection. Modern and versatile, the styles tend to remain simple, practical and sleek, featuring monochromatic separates including pants, button-down shirts and zip-up jackets. Contemporary cuts enhance a classic style sense that, like their rolling bags, can cross any time zone.
www.samsonite.com

020 7499 4239 **tube: Bond Street**
49-50 New Bond Street Mon-Sat 10-6 (Thurs 10-7)
London W1

Sasti

Guy Ritchie reportedly shops here, so there's reason enough to stop by, never mind the adorable assortment of children's clothing, booties, blankets and hats. Tiny camouflage pants, patchwork jeans that flare at the ankle, faux suede and sheepskin waistcoats and bright red silk pajamas come at prices that are less than a splurge. There's also a play area to distract the little ones while you shop. Well worth a visit.

020 8960 1125 **tube: Ladbroke Grove**
Portobello Green Arcade Mon-Sat 10-6
London W10

Savage London

Rough, tough fashion junkies craving streetwear should make the trip to Savage. Decal T-shirts denoting different local boroughs ("Hackney", "Peckham", "Chelsea"), express some London pride. Clubwear is also available, including tight leather pants and tons of denim. Go if you're cool enough. www.savagelondon.com

020 7439 1163 **tube: Oxford Circus**
14a Newburgh Street Mon-Sat 10:30-7
London W1 Sun 12-5

Scabal

Despite the ring-to-enter system, this London boutique of a Brussels-based international menswear chain has a more modern feel than many of its neighbors. The slick but slightly anodyne air to the shop's interior is reflected a little too well in the range of well made but somewhat unremarkable

made-to-measure and ready-to-wear suits. Uncut fabrics are also available. www.scabal.com

020 7734 8963 **tube: Piccadilly Circus/Oxford Circus**
12 Savile Row Mon-Fri 9-6, Sat 12-6
London W1

scorah pattullo

Johnny Pattullo and Frances Scorah are not afraid to tinker. If Sergio Rossi is offering a style of shoe they love but the color seems wrong, they'll order eight pairs in another color. The result is a unique selection of designer shoes that you won't find at large department stores. From Sonia Rykiel to Anya Hidmarch to Gucci McQueen, heels are high and stock numbers are low so when they run out of those eight pairs they won't order more. The flash of Tom Ford, the danger of Narciso Rodriguez, the panache of Christian Louboutin—it's all brought together in this special spot. What's more, Scorah and Pattullo recently launched their own collection.

020 7792 0100 **tube: Notting Hill Gate**
193 Westbourne Grove Mon-Fri 10:30-6:30
London W11 Sat 10-6, Sun 12:30-5:30

020 7226 9342 **tube: Angel**
137 Upper Street (opening times as above,
London N1 except Sat 10:30-6)

Sefton

One of a handful of the neighborhood's truly reputable boutiques, Sefton stocks a mix of backbone designers—Helmut Lang, Alexander McQueen, and Etro—as well as lesser-known labels like Gharani Strok or Eley Kishimoto, the husband-and-wife team gaining renown for their hand-printed designs. Everything has a quirky touch here, from T-shirts to suits with bright diagonal stitching and pleats in strange places. There's also Acqua di Parma perfume, Anya Hindmarch change purses and shoes by Marc Jacobs. If you've made the trip to Islington, Sefton is a must.

020 7226 9822 **tube: Highbury & Islington**
271 Upper Street (W) Mon-Sat 10-6:30 (Thurs-Fri 10-7)
London N1 Sun 12-5:30

020 7226 9822 (M) **tube: Highbury & Islington**
196 Upper Street (opening times as above)
London N1

☆ Selfridges

The best just keeps getting better. With a multimillion dollar refurbishment under its belt, Selfridges is the coolest department store in London. The mind-boggling mix of traditional designers, new talents and mainstream fashion satisfies even the most voracious of London's label hounds. Even the children's department is chock-full of designer names: Diesel, Ted Baker, Juicy Couture. For those shoppers long on style but short on time, the personal shopping service comes to the rescue. Add accessories, cosmetics, books, toys, homewares and the famous food hall, and you can see why Selfridges comes up trumps time and time again. www.selfridges.com

0870 837 7377 **tube: Bond Street**
400 Oxford Street Mon-Fri 10-8
London W1 Sat 9:30-8, Sun 12-6

☆ Semmalina

Emma Forbes's labor of love is a fantasyland of childrenswear, where fake trees flank a tiny film-set bridge and a castle façade leads to the back of the store. There are fairy costumes and tutus for playtime and, for young fashionistas in training, designer labels like Gertha DiSanto's kids' collection. Sizes run up to age eight, but the little St. Tropez baskets and hair accessories by Johnny Loves Rosie will suit every generation. Sweet down to the last detail, Semmalina will wrap your goodies in layers of tissue paper, with lollipops and hairpins hidden within. In the fall they will expand, with a clothing and accessories collection for girls aged 8-13. And listen here, moms, they will also solve your party bags problem! www.skstanding@aol.com

020 7730 9333 **tube: Sloane Square**
225 Ebury Street Mon-Sat 9:30-5:30
London SW1

Senso

Featuring ruched leather boots, girlish flats and sexy slingbacks, Senso offers a combination of designer and own-brand shoes for women, gleaning inspiration from modern and vintage looks. Among the other designers lining their shelves, you'll spot Rodolphe Menudier, Kim Meller and Johnny Barbato. There are some basic designs (leather moccasins and bright sneakers) but most of the selection tends to be more creative.

020 7499 9998 **tube: Bond Street**
6 South Molton Street Mon-Sat 10-6:30 (Thurs 10-7:30)
London W1 Sun 1-5

Serafina

Adult bridesmaids' dresses are a tricky issue. There are so many horror stories about elder bridesmaids being asked by a best friend to wear a hideous, unflattering peach ensemble that's never going to see the light of day after it's been worn once. Enter Serafina, a welcome addition to the London bridal scene. Clean-cut, simple and refined, the collection includes dresses in such luxurious fabrics as silk, duchesse satin and taffeta. Flowing chiffon makes for a romantic look and thick velvet is great for winter weddings. Styles are incredibly classic, many of them strapless with A-line skirts. Best of all, these dresses are lovely enough to be worn twice.

020 7731 5215 **tube: Fulham Broadway**
Studio 7, Redloh House (by appointment)
2 Michael Road
London SW6

Seraphine

When pregnant colleagues kept complaining about not being able to find decent maternity wear Cecile Reinaud saw a gap in the market. She quit her job in advertising, teamed up with Alexandra Sliosberg, a designer of nursery furniture, and Jacques Guilmard, formerly a designer for Armani, and set up Seraphine. The store is a haven for stylish new mums and offers refreshingly chic maternity wear, cute baby basics and sophisticated nursery furniture. Fresh fabrics and soft colors ensure that the clothing is far from stuffy. For everyday there are low-waist bootleg jeans and combat trousers; for a smarter look the pinstripe suits, blouses and linen trousers are elegantly comfortable, and for evenings and parties there are plenty of bias-cut dresses. The combination of practicality and prettiness is ideal and we're betting, and hoping, this store is here to stay.

020 7937 3156 **tube: High Street Kensington**
28 Kensington Church Street Mon-Sat 10:30-6, Sun 12-5
London W8

Sergio Rossi

He's a glamorous Italian hero, with an innate sense for sexy elegance that sends supermodels into spasms. Sleek and towering, his curved-heel stilettos put even petite women in the mile-high club. Shiny caramel slingbacks and black patent boots highlight the feminine collection and are perfect matches for the clothes of Gucci, who bought the company two years ago. They're certainly an investment, but they'll still be worth it long after Naomi, Claudia and Kate have teetered away from the catwalk. www.sergiorossi.com

020 7629 5598 **tube: Green Park/Piccadilly Circus**
15 Old Bond Street Mon-Sat 10-6 (Thurs 10-7)
London W1

Shanghai Tang

The store opening topped the hype meter, with Kate and Naomi in attendance and owner David Tang smiling from ear to ear for the glossies' paparazzi. No wonder. His Chinese-inspired home and clothing collection, a hit in Hong Kong, has made a smooth journey westward. The luxurious silk pajamas, velvet Chinese jackets and quilted silk slippers are a splurge. But there are some well priced prezzies, including teddy bears decked out in colorful eastern garb and a Dim Sum watch with dumplings denoting the hours (presented in its own bamboo basket). www.shanghaitang.com

020 7235 8778 **tube: Knightsbridge**
6a/b Sloane Street Mon-Sat 10-7, Sun 12-6
London SW1

Sharon Cunningham

Having worked with such top designers as Catherine Walker and Ben de Lisi, Sharon Cunningham opened her

own bridal shop in fashionable Marylebone in 1999. Her designs are simple, elegant, modern and well suited to an hourglass figure. Off the peg you'll find bias-cut gowns and column dresses enhanced with delicate embroidery or subtle beading, from £1,500. If you prefer to wear something unique expect to pay above £3,000 for bespoke designs.

www.sharoncunningham.com

020 7724 7002 — **tube: Marble Arch**
23 New Quebec Street — (by appointment)
London W1

Sheila Cook

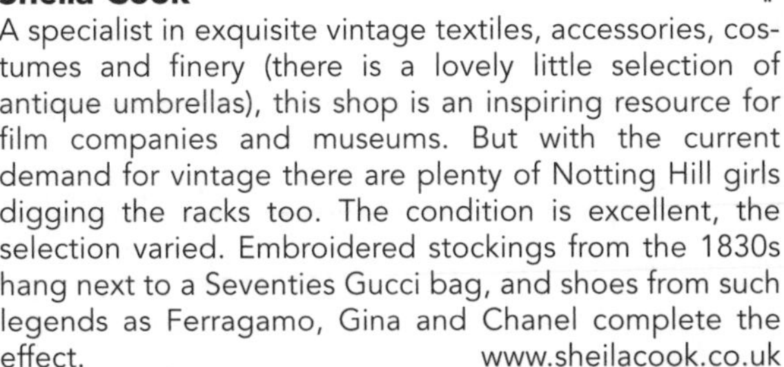

A specialist in exquisite vintage textiles, accessories, costumes and finery (there is a lovely little selection of antique umbrellas), this shop is an inspiring resource for film companies and museums. But with the current demand for vintage there are plenty of Notting Hill girls digging the racks too. The condition is excellent, the selection varied. Embroidered stockings from the 1830s hang next to a Seventies Gucci bag, and shoes from such legends as Ferragamo, Gina and Chanel complete the effect. www.sheilacook.co.uk

020 7792 8001 — **tube: Notting Hill Gate**
283 Westbourne Grove — Fri 10-6, Sat 18-6
London W11 — (Tues-Thurs by appointment)

Shellys

A big, buzzing footwear chain, Shellys won't win any design accolades but there's tons of variety on hand, all at good prices. With a staggering range, from high-heeled boots to standard loafers to sporty sneakers, there's a shoe here for everyone. The selection is easy to browse, organized by style and displayed on different levels of the store.

020 7287 0939 — **tube: Oxford Circus**
266-270 Regent Street — Mon-Sat 10-7
London W1 — (Thurs 10-8), Sun 12-6

020 7437 5842 — **tube: Oxford Circus**
159 Oxford Street — (opening times as above)
London W1

020 7240 3726 — **tube: Covent Garden**
14-18 Neal Street — (opening times as above)
London WC2

020 7581 5537 — **tube: Sloane Square**
124b King's Road — Mon-Sat 9:30-6:30
London SW3 — (Wed 9:30-7), Sun 11-6

020 7938 1082 — **tube: High Street Kensington**
40 Kensington High Street — Mon-Sat 9:30-6:30
London W8 — (Thurs 10-7), Sun 12-6

Shi Cashmere

Right in the expensive heart of Belgravia, this shop offers a slightly puzzling selection of made-to-measure eveningwear and Scottish cashmere for everyday, from an organza evening dress to cosy drawstring pants. We found some cuts too baggy and some colors too bold, but they, like the loose linen tunics, will probably please an older clientele. The chunky cashmere sweaters are the best of the bunch. www.shicashmere.com

020 7235 3829 **tube: Knightsbridge**
30 Lowndes Street Mon-Sat 9:30-6 (Wed 9:30-7)
London SW1

Shirin Guild

London-based Shirin Guild launched her own label in 1991 and now, at last, she's opened her own store. Inspired by the crisp simplicity of the traditional clothing in her native Iran, Guild's loose-layered designs are all about comfort and understated style. You'll find wide-leg trousers with wraparound belts, over-sized round-neck tops with square kimono sleeves and her ubiquitous box sweaters. Guild uses luxurious fabrics such as cashmere, tweed and flannel and her clothes come in subtle colors—brown, blue, gray, black and white. A small homeware selection rounds out the look with pebble-shaped soaps and light white china.

020 7351 2766 **tube: South Kensington**
241 Fulham Road Mon-Sat 10-6
London SW3

The Shirtsmith

This tiny shop, in a cobbled courtyard off Ledbury Road, is not quite as it sounds. The specialty is dressy, made-to-measure ladieswear—ruffled silk blouses, embroidered jackets, smart suits—though there is a small selection of ready-to-wear cotton shirts characterized by their crisp, pointy collars. Clientele is mature and primarily female, but men are happily accommodated.

020 7229 3090 **tube: Notting Hill Gate**
2a Ledbury Mews North Tues-Sat (by appointment)
London W11

Shop

Neon pink lighting leads the way to this basement Soho store where you'll find a cutting-edge combination of girly fashion and sexy kitsch. The list of labels is enough to tempt aspiring Carrie Bradshaws, with Sonia Rykiel, Marc by Marc Jacobs, Cacharel and Milk Fed. There are tight-fitting baby tees, frayed denim skirts and their own label of cute-but-naughty underwear sets. To top it all, plenty of sparkly accessories.

020 7437 1259 **tube: Piccadilly Circus**
4 Brewer Street Mon-Fri 10:30-6:30, Sat 11-6:30
London W1

Sigerson Morrison

This New York collection ranges from classic to fashion-inspired with slides, slingbacks, mules and boots in styles

that can border on just-so preciousness. Fabrics include leather, patent, corduroy and suede. There is also a small selection of handbags, French leather gloves and a new line of luggage. The selection is very pretty and starts at around £200. As we went to press they were within months of carrying a men's line as well.

020 7229 8465 **tube: Notting Hill Gate**
184 Westbourne Grove Mon-Fri 10-6, Sat 10-6
London W11 Sun 12-5

Sign of the Times

They aren't kidding when they tell you this is London's original dress agency. For 25 years Sign of the Times has offered high-end secondhand clothing and accessories. Designer names include (deep breath) Prada, Gucci, Chanel, Dolce & Gabbana, Yohji Yamamoto and Marc Jacobs, some still with the tags on. Upstairs you'll find Jimmy Choos and Manolos just begging to be broken in.

020 7589 4774 **tube: South Kensington**
17 Elystan Street Mon-Fri 10-6
London SW3 (Wed 10-7:30), Sat 10-5:30

Sisley

This is Benetton's big sister—a little more sophisticated and streamlined than her colorful counterpart. It's also a label best known for fine knitwear but the new London location carries every variation of men's and women's clothing, from coats to dyed denim to bikinis. We're betting it's best for ladies-in-training. www.sisley.com

020 7376 2437 **tube: High Street Kensington**
129-131 Kensington High Street Mon-Sat 10-7
London W8 (Thurs 10-8), Sun 12-6

Size?

If you're looking for the latest fashionable sneaker, look no further. All the top names are here—Adidas, Puma, Lacoste, Converse, Nike and Vans, in the season's most popular colors and styles. It's a treat not to have to trek up to heaving Oxford Street any more for sneakers, but be aware that this selection is more for posing than for sport.

020 7823 8182 **tube: Sloane Square**
104 King's Road Mon-Sat 9:30-7:30
London SW3 Sun 12-6

020 7240 1736 **tube: Covent Garden**
17-19 Neal Street Mon-Fri 9:30-7:30 (Thurs 9:30-8:30)
London WC2 Sat-Sun 10:30-6

020 7287 4016 **tube: Oxford Circus**
31 Carnaby Street Mon-Sat 10-7:30 (Thurs 10-8:30)
London W1 Sun 12-6

020 7792 8494 **tube: Ladbroke Grove**
200 Portobello Road Mon-Sat 9-6:30, Sun 11-5
London W11

Skin Machine

Famous among leather-loving celebrities, Skin Machine provides high-style hide off-the-peg or made-to-measure. For sexy sorts, there are tight red leather pants, black tube dresses and diamanté-studded halters with matching minis. If this sounds a bit too raunchy, you'll also find classic suede jackets and warm winter coats lined with wool. A solid selection of hats and goggles will please the biker buffs.

020 7937 3297 **tube: High Street Kensington**
25 Kensington Church Street Mon-Sat 10-6:30
London W8 Sun 12-5

Skins

Named for its humble beginnings in vintage leather, Skins now sells a range of new and secondhand goods. Students making the Portobello pilgrimage will love the Covent Garden-style streetwear, including Pussy Cat tracksuits, England team tank tops and bags by Punky Fish. An assortment of secondhand sneakers by Adidas and Puma are perfectly retro and nicely broken in.

020 7221 4203 **tube: Ladbroke Grove**
232 Portobello Road Mon-Fri 10-6, Sat 9:30-7
London W11 Sun 10:30-5:30

So aei kei

When Anna Krnajski, a Croatian fashion designer, teamed up with Djurdja Watson, a jewelry designer raised in what was Yugoslavia, the result was an ultra-hip new store in Portobello's up-and-coming Golborne Road. Although very different in style, Krnajski's pared-down clothing and Watson's semi-precious trinkets are perfect companions. Krnajski's designs are all about ladylike simplicity—sleeveless wraparound dresses, flattering bias-cut skirts, hand-printed silk vests and some sleek tops with low V-necks. Djurdja's decadent range of jewelry offers the perfect accompaniments in the form of jade and coral necklaces, dangly earrings and chunky bangles all the colors of the rainbow. This seamless match of minimalism and opulence is sure to succeed.

020 8960 8442 **tube: Ladbroke Grove/Notting Hill Gate**
357 Portobello Road Mon-Sat 11-6
London W10

Sole Trader

With a relaxed atmosphere and stagy lighting effects, Sole Trader is yet another Neal Street home of trendy shoes. The store carries a wide range of styles, from trainers to leather lace-ups to high-heeled boots. Shoes hark from such designers as DKNY, Dries Van Noten and Boss, and sneakers from Vans, Adidas and Nike. www.sole-trader.co.uk

020 7836 6777 **tube: Covent Garden**
72 Neal Street Mon-Sat 10:30-7 (Thurs 10:30-7:45)
London WC2 Sun 12-6

020 7361 1560 — **tube: High Street Kensington**
96a Kensington High Street — Mon-Sat 10-7
London W8 — (Thurs 10-8), Sun 12-6

Sonia Rykiel

She is a Grande Dame of chic Parisian fashion and her famous designs in knitwear have earned Sonia Rykiel the title Queen of Sweaters. Her soft fitted designs, often black or in primary colors, come enhanced with fun, eye-catching details—rainbow stripes, bright spots, sequins and rhinestones. While Rykiel is always in tune with fashion's ever-changing whims, her aesthetic remains reassuringly wearable. Her daughter Nathalie is now the company's creative director and is successfully making her presence felt in young, flirtier styles such as metal-studded handbags, sexy white linen suits and floppy felt hats.

020 7493 5255 — **tube: Bond Street**
27-29 Brook Street — Mon-Sat 10-6:30 (Thurs 10-7)
London W1

☆ Souvenir

Owners Anna Namiki and Anthony Manell capture the spirit of the Left Bank in Sixties Paris when fashion saw the collision of couture-house glamour and bohemian cool. Designers like Sara Berman, Paul & Joe, Les Prairies de Paris and Matthew Williamson create an inspired mix of new talents and luxury labels. The out-of-the-way location further enhances the magic of this tiny treasure-house.

020 7287 9877 — **tube: Piccadilly Circus/Oxford Circus**
47 Lexington Street — Mon-Fri 11:30-7
London W1 — (Thurs 11:30-7:30), Sat 12-7

Sox Kamen

This boutique offers a selection of Asian-inspired dresses, pants and tops made from silk specially chosen for its versatility and beauty. The designs are sophisticated but loose and comfortable. With a touch of eastern mystery, the range is colorful and unique.

020 7795 1830 — **tube: Sloane Square**
394 King's Road — Mon-Fri 10-5:30, Sat 10:30-5:30
London SW10

☆ SpaceNK

There's no doubt about it, shopping for beauty products can get ugly. Almost every woman has a horror story about buying cosmetics—domineering sales staff criticizing your skin, makeovers that leave you looking like a drag queen. Not so at SpaceNK, where the staff are more like sympathetic girlfriends than lip-linered lynch-women. All this, and the best of the hard-to-get brands including Laura Mercier, Stila and Kiehl's. Other highlights include Acqua di Parma perfume, Elemis creams and summer's must-have St. Tropez self-tanners. www.spacenk.com

020 7727 8063 — **tube: Notting Hill Gate**
127-131 Westbourne Grove — Mon-Sat 10-7
London W2 — (Wed-Thurs 10-8), Sun 12-6

020 7486 8791 **tube: Baker Street/Bond Street**
83a Marylebone High Street Mon-Fri 10-6:30
London W1 (Thurs 10-7), Sat 10-6, Sun 12-5

020 7355 1727 **tube: Bond Street**
45-47 Brook Street Mon-Sat 10-6:30 (Thurs 10-7)
London W1

020 7379 7030 **tube: Covent Garden**
4 Thomas Neals Centre Mon-Sat 10-7
37 Earlham Street (Thurs 10-7:30), Sun 12-5
London WC2

020 7256 2303 **tube: Liverpool Street**
137 Bishopsgate Mon-Wed 8:30-6:30
London EC2 Thurs-Fri 8:30-7

020 7589 8250 **tube: South Kensington**
307 Brompton Road Mon-Sat 10-6, Sun 12-5
London SW3

020 7351 7209 **tube: Sloane Square**
307 King's Road (opening times as above)
London SW3

020 7586 0607 **tube: St. John's Wood**
73 St. John's Wood High Street Mon-Sat 10-6
London NW8 Sun 12-6

020 7730 9841 **tube: Sloane Square**
27 Duke of York Square Mon-Tues, Sat 10-6:30
London SW3 Wed-Fri 10-7, Sun 12-6

020 7376 2870 **tube: High Street Kensington**
3 Kensington Church Street Mon-Tues, Sat 10-6:30
London SW3 Wed-Fri 10-7, Sun 12-6

Spaghetti

Walls painted with big bowls of pasta make a rather strange setting for couture. Chalk it up to homesickness for Italian designer Nadia La Valle whose dresses, tops, pants and wedding gowns are covered in hand embroidery and elaborate beading. Styles befit the more mature woman, and prices the more mature bank account. If the decor makes you crave carbonara, San Lorenzo is just across the street.

020 7584 0631 **tube: Knightsbridge**
32 Beauchamp Place Mon-Fri 9:30-6, Sat 10-6
London SW3

START

Situated in the cools of Shoreditch, where hip fashion is plentiful, this savvy boutique is a must. Owned by a former rock 'n' roll guitarist, the shop is quirky, spacious and full of character. The women's changing-room is strewn with red and purple velvet cushions, and luminous funfair signs from Blackpool Pier light the men's smaller nook. Meanwhile, the resident pug, Gromit, has his own hideaway doghouse built into the wall. The clothing is equally funky with Helmut Lang, Maharishi and Fake London intermingled with a casual collection of jeans by Seven and Paper Denim. A welcome respite from the surrounding pubs.

020 7739 3636 **tube: Old Street**
59 Rivington Street Mon-Fri 11-6, Sat 12-6
London EC2 Sun 1-5

☆ Steinberg & Tolkien

Fashion junkies with a few hours to kill will think they've died and gone to heaven. This is vintage designer clothing at its very best, featuring recovered relics from every decade from 1840 to 1980. The packed racks are organized by style (blazers, blouses, skirts) or designer (Pucci, Schiaparelli, Chanel). There's a wide range of accessories, including structured handbags, costume jewelry and Forties peep-toe pumps. The friendly sales staff will help you dig for your treasures.

020 7376 3660 **tube: Sloane Square**
193 King's Road Mon-Sat 11-7, Sun 12-6
London SW3

☆ Stella McCartney

In 1995 Stella McCartney, daughter of Beatle Paul, graduated from St Martin's London with a collection that revealed a rare designing talent and was almost immediately snapped up by Browns, Joseph and Neiman Marcus. Two collections later and with an established reputation for combining sharp tailoring with sexy femininity, Stella was appointed creative director of the house of Chloé in Paris. Now she's launched her own line, in partnership with the Gucci group, and has opened a shop on Bruton Street. Expect to see strong geometric patterns, a sexy sportswear sensibility and plenty of experimenting with construction, as seen in the fun "inside out" dress. This star is here to stay.

020 7518 3100 **tube:Green Park/Bond Street**
30 Bruton Street Mon-Sat 10-6 (Thurs 10-7)
London W1

Stephane Kélian

If you have a weakness for shoes you'll want to see what Stephane Kélian has been up to. Not one to chase the fashion pack, he sticks to the classics, so styles remain fairly constant from one season to the next but are never dull. From flowered mules to comfy flats, Kélian takes what works best in footwear and makes it one step better.

020 7235 9459 **tube: Knightsbridge**
48 Sloane Street Mon-Sat 10-6 (Wed 10-7)
London SW1

020 7629 8920 **tube: Green Park**
13 Grafton Street Mon-Sat 10-6 (Thurs 10-7)
London W1

Stewart Parvin

Stewart Parvin has come a long way. After graduating from Edinburgh College of Art, he trained in London with dressmaker Donald Campbell before designing eveningwear for high street chains such as C&A and Debenhams. Then he set up his own business in Knightsbrige and now nothing can hold him back. He has built up an impressive international clientele and designed several dresses for the Queen's Golden Jubilee tour. His new bridal boutique on Motcomb Street, decorated with ivory walls, leather sofas and sparkling mirrors, houses a signature collection of romantic contemporary styles infused with a touch of Fifties glamour. A couture service is also on offer, along with going away outfits and plenty of pretty accessories. Prices start from £1,600 and rise-to around £6,500. www.stewartparvin.com

020 7235 1125 **tube: Hyde Park Corner**
14 Motcomb Street Mon-Fri 10-6, Sat by appointment
London SW1

Still...

The emphasis at this vintage store is on dresses from the Fifties and Sixties but you can also find other retro relics, from roller-skates to pre-Calvin Klein underwire bras. On a recent visit we found a crocheted, patchwork sweater dress, a caramel-colored leather blazer, and an assortment of small-waisted circle skirts. In an area rife with vintage, the selection here is obviously from the attic, but also appropriately "now".

020 7243 2932 **tube: Ladbroke Grove**
61d Lancaster Road Mon-Sat 11-6, Sun 12-5
London W11

Strada

Not exactly the stuff that fetishes are made of, but the shoes here do fill occasional needs (i.e. when you have a dress with nothing to match and time is running out). The selection includes both classic and current designs, from slip-on loafers to zebra-hair boots, as well as some simple strappy sandals. The good news: prices won't do much damage.

020 7823 5497 **tube: Sloane Square**
63 King's Road Mon-Sat 10-7, Sun 11-6
London SW3

Stüssy

Once just a California T-shirt brand, Stüssy was among the first to mass-market skateboard style back in the Eighties. Today, the clothing collection is more diversified, incorporating skate and preppy influences (cargo pants, baseball shirts, camouflage caps and wide-leg jeans) but the name still suggests cool urban gear. www.stussystore.co.uk

020 7836 9418 **tube: Covent Garden**
19 Earlham Street Mon-Sat 11-7
London WC2 Sun 1-5:30

Sub Couture

There's nothing substandard about this popular Notting Hill shop, where the atmosphere is casual and the designer

selection hip...Nolita, Stephane Kélian, Les Prairies de Paris and Kenzo Jungle. But here big names do not mean big attitude. The staff are friendly and promote a villagey feel—if you find a skirt but no top to match, they'll call round the other neighborhood shops for you. The effect is completed with sunglasses, bags and shoes to suit every woman in the hunt for a refined look.

020 7229 5434 | **tube: Notting Hill Gate**
204 Kensington Park Road | Mon-Sat 10:30-6:30
London W11 | Sun 12-5

Sukie's

It's not often you find glass-blown vases for sale in a shoe shop, but such is the eclectic character of this one-off store whose owner H. Salimian commissions his own quirky interpretations of high-street style. For men there are Camper-style trainers, handmade ostrich lace-ups and rubber-soled boots with upturned toes. Women will find pointy mules, colorful slingbacks and comfy loafers with striking character. It's all a bit hit-and-miss, and definitely not for buttoned-up City types.

020 7352 3431 | **tube: Sloane Square**
285 King's Road | Mon-Sat 10-7, Sun 1-6
London SW3

Super Lovers 

Part of a Japanese chain, this shop with its bright turquoise exterior is difficult to miss. Inside you'll find kitsch streetwear with club roots, including an extensive collection of colorful logo'd merchandise. Tie-dyed T-shirts declaring "Love is the Message" and tank tops stating "non-violence" will appeal to club-kids with a Seventies sensibility.

www.superlovers.co.jp

020 7240 5248 | **tube: Covent Garden**
64 Neal Street | Mon-Sat 11-7
London WC2 | (Thurs 11-8), Sun 12-6

Swaine Adeney Brigg/Herbert Johnson 

Swaine sells sumptuous traditional leather luggage, small leathers and luxury items including champagne bottle holders alongside its renowned umbrellas and walking sticks. Herbert Johnson purveys a large range of formal and casual hats for both men and women, which for many will call to mind a period drama.

020 7409 7277 (Swaine Adeney Brigg) | **tube: Green Park**
020 7408 1174 (Herbert Johnson)
54 St. James's Street | Mon-Sat 10-6
London SW1

Swear 

The bright orange shop exterior sets the tone for the collection within, where purple ponyskin slip-ons are branded with a swirly motif and camouflage shoes feature Velcro straps. Ked-style sneakers with kitten heels and unusually pointy wingtips give the collection a cartoonish feel. Chunky rubber-soled shoes from the Skateboarder collection look like something that Goofy might wear.

www.swear-net.net

020 7240 7673 — **tube: Covent Garden**
61 Neal Street
London WC2
Mon-Sat 11-7, Sun 2-6

020 7734 1690 — **tube: Oxford Circus**
22 Carnaby Street
London W1
(opening times as above)

020 7485 7182 — **tube: Camden Town**
Unit 6, Stables Market
Chalk Farm Road
London NW1
Mon-Fri 11-6
Sat-Sun 10:30-6:30

Sweatshop

Think function not fashion at this small sports shop that carries a selection of top action brands—Venice Beach, USA Pro, Nike and Adidas. Choose from a large assortment of logo'd T-shirts, cozy hooded sweatshirts, running shoes and sleek tank tops. There are also Speedo swimsuits—better for doing laps than turning heads—and baggy cream T-shirts with matching leggings for yogis. Backpacks, goggles, sunglasses and a huge variety of socks round out the sporty selection. Not as trendy as Sweaty Betty, but it does the job.

020 7351 4421 — **tube: Gloucester Road**
188 Fulham Road
London SW10
Mon-Fri 10-8
Sat-Sun 10-6

020 7497 0820 — **tube: Covent Garden**
9a Endell Street
London WC2
Mon-Thurs 11-8, Fri 11-6:30
Sat 10-6, Sun 10-4

Sweaty Betty

Welcome to London's first fashion-savvy sportswear shop, where the final score is a tie between being comfortable and looking cute. For those who actually make it to the gym, there are Adidas stretch tops with matching pants, USA Pro biking shorts and shock-absorbing bras by Berlei, while gym-at-home types could reach for the stretching mats, skipping ropes and yoga travel kits. If you'd rather just look the part, you'll find Nike trainers, Puma bags, Quiksilver cropped trousers, diamanté halternecks and a wide assortment of bikinis and swimwear for posing by the pool.

www.sweatybetty.com

020 7937 5523 — **tube: High Street Kensington**
5 Kensington Church Street
London W8
Mon-Fri 10:30-7
Sat 10:30-6:30, Sun 12-5

020 7751 0228 — **tube: Parsons Green**
833 Fulham Road
London SW6
Mon-Fri 10-6:30
Sat 10-6, Sun 12-5

T&G Clothing

It's meant to be worn on boats but there are desperate wannabe yachtsmen and women wearing this nautical clothing around Fulham. The selection for men includes solid polo shirts with a single stripe across the front, sailing jackets and khaki pants. For women there are blue-and-white-striped polo dresses, three-quarter length clamdiggers and navy sweaters (for knotting around one's neck). If you're setting sail, feel free; otherwise, please don't do it. www.tandg.co.uk

020 7736 7776 — **tube: Parsons Green**
783 Fulham Road — Mon-Sat 10-6, Sun 11-5
London SW6

T.M.Lewin

Although it's one of London's longest established shirtmakers (since 1898), T.M.Lewin is also one of those leading the charge to attract a younger, more trend-conscious customer. This is achieved mainly through opening up the shops with brighter, cleaner shopfits and introducing younger, friendly staff without compromising quality—and it works. No fewer than 10 branches in the City show just how much businessmen and women like their Lewin shirts. Casualwear and accessories are also available.

www.tmlewin.co.uk

020 7930 4291 — **tube: Piccadilly Circus/Green Park**
106 Jermyn Street (M&W) — Mon-Sat 9:30-6
London SW1 — (Wed 10-6, Thurs 10-7)

020 7283 1277 (M) — **tube: Bank**
34-36 Lime Street — Mon-Fri 9:30-6
London EC2

020 7920 0787 (M) — **tube: Liverpool Street**
32-33 Blomfield Street — (opening hours as above)
London EC2

020 7256 6584 (M) — **tube: Moorgate**
67 Moorgate — (opening hours as above)
London EC2

020 7242 3180 (M) — **tube: Chancery Lane**
27a Chancery Lane — (opening hours as above)
London WC2

020 7242 1409 (W) — **tube: Chancery Lane**
9a Chichester Rents — (opening hours as above)
London WC2

020 7329 5337 (M&W) — **tube: St. Paul's**
59 Ludgate Hill — (opening hours as above)
London EC4

020 7329 2258 (W) — **tube: Bank**
49 Bow Lane — (opening hours as above)
London EC4

020 7588 4460 (W) — **tube: Liverpool Street**
77 London Wall — (opening hours as above)
London EC2

020 7623 0486 (W, casual) **tube: Bank**
9-9a Cullum St (opening hours as above)
London EC3

020 7606 2995 (M, casual) **tube: Bank**
85 Cheapside (opening hours as above)
London EC3

Tabio

Before we'd visited this new Japanese shop, we didn't realize the creative potential of the humble sock. There's every conceivable style (long or short, stripy or spotty, cotton or wool, fishnet or crocheted) minus the cartoon characters and geometric patterns that seem to haunt most sock shops. If you treasure absolute freedom of movement, some even come with separated toes. Quality fabrics and reasonable price range make this a reliable choice for the well heeled.

020 7591 1960 **tube: Sloane Square**
94 King's Road Mon-Sat 10-7, Sun 12-6
London SW3

Talbots

This American import will never turn heads, so if you dress to get noticed, move on. But Talbots has its niche for its wide selection of classic business and casualwear, particularly among conservative, mature dressers. Sensible suits, pants, dresses and skirts are mixed with T-shirts and soft knitwear. Petite sizes, accessories and shoes are also available. www.talbots.com

020 7494 9272 **tube: Piccadilly Circus**
115 Regent Street Mon-Sat 10-7
London W1 (Thurs 10-8), Sun 12-6

Tanner Krolle

This small handbag and luggage shop offers stylish, colorful cases for the fashionably high-minded. Durability is guaranteed and, with proper care, fabrics are liable to last a lifetime—this is the stuff that fashion heirlooms are made of. From alligator to plaid, from small and structured to giant weekender bag, the range of colors and styles makes choosing tough. If crowds clog your concentration, opt for the private client suite where you can shop in peace. www.tannerkrolle.com

020 7491 2243 **tube: Green Park**
3 Burlington Gardens Mon-Sat 10:6:30
London W1

020 7493 6302
Private Client Suite (by appointment)

Tartine et Chocolat

Stepping into this shop is like stepping back in time, with linen pinafores of a quality not seen since our grandmothers were girls. From pastel smock dresses to tiny twill pants, this is childrenswear at its most adorably refined. Mothers-to-be can prep with the small selection of baby blankets, booties and bibs. Sizes run from newborn to age 10.

020 7629 7233 — **tube: Bond Street**
66 South Molton Street — Mon-Sat 10-6
London W1

Tashia

It's a bit like a recipe that mysteriously fails: the ingredients are all there, but the mixture doesn't quite work. Calypso, Gharani Strok, Roland Mouret and Matthew Williamson are great labels, but cobbled together in this newish boutique, the end result is a bit too potent—too many different colors, too many different looks. That said, it may still be a good place to buy one thing at a time, such as a gemstone necklace by Sage.

020 7589 0082 — **tube: South Kensington**
178 Walton Street — Mon-Sat 10-6
London SW3

Tatters

When an off-the-rack just won't cut it, grab your fairy godmother and head to Tatters for made-to-measure eveningwear. Alas, it's not quite as simple as a touch of the magic wand. There are plenty of decisions to make: a satin or chiffon skirt? a beaded or sequined bodice? a simply-hemmed dress or one trimmed with lace? Be careful what you wish for: elaborate designs may take more than six months. But a simple dream dress could come to life within four weeks.

020 7584 1532 — **tube: South Kensington**
74 Fulham Road — Mon-Fri 10-6, Sat 10-5
London SW3

Ted Baker

For those who are fashion-conscious but don't feel compelled to prove it, Ted Baker is more sophisticated than the high street shops but not quite dashing designer. The clothing is modern and grounded, with his especially popular linen and cotton shirts, wool suits and a women's collection that includes comfortable denim, trendy silk tops and decal T-shirts. A full range of accessories is also available. All in all, more exciting than the prosaic name might suggest. www.tedbaker.co.uk

020 7836 7808 — **tube: Covent Garden**
9-10 Floral Street — Mon-Sat 10-7 (Thurs 10-8), Sun 12-6
London WC2

020 7497 8862 — **tube: Covent Garden**
1-4 Langley Court — Mon-Fri 10-7 (Thurs 10-7:30)
London WC2 — Sat 10-6:30, Sun 12-5

020 7437 5619 — **tube: Oxford Circus**
5-7 Foubert's Place — (opening times as above)
London W1

020 7351 6764 — **tube: Sloane Square**
75-77 King's Road — (opening times as above)
London SW3

Texier

It's leather goods as we like 'em—of impeccable quality and classic design. The business has been family-owned since 1951 and the folks have spent half a century perfecting their craft. The result is a collection of briefcases, travel bags, handbags and wallets that the French have been known to go mad for.

020 7935 0215 **tube: Bond Street/Baker Street**
6 New Cavendish Street Tues-Sat 9:30-5:30
London W1

Thailandia

From Bombay to Bali, this is an unexpected Aladdin's Cave in otherwise mundane Munster Road. It all began when Old Etonian Jeremy Reiss took a business trip to northern Thailand and noticed how beautiful everything was, from the people to the clothes. Now he travels to India, Vietnam, Indonesia and other Asian lands to seek out the beautiful and unique for this surprising store. Ethnic clothing doesn't get much better than this, not to mention Indian crystals, south-east Asian Buddhas and much more. And if you're stressed out, try an hour in the flotation tank downstairs; it's particularly popular with the tennis players during Wimbledon.

020 7610 2003 **tube: Parsons Green**
222 Munster Road Mon-Sat 11-6, Sun 12-4:30 (roughly)
London SW6

Thierry Mugler

Mugler is a fashion force unto himself. His women's collection exudes Ivana Trump-style drama, with massive, jutting shoulder pads, collars cut at sharp angles and teeny, tapered waists. Some might consider the funky cuts and bold colors a bit too eurotacky, but where else can you find a bright purple suit with a silver collar for £1,200? Understated dressers need not apply.

020 7629 7020 **tube: Bond Street**
134 New Bond Street Mon-Sat 10-6 (Thurs 10:30-6:30)
London W1 Sat 10:30-6

Thomas Pink

The most forward-looking of the traditional shirtmakers on Jermyn street, Thomas Pink has modern, open-plan stores and non-stuffy staff to guide you through the awesome selection of shirts and ties on display. Pink shirts have stiff, semi-cutaway collars and consequently look better worn with a tie, although some complain that the collars can crease badly. This is the company that has been largely responsible for attracting younger customers, men and women, to the joys of English shirtmaking and that has also been expanding in the City. Good mail-order service. www.thomaspink.co.uk

020 7930 6364 **tube: Piccadilly Circus/Green Park**
85 Jermyn Street Mon-Fri 10-7, Sat 9:30-6:30
London SW1 Sun 12-5

020 7245 0202 — **tube: Knightsbridge/Sloane Square**
74 Sloane Street — Mon-Fri 10-7 (Wed 10:30-7:30)
London SW1 — Sat 9:30-6:30, Sun 12-5

020 7730 5967 (W) — **tube: Sloane Square**
161 Sloane Street — Mon-Sat 10-6:30
London SW1 — (Wed 10-7), Sun 12-5

020 7499 4580 — **tube: Bond Street**
18 Davies Street — Mon-Sat 10-6:30 (Thurs 9:30-7)
London W1

020 7329 2248 (W) — **tube: Mansion House/Bank**
2 Bow Lane — Mon-Fri 9:30-6
London EC4

020 7374 2800 — **tube: Liverpool Street/Moorgate**
16 Blomfield Street — Mon-Fri 9:30-6
London EC2

020 7513 0303 — **tube: Canary Wharf**
Cabot Place East — Mon-Fri 8:30-7 (Thurs 8:30-7:30)
London E14 — Sat 10-6, Sun 11-5

Tim Little

Worn leather club chairs, an antique rug and blues playing in the background—not exactly what you'd expect in a shoe store. But the Fifties bachelor vibe is a perfect complement to Tim Little's traditional men's footwear—all made from superior French calfskin and each named after a song of the era. There's the "Whisky and Women" loafer, the "Stormy Monday" ankle boot, and their bestseller, the "Red House" lace-up, as well as a made-to-measure service. Women will find a similar selection in smaller sizes. The sleek, classic aesthetic is Terence Conran for the feet. No surprise then that the home guru himself created his own shoe for the collection, a slip-on loafer made from kangaroo.

020 7736 1999 — **tube: Fulham Broadway**
560 King's Road — Mon-Sat 10-6, Sun 11-5
London SW6

Timberland

The clothing here is tough enough for a mountain trek, a river crossing or even a stroll through Piccadilly Circus. Once an American outpost for durable waterproof boots, Timberland has grown into a major source of outdoor wear divided into three lines, Trek Travel, Rugged Casual and The Classic Line. There are state-of-the-art entron jackets, fleeces and dense wool socks, as well as simple thick sweaters, oxford shirts and soft chinos. The hiking boots top the lot, guaranteed to withstand the rigors of nature. www.timberland.com

020 7495 2133 — **tube: Bond Street**
72 New Bond Street — Mon-Sat 10-6
London W1 — (Thurs 10-7), Sun 12-6

Timothy Everest

One of London's foremost tailors, Everest is a pioneer in the revival of British bespoke tailoring. He makes suits for the great and the good, including Tom Cruise, from his base in a beautiful Georgian townhouse in the newly trendy neighborhood of Spitalfields. Everest favors a classic, waisted English style, although with bespoke anything is possible. He also sells a small selection of non-tailored ready-to-wear and accessories. Appointments are recommended, especially for bespoke services, but visitors are welcome to look around.

020 7377 5220 | **tube: Liverpool Street**
32 Elder Street | Mon-Fri 9-6, Sat 10-4
London E1

Titri

Antique botanical motifs, inspired by 17th-century northern India, are hand-printed onto Titri's selection of soft home furnishings and clothing. Peonies, poppies and cypresses cover cotton housecoats, silk Cholo jackets and sarongs. There are also silk/pashmina dressing-gowns and shawls, hand-dyed in India, in such cheerful colors as lavender, forest-green and red. A welcome respite from the vintage overload on Portobello. www.titri-online.com

020 7229 2023 | **tube: Notting Hill Gate**
82d Portobello Road | Tues-Sat 10-5
London W11

Tod's

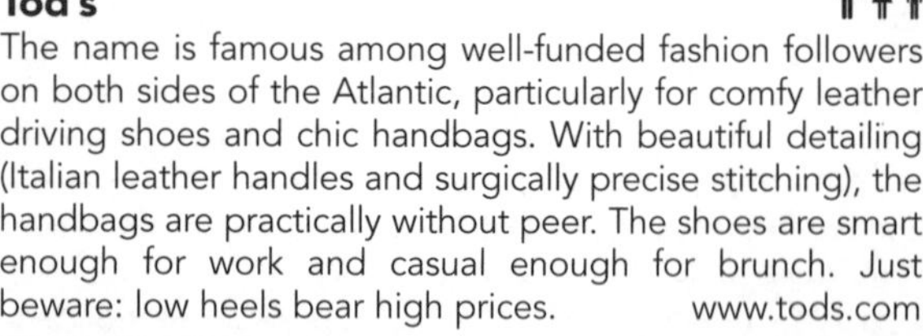
The name is famous among well-funded fashion followers on both sides of the Atlantic, particularly for comfy leather driving shoes and chic handbags. With beautiful detailing (Italian leather handles and surgically precise stitching), the handbags are practically without peer. The shoes are smart enough for work and casual enough for brunch. Just beware: low heels bear high prices. www.tods.com

020 7235 1321 | **tube: Knightsbridge**
35-36 Sloane Street | Mon-Fri 10-6 (Wed 10-7)
London SW1 | Sat 10:30-6

Tomasz Starzewski

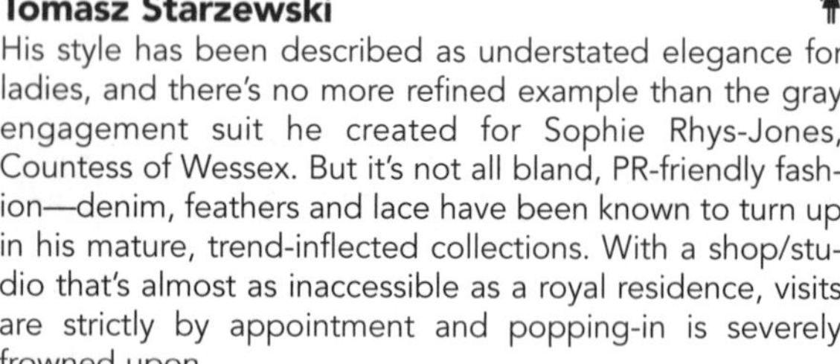
His style has been described as understated elegance for ladies, and there's no more refined example than the gray engagement suit he created for Sophie Rhys-Jones, Countess of Wessex. But it's not all bland, PR-friendly fashion—denim, feathers and lace have been known to turn up in his mature, trend-inflected collections. With a shop/studio that's almost as inaccessible as a royal residence, visits are strictly by appointment and popping-in is severely frowned upon.

020 7244 6138 | **tube: Gloucester Road**
14 Stanhope Mews West | Mon-Fri 10-6 (by appointment)
London SW7

Tommy Hilfiger

Bringing the American spirit to London, Tommy Hilfiger features bold-colored casualwear with Ivy League style.

There's a crisp sense of clean living to the classic button-down shirts, knitwear, pants and skirts. The wide selection of Tommy accessories, from shoes and socks to perfume, offers Londoners, or visitors, the chance to snap up a piece of American prep. www.tommy.com

020 7235 2500 **tube: Knightsbridge**
6 Sloane Street Mon-Sat 10-6
London SW1 (Wed 10-7), Sun 1-6

Top Gun

The name may be a little dated but it pays homage to Tom Cruise's big-screen rebel who helped bring back the bomber jacket, here in all its macho glory at this made-to-measure leather shop. It may not be the danger zone but you'll still find a racy range of styles, from turquoise snake-skin to black suede. Long or short, shiny or weathered, zip-up or button-down—you want it, they got it.

020 7376 0823 **tube: High Street Kensington**
23 Kensington High Street Mon-Sat 10-7 (Thurs 10-8)
London W8 Sun 12:30-6:30 (but call beforehand)

☆ Top Shop/Top Man

This store has earned accolades for the trendiest and most affordable designs to hit the high street. Three giant floors feature sleek and cheap designer copies and basic mix-and-match separates for women and men. The bottom floor features one-off designer and vintage pieces, while upstairs you'll find a massive selection of accessories, extending beyond the basic belts and bags to include cosmetics, Kangol visors, body jewelry and every other conceivable club-kid treat. The buzz of the Oxford Circus flagship is compounded by loud music and hordes of teens, but with rock-bottom prices and dead-on designs you'd be crazy not to join in the fun.

020 7636 7700 **tube: Oxford Circus**
214 Oxford Street Mon-Sat 9-8 (Thurs 9-9)
London W1 Sun 12-6

Tops & Bottoms

Girls blessed with God-given figures might find something suitable in this store where the theme seems to be the tighter, the better. There are skin-hugging bodysuits, suede pants with barely enough room to breathe and tiny tees by Anti-flirt that will do the strutting for you.

020 7349 8822 **tube: South Kensington**
3 Cale Street Mon-Fri 10-6, Sat 11-4:30
London SW3

Travelling Light

The Riviera, the Costa Smeralda, Malaga—all are just a few hours away but beachwear is often difficult to come by in London. Not so at Travelling Light, where the slogan is "hot weather clothing all year round" and the specialty is travel, safari, cruise and beachwear. The clothes are bright and the fabrics light and comfortable. The styles may be a bit dowdy, but if you're going on safari you won't be glamming up anyway. Accessories are also available. www.travellinglight.com

020 7629 7000 **tube: Green Park**
35 Dover Street Mon-Fri 10-6, Sat 10-5
London W1

Trésor

Want to look fab, dahling, but find yourself without the funds? This cramped secondhand store (decorated with 19th-century paintings and Russian icons, also for sale) is packed with dresses from Christian Dior, Emanuel Ungaro and Eskimo. Top it all off from their selection of fur coats, crocodile bags and Manolo Blahniks and you'll leave friends guessing at your net worth. Our tip: don't skip lunch...Trésor like to lunch too, and close the store most days from 1:15 to 2:15.

020 7349 8829 **tube: South Kensington/Sloane Square**
13 Cale Street Mon 2:30-6, Tues-Sat 11-6
London SW3

☆ Tricker's

One of the giants of traditional English shoemaking (since 1829) and one of the few remaining family-owned independents since Prada's purchase of Church's. In addition to brogues, derbys, oxfords, buckled monk shoes and boots, they also feature their unique monogrammed velvet slippers, which are lined in leather and can be customized with any motif, from dragons to camels to family crests. (A proportion of their considerable American clientele, specifically those from the sunnier cities like Los Angeles and Miami, are known to wear the slippers as streetwear.) This small, intimate store with its old-fashioned interior and great service provides the ideal environment for purchasing. Shoemakers by royal appointment to the Prince of Wales.

020 7930 6395 **tube: Piccadilly Circus/Green Park**
67 Jermyn Street Mon-Fri 9:30-6, Sat 9:30-5:30
London SW1

Trotters

A bright and bubbly source for extremely wearable children's clothing. Offering a standard selection (dresses, pants and matching tops) for babies and kids, it's the patterns that bring these looks to life. The staff also do expert shoe fittings. www.trotters.co.uk

020 7259 9620 **tube: Sloane Square**
34 King's Road Mon-Sat 9-7
London SW3 Sun 10-6:30

020 7937 9373 **tube: High Street Kensington**
121 Kensington High Street Mon-Sat 9-7
London W8 Sun 10:30-6:30

Trudy Hanson 

Whether you want a slim, sexy gown reminiscent of a glamorous evening dress, or a full princess-line skirt teamed with a strapless bodice, Hanson's creations range from the sleek to the opulent. Her salon, situated on trendy All Saints Road, is airy and friendly with over 40 display dresses to draw inspiration from. Handmade veils and tiaras are designed to match the dresses and a tiny blue bow is sewn inside each made-to-measure gown as a token of good luck. www.trudyhanson.co.uk

020 7792 1300 **tube: Westbourne Park**
25 All Saints Road Mon-Sat 10-5:30 (Thurs 10-7:30)
London W11 (by appointment)

☆ Turnbull & Asser  

Shirtmakers to the Prince of Wales, T&A are a contender for the best on Jermyn Street but definitely have the most beautiful windows. This is a treasure-house for lovers of traditional British menswear, not only selling some of the finest bespoke and off-the-peg shirts in the world but also a stunning, colorful range of dressing-gowns, ties, cufflinks, suspenders, socks, handkerchiefs and sweaters. The country-house interior has wooden cabinets stuffed with countless goodies.

020 7808 3000 **tube: Piccadilly Circus/Green Park**
71-72 Jermyn Street Mon-Fri 9-6, Sat 9:30-6
London SW1

Uniqlo 

It's been described as Japan's answer to Gap, and hopes were high that their wild success would spread west with the opening of the giant Brompton Road store, but so far it's been a bit of a disappointment. The extensive selection of casualwear, from fleece pullovers to corduroy pants, plus tote bags, belts and Birkenstock-style sandals, come at prices that rival London's favorite high street depots, but fabrics can be cheap and styles border on boring.
www.uniqlo.com

020 7584 8608 **tube: Knightsbridge**
163-169 Brompton Road Mon-Sat 10-7 (Wed-Thurs 10-8)
London SW3 Sun 12-6

020 7434 9688 **tube: Piccadilly Circus**
84-86 Regent Street Mon-Sat 10-7 (Thurs 10-8)
London W1 Sun 12-6

United Colors of Benetton 

Shoppers of a certain generation will remember when the green and blue Benetton rugby shirts were ubiquitous. At times this Italian company makes more headlines for its controversial ad campaigns than for its designs, but it continues to be a reliable source of well-made knitwear in a brilliant spectrum of solid colors. Sweaters, dresses, pants and skirts are the staples of the women's selection; men can choose from suits and casualwear. For the color-shy there is even the odd bit of black, white and brown. www.benetton.com

020 7647 4200 **tube: Oxford Circus**
255-259 Regent Street Mon-Wed 10-7:30, Thurs 10-9
London W1 Fri-Sat 10-8, Sun 10-6

020 7591 0925 **tube: Knightsbridge**
23 Brompton Road Mon-Sat 10-7
London SW3 Sun 12-6

020 7937 3034 **tube: High Street Kensington**
147-153 Kensington High Street Mon-Sat 10-7
London W8 (Thurs 10-8), Sun 12-6

020 7297 6260 **tube: Bond Street**
415-419 Oxford Street Mon-Wed, Sat 10-7:30, Thurs 10-9
London W1 Fri 10-8, Sun 12-6

Urban Outfitters

The English cousin of the American chain, this store is a huge industrial-style warehouse for retro/modern culture. You may go in looking for just one thing, but you're liable to leave with credit card damage. The basement houses a men's garage-meets-grunge clothing collection with a secondhand effect. Thumping music will draw you to the DJ booth where you can purchase the latest sounds. Upstairs, the women's section offers a variety of styles, from too-cool-to-care T-shirts to Sixties striped sweaters to basic button-downs. Throw in bohemian skirts and hippy jewelry and the overall effect is mismatched and proud of it. Huge Chinese lanterns, velvet pillows, "Playmate of the Year" pint glasses and suede ottoman cubes will perk up any drab pad.

020 7761 1001 **tube: High Street Kensington**
36-38 Kensington High Street Mon-Sat 10-7
London W8 (Thurs 10-8), Sun 12-6

Valentino

Few people signify legendary, elegant couture like Valentino. Women can select from sophisticated ready-to-wear including knitwear, separates, pants and suits. Men who prefer dressing down can bypass the business section for a collection of casual but equally well crafted clothes. Known around the world for razor-sharp suits and glamorous evening gowns, the Valentino label is the mark of chic opulence. www.valentino.it

020 7235 5855 **tube: Knightsbridge**
174 Sloane Street Mon-Fri 10-6, Sat 10:30-6
London SW1

Van Heusen

Van Heusen has been a prominent brand in both the US and Britain since 1881. It has changed hands several times but retains its position as a venerable name within classic menswear circles. The Van Heusen brand covers sportswear too, but this small store focuses on shirts and ties and does a very good job of it. They have recently begun to carry a ladies line as well.

020 7930 1927 **tube: Piccadilly Circus/Green Park**
112 Jermyn Street Mon-Fri 9:30-6, Sat 10:30-6:30
London SW1

Vent

You'd be wise to plan your visit to Vent in advance as this Notting Hill vintage outpost is open only two days a week. The owner, an architect by trade, has a passion for fashion treasures of all sorts, including homeware. If you want to incorporate a touch of boho or retro cool into a modern wardrobe, this is the perfect place to start.

(no phone) **tube: Notting Hill Gate**
178a Westbourne Grove Fri-Sat 9-5
London W11

Ventilo

It may be all over Paris, but there's only one London home for Armand Ventilo's sophisticated collection, where French classicism finds eastern flair. Gold-colored scarves in sheer chiffon are edged with bands of ribbon and long skirts are swirled with bright beading. For more practical pursuits, linen suits and silk knits in earthy tones like aubergine and caramel are cut forgivingly without looking dowdy. There are also black ruffled tank tops with matching trousers, crisp shirts and red denim skirts with white ribbon piping. Soft leather bucket bags in vibrant red and orange round out the fun but smart selection. www.ventilo.fr

020 7491 3666 **tube: Bond Street**
70 New Bond Street Mon-Fri 10:30-6 (Thurs 10-7)
London W1 Sat 10-6:30

Versace

The perennially tanned and bottle-blonde Donatella has worn the mantle since her brother Gianni's murder in 1995, churning out a signature collection that gets flashier and trashier with every passing season. The new HQ on Bond Street combines all things Versace under one palatial roof: Gianni Versace, Versus, Versace Jeans Couture, Versace Sport, Versace Young and Versace Intensive (swim- and underwear), as well as the home and jewelry collections. www.versace.com

020 7355 2700 **tube: Bond Street/Oxford Circus**
113-115 New Bond Street Mon-Sat 10-6 (Thurs 10-7)
London W1

020 7259 5700 **tube: Knightsbridge**
183-184 Sloane Street Mon-Sat 10-6
London SW1

Vertice Uomo

An approachable boutique featuring designer menswear without the hype. Labels include Allessandrini, Roberto Cavalli, Romeo Gigli, Costume National and Dsquared. Styles are wearable and prices within reason. Worth a glance if you're walking by.

Directory

020 7408 2031 **tube: Bond Street**
16 South Molton Street Mon-Sat 10-6:30
London W1 (Thurs 10-7)

The Vestry

If you're making the style leap into cheap-chic, the Vestry is a good place to start your transformation. The racks are lined with a trendy variety of hip-hugging denim, gypsy tops and belts with tassels, all very timey if not built to last. If you like Miss Selfridge, you'll be happy here.

020 7225 1323 **tube: Sloane Square**
120 King's Road Mon-Thurs 10-6:30 (Wed 10-7:30)
London SW3 Fri-Sat 10-7, Sun 12-6

Via Venise

Relatively new to the block, Via Venise has already established a following among Chelsea's abundant style seekers. The French footwear designs are sometimes quirky, sometimes classic, but always wearable. Find towering boots, jeweled slingbacks and court shoes with demoniacally pointed toes—all at good prices.

020 7351 7707 **tube: Sloane Square**
163 King's Road Mon-Sat 10-7, Sun 12-6
London SW3

Virginia

John Galliano might drop by to discuss the finer points of corsetry, such is the esoteric character of Virginia and her vintage shop which features women's clothing from the 1880s to the 1930s. It's all displayed in an over-the-top boudoir where literally everything is pink—imagine a grandmother's crowded dressing-room, her frilly knickers resting on a day-bed that's draped with an embroidered piano shawl. There's no rhyme or reason to the selection, it's whatever Virginia likes...evening gowns, lingerie, hats, bags and decorative objets. One thing she definitely doesn't like: customers who gripe about her prices, which generally start around £200.

020 7727 9908 **tube: Holland Park**
98 Portland Road Mon-Fri 11-6, Sat by appointment
London W11

Vivienne Westwood

Her approach may be outlandishly wild but that doesn't deter the legions (mainly Japanese) who swear by her designs. In business since the early Seventies, this true fashion legend has established four labels: Vivienne Westwood Gold Label, Red Label by Vivienne Westwood, Anglomania, and MAN. Her outrageous dresses, suits, skirts and shirts portray a bold sense of drama that will definitely turn heads at the supermarket.

020 7439 1109 **tube: Oxford Circus**
44 Conduit Street Mon-Sat 10-6 (Thurs 10-7)
London W1

020 7629 3757 **tube: Bond Street**
6 Davies Street (opening times as above)
London W1

020 7352 6551 **tube: Sloane Square**
430 King's Road Mon-Sat 10-6 (Wed 10-7)
London SW10

Viyella

Elastic waistband trousers, basic blouses and long, roomy skirts take no apparent notice of the latest fashion trends. The mixed separates and suits at Viyella feature basic fabrics like cotton and linen, and mostly solid shades of beige, brown and navy. We were bored stiff here, but there's bound to be someone looking for such safe, practical casualwear.

020 7734 7524 **tube: Oxford Circus**
179-183 Regent Street Mon-Fri 10-6:30 (Thurs 10-8)
London W1 Sat 10-6, Sun 12-5

Voyage

First Voyage was well in with fashion luvvies, then it was well and truly out. The boho-chic clothing in lush fabrics was popular, but a discriminating entrance policy and unfriendly staff were distinctly off-putting. Now, after a year's break, the Mazzilli clan are back, with a new flagship store in Mayfair and a diffusion shop, I Love Voyage, in Covent Garden. Thankfully there is no door policy at either location and service is much less intimidating, although shopping here is still an experience. The flagship store has a wonderfully eye-catching exterior exactly like a Fifties movie house, and the film on show is "Voyage: directed by Tatum and Rocky", the brother-sister duo behind the label. Inside awaits a dramatic couture collection. Recent highlights include faded jeans covered in multi-colored buttons, shirts decorated with fluorescent stripes, handbags covered in fringing and beading, and T-shirts declaring "Sleep with the Best". The Voyage look is slightly outlandish and, despite the shop's more welcoming vibe, the styles on offer are not for the faint-hearted.

020 7287 9989 **tube: Oxford Circus/Green Park**
50 Conduit Street Mon-Sat 9:30-6 (Thurs 9:30-7)
London W1

020 7836 5309 **tube: Covent Garden/Leicester Square**
33 Monmouth Street Mon-Wed 10-6:30, Thurs-Sat 10-7
London WC2

Wall

Influenced largely by Peruvian and Tibetan designs, the womenswear here reflects an earthy, organic style sense in such materials as Pima cotton, alpaca wool and Irish linen. Colors are inspired by the great outdoors, with sea-green shirts, sky-blue tunic dresses and sandy-beige cropped pants. Best for a mature shopper with a boho bent. They are also a mail order company, if you're too tired to make it over to Notting Hill. Order a catalog or shop online at www.wall-london.com

020 7243 4623 **tube: Notting Hill Gate**
1 Denbigh Road Mon-Fri 10:30-6:30, Sat 10-6
London W11 (for mail order, 020 7372 7373)

Wallis

If making the style pages has never been at the top of your to-do list, you might find this a good source for benign basics. It's certainly a place to visit for the seasonal changing of the guards, when a glance through your wardrobe reveals nothing reliable to wear. Bright tops, perennial pants and sexy evening bits achieve the look of the moment without risking much, but the classic cuts and commendable petite selection really make it worth stopping by.

020 7408 0639 **tube: Marble Arch**
532-536 Oxford Street Mon-Fri 9-8 (Thurs 9-9)
London W1 Sat 9-6, Sun 12-6

020 7938 1534 **tube: High Street Kensington**
42-44 Kensington High Street Mon-Sat 10-7
London W8 Sun 12-6

Wardrobe

Susie Faux offers women a uniquely individualized shopping experience. Meeting with customers one-on-one, she helps working women build their core business wardrobe—a great service for the shopping illiterate and those who don't have time to learn the tricks. The emphasis is on Italian designers such as Sergio Rossi, TSE, Piazza Sempione and many others. Beyond business, there are dresses and eveningwear as well. If you want to overhaul more than your closet, there's also a hair studio, beautician and shiatsu practitioner on hand. www.wardrobe.co.uk

020 7494 1131 **tube: Oxford Circus**
42 Conduit Street Mon-Sat 10-6 (Fri 8-6)
London W1

Warehouse

Tapping into the under-25 market and feeding its rabid appetite for trend, Warehouse brings the latest runway looks to the masses. Girls love the tight tanks and black pants, as well as the more casual line of sporty shirts and denim. Designs are primarily flashy and bright (but not of exceptional quality) and the latest trends are well represented. If Kookaï and Oasis are your guilty pleasures, this will also please.

020 7436 4179 **tube: Oxford Circus**
The Plaza, 120 Oxford Street Mon-Sat 10-7
London W1 (Thurs 10-8), Sun 12-6

020 7240 8242 **tube: Covent Garden**
24 Long Acre Mon-Fri 10-7:30 (Thurs 10-8)
London WC2 Sat 10-7, Sun 12-6

020 7584 0069 **tube: Sloane Square**
96 King's Road Mon-Sat 10-6:30
London SW3 (Wed 10-7), Sun 12-6

020 7437 7101 — **tube: Oxford Circus**
19-21 Argyll Street — Mon-Sat 10-7
London W1 — (Thurs 10-8), Sun 12-6

020 7519 1662 — **tube: Canary Wharf**
14 Canada Square — Mon-Fri 8:30-7
London E14 — Sat 9-6, Sun 11-5

020 7256 8976 — **tube: Liverpool Street**
26 Blomfield Street — Mon-Fri 8:30-6:30
London EC2

Welsh & Jefferies

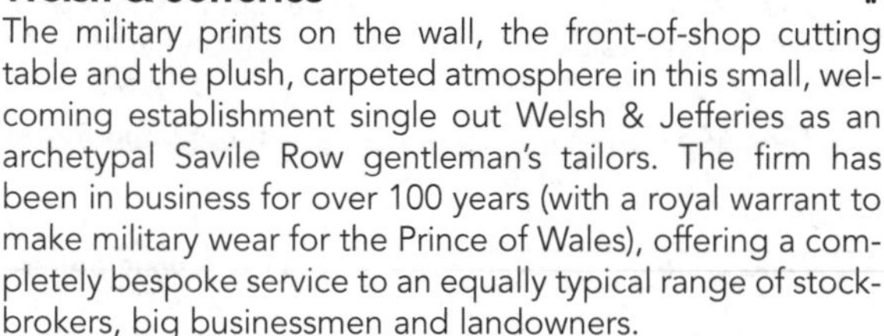
The military prints on the wall, the front-of-shop cutting table and the plush, carpeted atmosphere in this small, welcoming establishment single out Welsh & Jefferies as an archetypal Savile Row gentleman's tailors. The firm has been in business for over 100 years (with a royal warrant to make military wear for the Prince of Wales), offering a completely bespoke service to an equally typical range of stockbrokers, big businessmen and landowners.

www.welshandjefferies.co.uk

020 7734 3062 — **tube: Piccadilly Circus/Oxford Circus**
20 Savile Row — Mon-Fri 9-5
London W1

West Village

Named after one of Manhattan's most celebrated neighborhoods, West Village hocks an eclectic selection of international designers. Style fanatics will swoon for the selection, featuring names like Anne Mary Roswald, Susan Rose Mary and the signature label, The West Village. If you're looking for a girly gift, pick up one of the popular West Village White T's pre-packed in its own cute box. Candles, beaded bracelets and flowery hairclips are also on hand. It's all very cool, but we reckon the new store location, in the heart of Notting Hill, has sent prices soaring a bit too high.

020 7243 6912 — **tube: Notting Hill Gate**
35 Kensington Park Road — Mon-Sat 10-6, Sun 12-5
London W11

What Katy Did

With lollipops strung from the ceiling and teddy bears posing in a miniature vintage car, this store is a perfect playland for kids. While they play, you can buy: swimsuits trimmed in flowers and striped swim trunks, cropped trousers, T-shirts declaring "I love parties" and tiny sheepskin slippers. Babies can be swaddled in sweet gingham sleeping bags or kitted out in their own handmade booties. There are plenty of rompers for crawlers and, for the older ones, stylish lambskin jackets and embroidered Alice bands. Shower gift baskets and velvet changing bags offer treats for mom, too.

020 7937 6499 — **tube: High Street Kensington**
49 Kensington Church Street — Mon-Sat 10:30-5:30
London W8

☆ Whistles

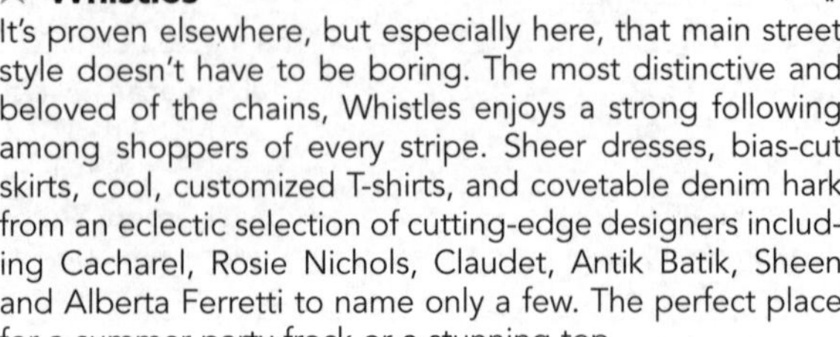

It's proven elsewhere, but especially here, that main street style doesn't have to be boring. The most distinctive and beloved of the chains, Whistles enjoys a strong following among shoppers of every stripe. Sheer dresses, bias-cut skirts, cool, customized T-shirts, and covetable denim hark from an eclectic selection of cutting-edge designers including Cacharel, Rosie Nichols, Claudet, Antik Batik, Sheen and Alberta Ferretti to name only a few. The perfect place for a summer party frock or a stunning top.

020 7823 9134 — **tube: South Kensington**
303 Brompton Road — Mon-Sat 10-6:30
London SW3 — (Wed 10-7), Sun 12-5

020 7487 4484 — **tube: Bond Street**
12 St. Christopher's Place — Mon-Sat 10-6
London W1 — (Thurs 10-7), Sun 12-5

020 7730 2006 — **tube: Sloane Square**
31 King's Road — Mon-Tues 10-6, Wed-Thurs 10-7
London SW3 — Fri-Sat 10-6:30, Sun 12-6

020 7379 7401 — **tube: Covent Garden**
20 The Market — Mon-Wed 10:30-6:30, Thurs 10:30-7:30
London WC2 — Fri-Sat 10:30-7, Sun 12-6

020 7935 7013 — **tube: Bond Street**
1 Thayer Street — Mon-Sat 10-6
London W1 — (Thurs 10-7), Sun 12-5

020 7431 2395 — **tube: Hampstead**
2-4 Hampstead High Street — Mon-Sat 10-6
London NW3 — (Thurs 10-7), Sun 12-6

020 7586 8282 — **tube: St. John's Wood**
51 St. John's Wood High Street — Mon-Sat 10-6, Sun 12-5
London NW8

020 7226 7551 — **tube: Highbury & Islington/Angel**
135 Upper Street — Mon-Sat 10:30-6:30 (Thurs 10:30-7:30)
London N1 — Sun 12-6

White Stuff

It all started when two Englishmen set off to sell T-shirts in the French Alps. Fifteen stores later, selection is still inspired by the alpine tourist seasons—skiwear in the winter and beachwear when the sun shines. Capri pants and tank tops, snowboarding jackets and slick goggles all get their turn on the floor. Emphasis is on fun fashion rather than function. www.white-stuff.com

020 7371 0174 — **tube: Parsons Green**
845 Fulham Road — Mon-Sat 10-6, Sun 12-5
London SW6

020 7228 7129 — **Overland train to Clapham Junction**
49 Northcote Road — (opening times as above)
London SW11

020 7354 8204 — **tube: Angel**
12-14 Essex Road — (opening times as above)
London N1

020 7313 9544 **tube: Bayswater/Notting Hill Gate**
66 Westbourne Grove (opening times as above)
London W2

Wigwam

East meets West at this bohemian Notting Hill shop. Inspired by her travels through Asia, Sioned Mclean has culled a lifestyle collection complete with beaded bags, embroidered cushions and brilliant-hued bedspreads. Indian-inspired clothing, including spice-colored pieces from labels Noa Noa and Resource, round out the ethnic mix.

020 7727 8888 **tube: Notting Hill Gate**
25 Kensington Park Road Mon-Sat 10:30-5:30
London W11

Wild Swans

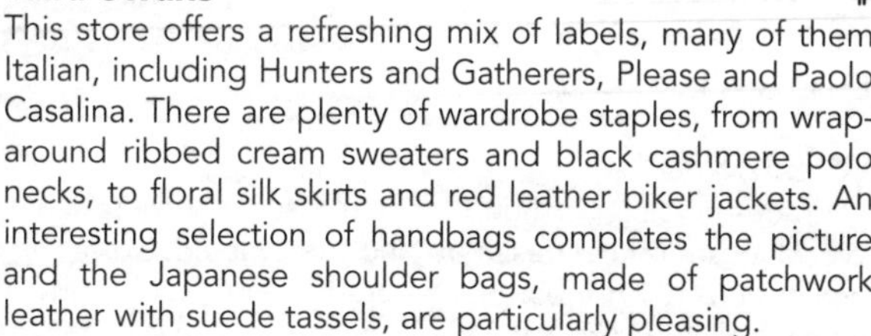

This store offers a refreshing mix of labels, many of them Italian, including Hunters and Gatherers, Please and Paolo Casalina. There are plenty of wardrobe staples, from wrap-around ribbed cream sweaters and black cashmere polo necks, to floral silk skirts and red leather biker jackets. An interesting selection of handbags completes the picture and the Japanese shoulder bags, made of patchwork leather with suede tassels, are particularly pleasing.

020 7801 9299 **Overland train to Clapham Junction**
70 Battersea Rise Tues-Sat 10-6 (Thurs 10-7), Sun 12-5
London SW11

William Hunt

William Hunt, even more so than Richard James, plays the Savile Row upstart with aplomb. The utterly, instantly flamboyant appearance of his brilliantly bohemian shop is perfect for the larger-than-life clothes with which he has made his name over the past few years. Bespoke and ready-to-wear suits boast signature flared cuffs and theatrical linings while a superb range of high-collared, full-color, fitted shirts fight for attention with casual (but no less colorful) pants and half-sleeve shirts.

020 7439 1921 **tube: Piccadilly Circus/Oxford Circus**
41 Savile Row Mon-Sat 10-6
London W1

020 7836 0809 **tube: Covent Garden**
68 Neal Street Mon-Sat 10:30-7, Sun 1-6
London WC2

Willma

After more than two years in business, this Notting Hill hotspot has lasted longer than the average fashion whim. There's little in the way of clothing here but you can hardly do better for cool accessories, from jewelry by star magnets Me&Ro or Isabelle Marant to underwear from Frost French.

www.willma.co.uk

020 8960 7296 — **tube: Ladbroke Grove**
339 Portobello Road — Tues-Sat 11-6
London W10

Wolford

Where there are stockings there will be runs, right? Not so for Wolford, whose high-tech stretch hosiery is said to withstand the rigors of repeated wear. Classic tights or naughty fishnets, support hose or knee-highs, sheer or opaque—Wolford has a leg up on the stocking trend. Best of all, they've eliminated waistbands from their designs, thereby banishing the embarrassing belly-bulge effect. Samples are hung throughout the store so customers can pull and stretch to their heart's content, and the staff are knowledgeable and helpful. You'll never have another clear nail polish emergency. www.wolfordboutiquelondon.co.uk

020 7499 2549 — **tube: Bond Street**
3 South Molton Street — Mon-Sat 10-6 (Thurs 10-7)
London W1

Woodhouse

A grade-A training ground for that fashion-clueless male, Woodhouse offers designer and designer-inspired top-quality basics including structured suits, plaid button-downs, jeans and khakis. Men in the know shouldn't be discouraged—there are plenty of higher-minded goods to be had here, from such designers as Armani, Stone Island, Hugo Boss and Kenzo.

020 7823 3014 — **tube: Sloane Square**
97 King's Road — Mon-Sat 10-6:30
London SW3 — (Wed 10-7), Sun 12-6

020 7240 2008 — **tube: Covent Garden**
138 Long Acre — Mon-Sat 10-7 (Thurs 10-8)
London WC2 — Sun 12-6

020 7486 1099 — **tube: Bond Street**
28-32 St. Christopher's Place — Mon-Sat 10-6:30
London W1 — (Thurs 10-7), Sun 12-5:30

020 7937 2420 — **tube: High Street Kensington**
141 Kensington High Street — Mon-Sat 10-6:30
London W8 — (Thurs 10-7:30), Sun 12-6

Yohji Yamamoto

His name is synonymous with cutting-edge Japanese fashion. Yamamoto's modern, architectural designs come from a mostly black, white and beige palette. Men can choose from suits while women browse among tailored pants, shirts, jackets and wrap skirts. The pieces in this ready-to-wear collection are structural works of art. Naturally, creative genius comes at a price.

020 7491 4129 — **tube: Oxford Circus**
14-15 Conduit Street — Mon-Sat 10-6 (Thurs 10-7)
London W1

Young England

Manager Barbara Barnes—Princess Diana's former nanny—can be sour as clotted cream gone off, but her balloon-sleeved pinafores couldn't be sweeter. Traditional children's clothes are the specialty here, with sizes ranging from new-born to 10. In addition to classic cotton frocks with bows at the back, there are little sleeveless pink chiffon dresses, black trousers with tiny rhinestones on the cuffs and, for boys, plaid shorts. The Trussardi Baby and Baby Graziella labels are on hand, as well as colorful booties, embroidered bed sheets, tiny straw handbags and a small selection of toys. All this, plus a made-to-measure service (for brides-maid dresses and mini cutaways), makes Young England one of the best kids' shops in London.

020 7259 9003 — **tube: Victoria/Sloane Square**
47 Elizabeth Street — Mon-Fri 10-5:30, Sat 10-3
London SW1

Yves Saint Laurent: Rive Gauche

Fashion master Tom Ford adds another feather to his cap: his ready-to-wear collection for the legendary French label is hipper and sexier than ever. The tailoring is vintage YSL, perfectly fitted for a super-sleek look. Pants and skirts, suits and matching blouses remain staples of the incomparable women's selection. www.ysl-hautecouture.com

020 7493 1800 (W) — **tube: Bond Street**
33 Old Bond Street — Mon-Sat 10-6 (Thurs 10-7)
London W1

020 7235 6706 (M/W) — **tube: Knightsbridge**
171-172 Sloane Street — Mon-Sat 10-6 (Wed 10-7)
London SW1

☆ Zara

Zara has hit London's shopping streets in a big way. Women of every age love this Spanish chain for its low prices and high style sense. With a selection that ranges from sporty to girlishly hip to downright classic, they recreate every major seasonal look, often before anyone else. Jeans and baby tees are mingled with leather skirts and sleek business suits. There's so much good stuff, you can't try it on fast enough. Accessories are the icing on the cake. Keep coming back—the selection changes constantly. www.zara.com

020 7534 9500 — **tube: Oxford Circus**
118 Regent Street — Mon-Sat 10-7
London W1 — (Thurs 10-8), Sun 12-6

020 7318 2700 — **tube: Oxford Circus**
242-248 Oxford Street — (opening times as above)
London W1

020 7368 4680 — **tube: High Street Kensington**
48-52 Kensington High Street — (opening times as above)
London W8

020 7518 1550 | **tube: Bond Street**
333 Oxford Street | (opening times as above)
London W1

020 7438 9900 | **tube: Covent Garden**
52-56 Long Acre | (opening times as above)
London WC2

Zibba

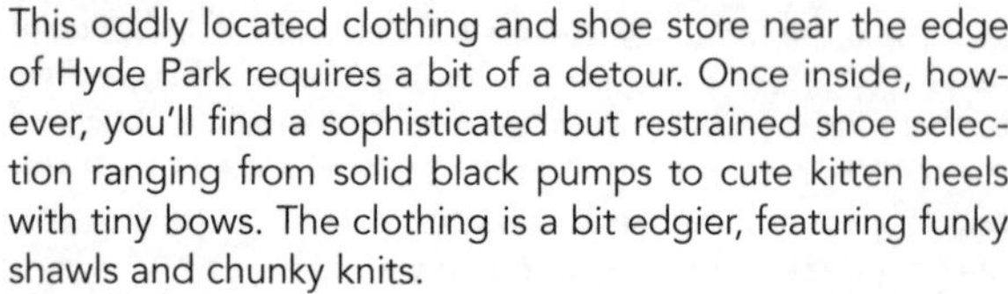
This oddly located clothing and shoe store near the edge of Hyde Park requires a bit of a detour. Once inside, however, you'll find a sophisticated but restrained shoe selection ranging from solid black pumps to cute kitten heels with tiny bows. The clothing is a bit edgier, featuring funky shawls and chunky knits.

020 7235 3344 | **tube: Knightsbridge/Hyde Park Corner**
61 Knightsbridge | Mon-Sat 10-6:30
London SW1 | (Wed 10-7), Sun 11-5

MAIL ORDER / INTERNET

Adore 

The selection isn't huge but this mail order company sources girly fashion from London's coolest markets, including Portobello and Brick Lane, so you can be sure you'll discover something desirably different. Perhaps a bright pink velour tracksuit from the "Sporty Chic" section, a silk crepe skirt with fishtail hem for a "Grown-Up Glamour" look. Or for a more romantic image how about a soft needlecord jacket with vintage lace trim and flute sleeves? The "mini me" selection is for children and we were particularly taken by a cute linen cowgirl dress with suede fringe and blanket stitching. You'll also find a small selection of accessories including beeswax candles, leather cuffs and a semi-precious charm necklace. www.adorelondon.co.uk

0906 302 0321
237 Kensington High Street | Mon-Fri 9:30-6
London W8

Boden 

Boden is the mail-order clothes catalog that has taken Britain by storm. Designs are fun, colorful and good quality and there's something for everybody—from pretty ruffled T-shirts for women, soft linen shirts for men and basic cotton trousers from Mini Boden for kids. There is no need to worry about buying something without seeing it first. Sizing is spot-on, the clothes are modeled by real people, and if you decide you don't like what you've ordered simply return it and get the refund. Shopping from the comfort of your armchair has never been easier. www.boden.co.uk

0845 357 5000
Boden — Mon-Sat 8-8
Meridian West
Meridian Business Park
Leicester
LE 19 1PX

Harry Duley

She did not set out to be a maternity designer but Harry Duley's clothes are the perfect pregnancy wear. They're soft, comfortable and flattering; most important of all, they're made of a brilliant stretch fabric that will expand over your tummy and then bounce back after the baby is born. Styles are simple and lovely enough to be worn whether you're pregnant or not. Signature items include a ruche-sided top with three-quarter-length sleeves, a below-the-knee skirt and a simple frill dress. A new clothing capsule for babies offers hand-knitted tank tops, cardigans and jumpers in contrasting colors and a children's collection is about to appear. Every Harry Duley piece comes decorated with a small embroidered spider, so arachnophobics beware. www.harryduley.co.uk

020 7485 5552
Unit 2 — Mon-Fri 10-6
77 Fortess Road
London NW5

Peruvian Connection

Peru is renowned for two luxurious fabrics, hand-harvested pima cotton, velvety soft and smooth, and silky precious alpaca. This mail order company offers the best of both. The team of UK-based designers produces detailed sketches, inspired by everything from Andean textiles to Turkoman carpets. Skilled Andean knitters in South America, who employ a range of knit and crochet techniques, then translate these sketches into reality. The resulting garments are soft, bold and full of character. Strong geometric patterns and warm rustic shades may be a bit too dowdy for the younger generation, but who can resist the warm, weightless long-haired alpaca blankets. www.peruvianconnection.com

0800 550000
3 Thames Court — Mon-Fri 8-7, Sat 9-5
Goring on Thames
Berkshire RG8 9AQ

Plumo

Plumo has been going strong for a few years now and its colorful catalog still offers an eclectic range of inspiring goodies sourced from all over the world. There are Vietnamese flower bags, Moroccan lanterns, orchid bowls from Japan, super-soft Mongolian rugs and embroidered

North African cushions. The Russian Swarovski crystal bracelets are wonderful gifts and the pretty Venetian wine goblets made of plastic are perfect for elegant picnics. Clothing highlights include cotton paisley pajamas, a reversible oriental jacket, napa leather espadrilles and a black silk caftan. You'll be tempted by something if you're in the spending mood. www.plumo.com

0870 241 3590
Leroy House, Unit 30 — 24-hour ordering service
436 Essex Road
London N1

Toast

Simple, subtle and yet always interesting, the clothing offered by mail order company Toast is apparently favored by David Beckham, Nigella Lawson and Kate Winslet. Styles are a combination of vintage, eastern and classic and come in lovely soft colors such as sage blue, dusty plum and ivory. For women there are pearl button sandals, embroidered cotton tunics, toweling caftans and gathered skirts; a new capsule collection for men features poplin shirts, cargo pants, suede jackets and boat-neck sweaters. The overall look is understated and informal and is continued in a seductive selection of homewares: Mexican hammocks, Irish bed linens, hammam towels from Turkey and block-printed sleeping bags. www.toastbypost.co.uk

0870 240 5200
Unit D, Lakeside — Mon-Fri 9-8, Sat 10-6
Llansamlet
Swansea SA7 9FF

Dromedary

Don't be put off by the home-made look of the brochure; low-key coziness is exactly what appeals about this Northumberland-based mail order company. The clothing is mostly for children, (although some popular designs are now available for adults) and the range starts at 12 months and goes up to 12 years. There is a strong emphasis on stripes, ginghams, florals and denims and the overall look is old-fashioned country garden. The selection includes baby bloomers, sailor suits, Hero shirts, Yum Yum sundresses and toggle fleeces. If only everything was this sweet.

0143 467 3961
Healey Hall — Mon-Fri 9-5:30
Riding Mill NE44 6BH

The White Company

It's a simple concept: a mail order company that specializes in a stylish collection for the home—cotton bed linen, throws, bedspreads, towels, bathrobes and china—all predominantly in white. So successful has the idea proved that The White Company now has two shops in London and has incorporated a small casual selection of clothing also in white, but with a few pieces in sky blue, beige and black thrown in. The jerseywear is soft and comfortable with simple T-shirts, cami tops and bottoms, all great for lounging around at home in. The linen nightwear—pajamas, nightdresses and gowns—is fresh and crisp, and the active wear is reminiscent of Gap, but without the logos: cotton hooded jackets, jersey shorts and sporty T-shirts. www.thewhiteco.com

020 7823 5322 **tube: Sloane Square**
8 Symons Street Mon-Sat 10-7
London SW3

020 7935 7879 **tube: Bond Street**
12 Marylebone High Street Mon-Sat 10-7, Sun 11-5
London W1

Returns:
Unit 30
Perivale Industrial Park
Horsenden Lane South
Greenford
Middlesex UB6 7RJ

Stores by Neighborhood

London Area Map

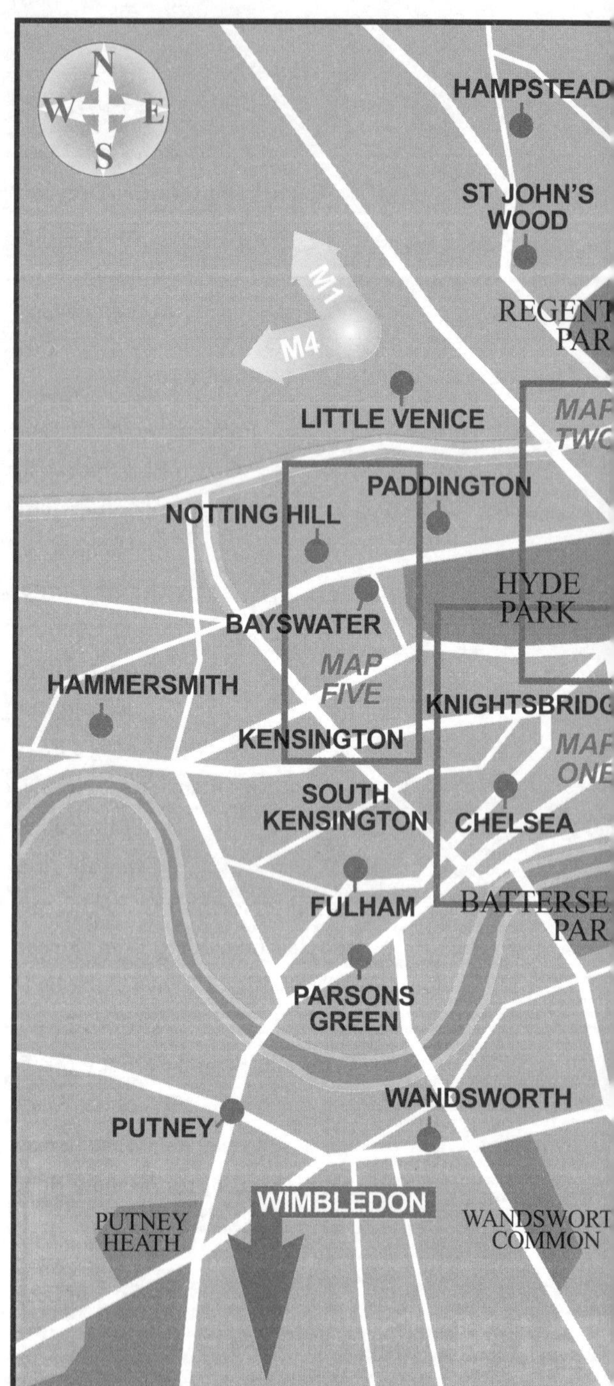

London Area Map

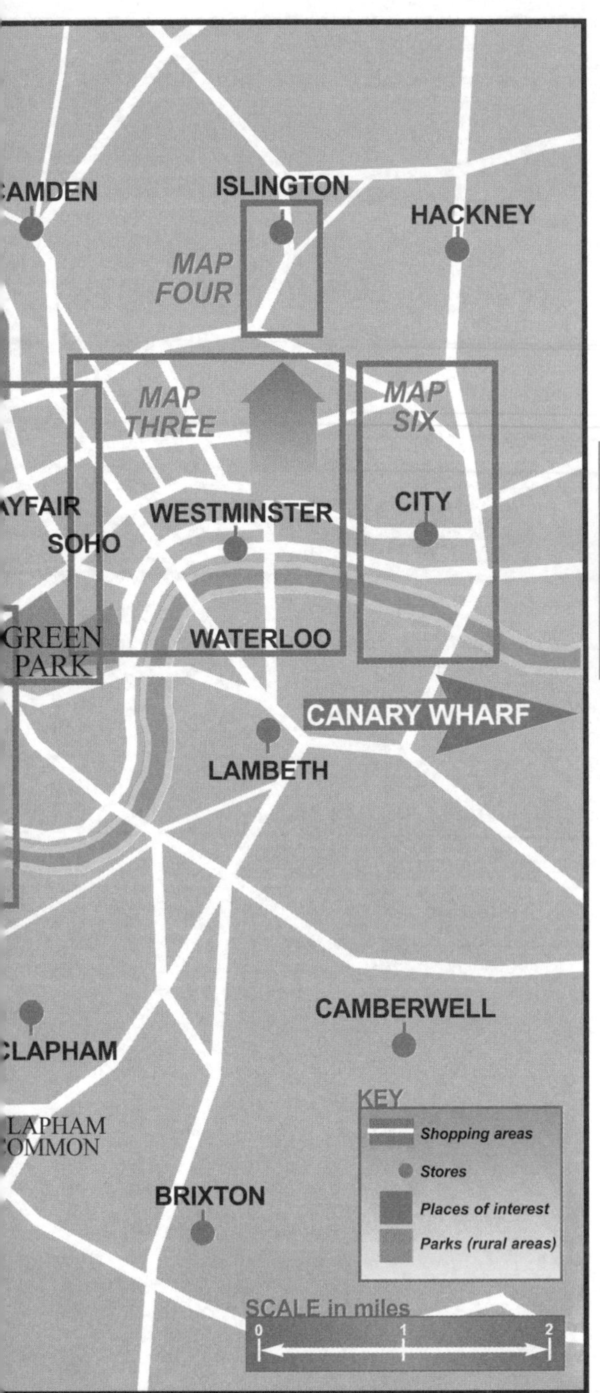

AMDEN
ISLINGTON
HACKNEY
MAP FOUR
MAP THREE
MAP SIX
YFAIR
SOHO
WESTMINSTER
CITY
GREEN PARK
WATERLOO
CANARY WHARF
LAMBETH
CAMBERWELL
LAPHAM
LAPHAM OMMON
BRIXTON
KEY
Shopping areas
Stores
Places of interest
Parks (rural areas)
SCALE in miles
0
1
2

Beauchamp Place / King's Road / South Ken

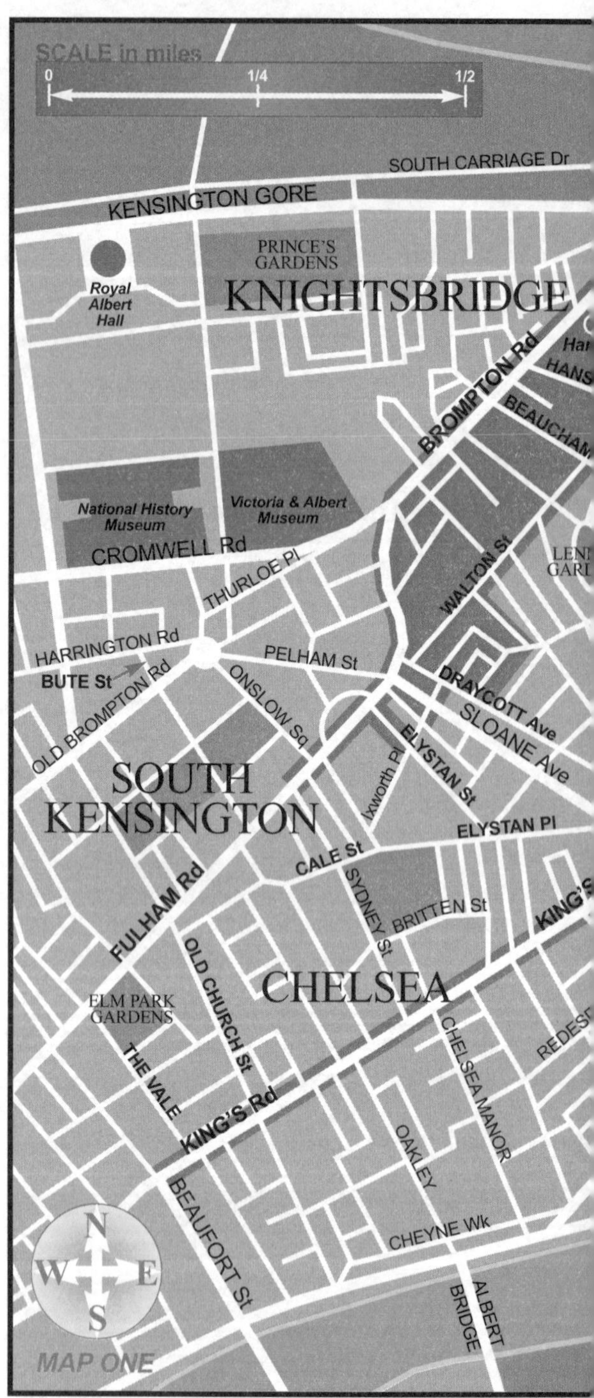
SCALE in miles
0
1/4
1/2
SOUTH CARRIAGE Dr
KENSINGTON GORE
Royal Albert Hall
PRINCE'S GARDENS
KNIGHTSBRIDGE
BROMPTON Rd
National History Museum
Victoria & Albert Museum
CROMWELL Rd
THURLOE Pl
WALTON St
HARRINGTON Rd
BUTE St
PELHAM St
OLD BROMPTON Rd
ONSLOW Sq
DRAYCOTT Ave
SLOANE Ave
Ixworth Pl
ELYSTAN St
SOUTH KENSINGTON
ELYSTAN Pl
CALE St
SYDNEY St
BRITTEN St
FULHAM Rd
OLD CHURCH St
CHELSEA
ELM PARK GARDENS
THE VALE
CHELSEA MANOR
KING'S Rd
OAKLEY
BEAUFORT St
CHEYNE Wk
ALBERT BRIDGE
N
W
E
S
MAP ONE

Knightsbridge / Belgravia

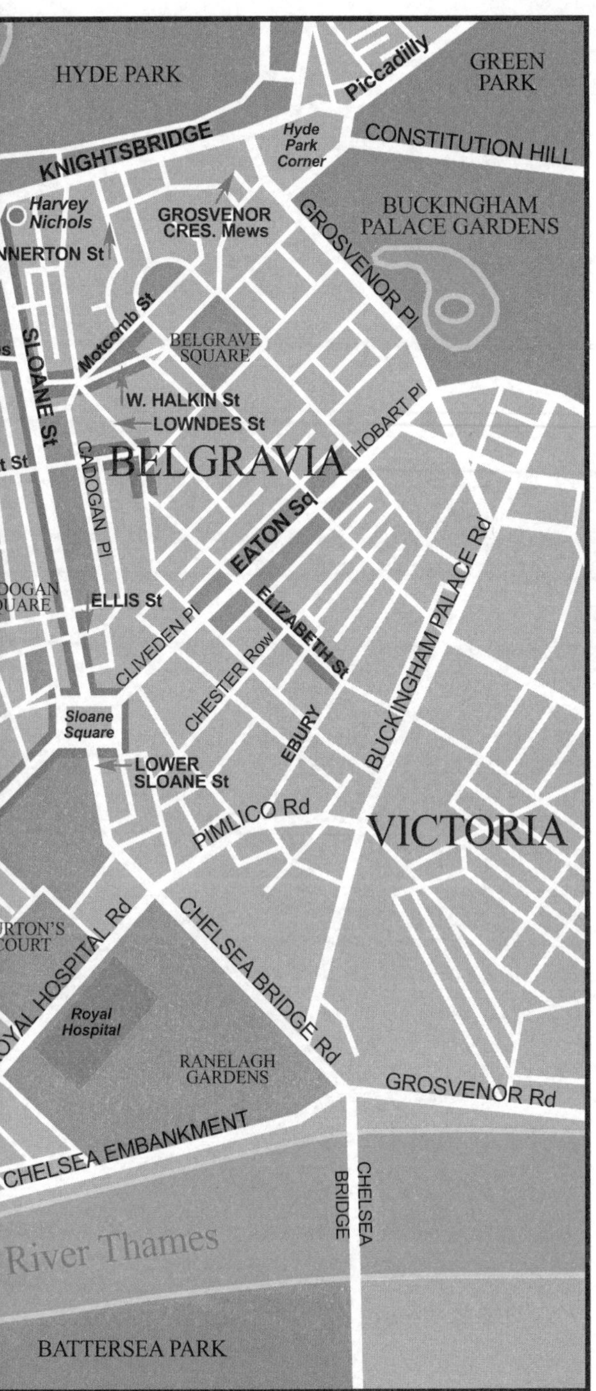

Mayfair / Oxford Street / Marylebone

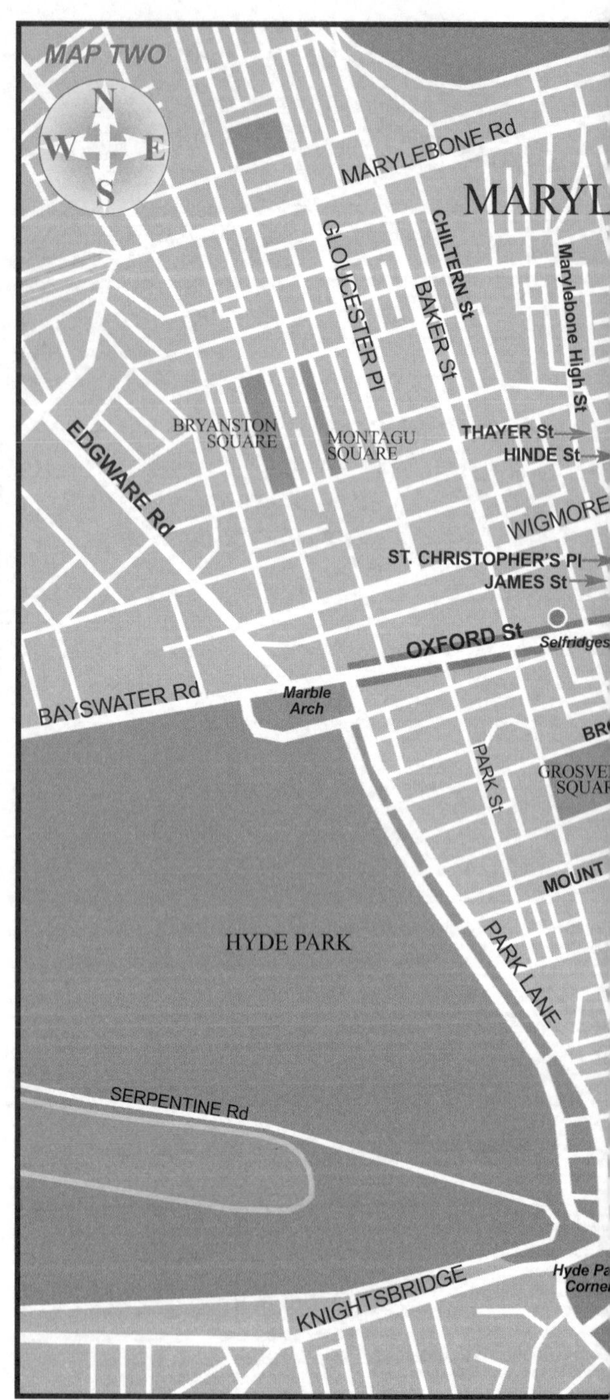

Bond Street / Regent Street / Jermyn Street

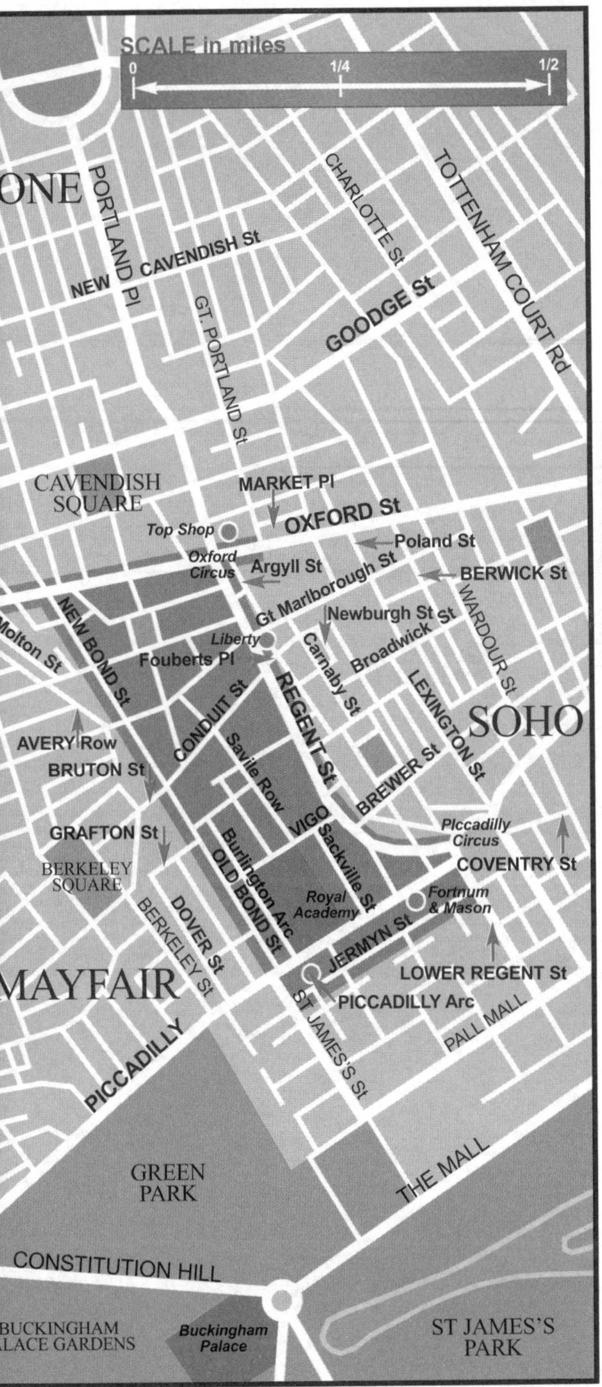

Covent Garden / Soho

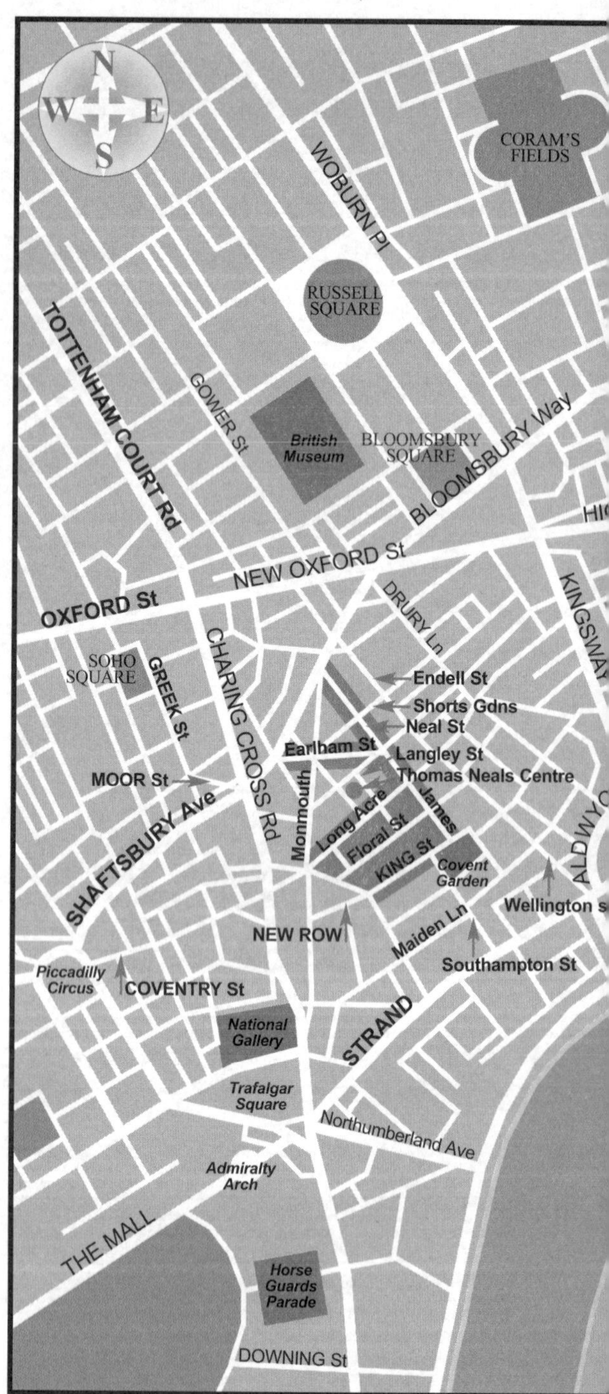

The Strand / Islington

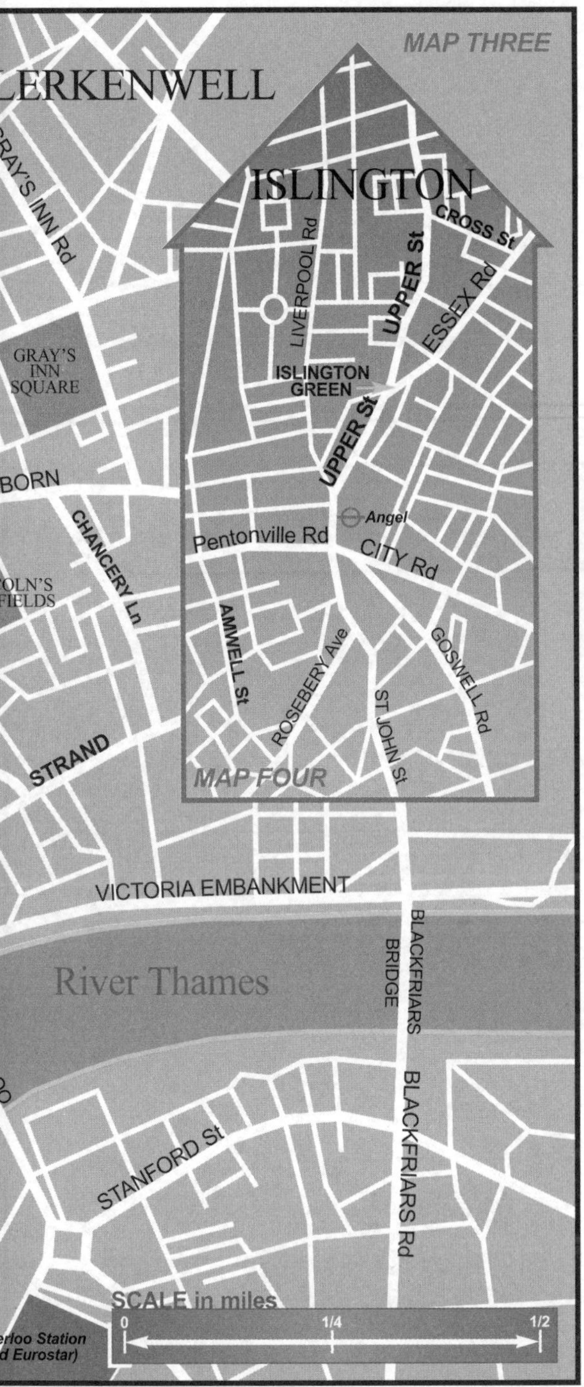
MAP THREE
LERKENWELL
ISLINGTON
GRAY'S INN Rd
CROSS St
UPPER St
LIVERPOOL Rd
ESSEX Rd
GRAY'S INN SQUARE
ISLINGTON GREEN
UPPER St
BORN
CHANCERY Ln
Angel
Pentonville Rd
CITY Rd
OLN'S FIELDS
AMWELL St
ROSEBERY Ave
GOSWELL Rd
ST JOHN St
STRAND
MAP FOUR
VICTORIA EMBANKMENT
BLACKFRIARS BRIDGE
River Thames
BLACKFRIARS Rd
STANFORD St
SCALE in miles
0
1/4
1/2
erloo Station
d Eurostar)

Notting Hill / Kensington

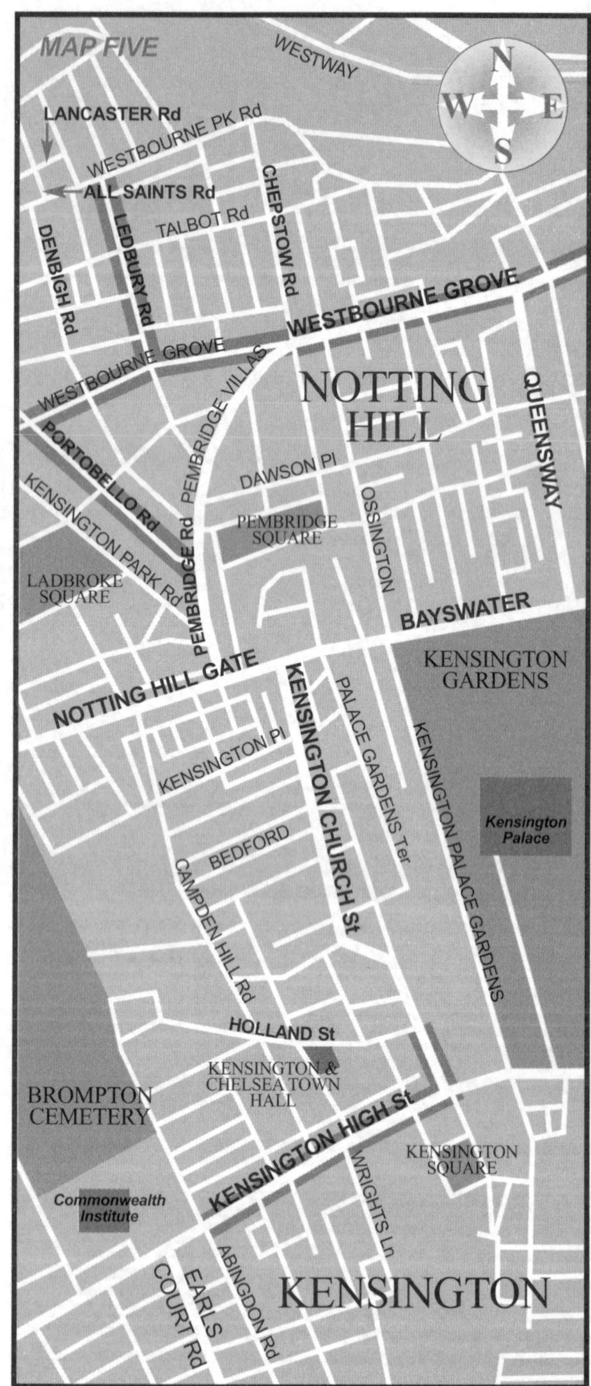

City

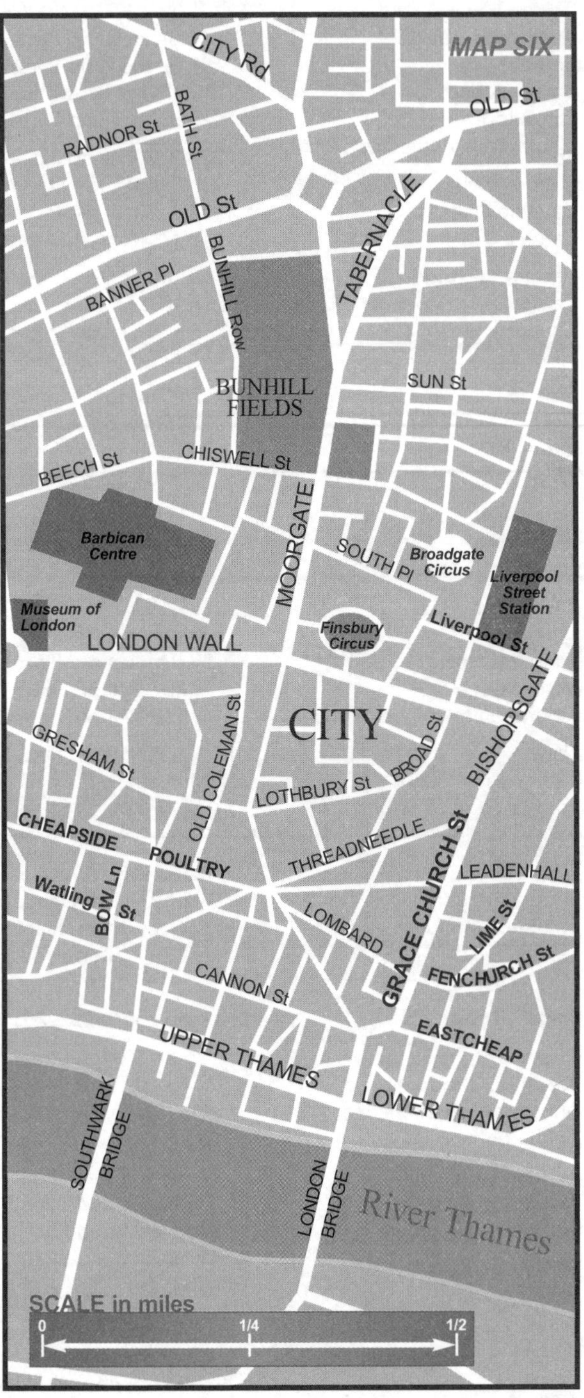
MAP SIX
CITY Rd
OLD St
BATH St
RADNOR St
TABERNACLE
OLD St
BUNHILL Row
BANNER Pl
SUN St
BUNHILL FIELDS
CHISWELL St
BEECH St
MOORGATE
Barbican Centre
SOUTH Pl
Broadgate Circus
Liverpool Street Station
Museum of London
Finsbury Circus
Liverpool St
LONDON WALL
BISHOPSGATE
CITY
OLD COLEMAN St
BROAD St
GRESHAM St
LOTHBURY St
CHEAPSIDE
POULTRY
THREADNEEDLE
GRACE CHURCH St
LEADENHALL
Watling St
BOW Ln
LOMBARD
LIME St
FENCHURCH St
CANNON St
EASTCHEAP
UPPER THAMES
LOWER THAMES
SOUTHWARK BRIDGE
LONDON BRIDGE
River Thames
SCALE in miles
0
1/4
1/2

Beauchamp/Walton/Draycott (SW3)

See map pages 200–201

Anello and Davide	47 Beauchamp Place
Bertie Golightly	48 Beauchamp Place
Betsey Johnson	106 Draycott Avenue
The Bridge	25 Beauchamp Place
Bruce Oldfield	27 Beauchamp Place
Butterscotch	172 Walton Street
Caroline Charles	56-57 Beauchamp Place
Caroline Holmes	176 Walton Street
Cashmere London	180 Walton Street
Caz	177 Draycott Avenue
Charlotte Smith	160 Walton Street
Eliot Zed	117-119 Walton Street
Galerie Gaultier	171-175 Draycott Avenue
Gigi	124 Draycott Avenue
Isabell Kristensen	33 Beauchamp Place
Janet Reger	2 Beauchamp Place
Jimmy Choo	169 Draycott Avenue
Kruszynska	35 Beauchamp Place
Laurence Tavernier	77 Walton Street
Liola	69 Walton Street
M-A-G	20 Beauchamp Place
Margaret Howell	29 Beauchamp Place
Mikihouse	107 Walton Street
Monogrammed Linen Shop	168 Walton Street
Nara	8 Beauchamp Place
Paddy Campbell	17 Beauchamp Place
Patrizia Wigan Designs	19 Walton Street
Paul Costelloe	10 Beauchamp Place
Plein Sud	151 Draycott Avenue
Robert Clergerie	122 Draycott Avenue
Spaghetti	32 Beauchamp Place
Tashia	178 Walton Street

Bond Street (W1)

See map pages 202–203

Aftershock	12 South Molton Street
Alexander McQueen	4 Old Bond Street
Anna Molinari Blumarine	11a Old Bond Street
Anne Fontaine	30 New Bond Street
Armand Basi	48 Conduit Street
Avi Rossini	46 New Bond Street
Ballantyne Cashmere	153a New Bond Street
Bally	116 New Bond Street
Bally	30 Old Bond Street
Berluti	43 Conduit Street
Bernini	95-96 New Bond Street
Bertie	36 South Molton Street

Brioni	131-133 New Bond Street
Browns	23-27 South Molton Street
Browns Focus	38-39 South Molton Street
Browns Labels For Less	50 South Molton Street
Burberry	21-23 New Bond Street
Butler & Wilson	20 South Molton Street
Calvin Klein	53-55 & 65 New Bond Street
Calvin Klein	67 South Molton Street
Camper	8-11 Royal Arcade, Old Bond Street
Canali	122 New Bond Street
Catimini	52a South Molton Street
Cecil Gee	92 New Bond Street
Celia Loe	68 South Molton Street
Céline	160 New Bond Street
Chanel	26 Old Bond Street
Charles Jourdan	27 New Bond Street
Church's	133 New Bond Street
Cleverley	13 The Royal Arcade
Clio	75 New Bond Street
Coccinelle	44 South Molton Street
Collezioni: Giorgio Armani	43 New Bond Street
Comme des Garçons	59 Brook Street
Connolly	41 Conduit Street
DKNY	27 Old Bond Street
Daks	10 Old Bond Street
Dolce & Gabbana	6-8 Old Bond Street
Donna Karan	19-21 New Bond Street
Dune	18 South Molton Street
Dunhill	21 Old Bond Street
Eda Lingerie	49 South Molton Street
Edward Green	12-13 Burlington Arcade
Eliot Zed	4 Avery Row
Emanuel Ungaro	150-151 New Bond Street
Emporio Armani	112a New Bond Street
Episode	69 New Bond Street
Ermenegildo Zegna	37-38 New Bond Street
Escada	66-67 New Bond Street
Etro	14 Old Bond Street
Fenwick	63 New Bond Street
Formes	33 Brook Street
F.Pinet	47-48 New Bond Street
Fratelli Rossetti	177 New Bond Street
French For Less	8 South Molton Street
Furla	31 New Bond Street
Gérard Darel	31 Old Bond Street
Gibo	47 Conduit Street
Gina	9 Old Bond Street
Gordon Scott	29 New Bond Street
Hermès	155 New Bond Street

Hobbs	47-49 South Molton Street
Holland & Holland	31-33 Bruton Street
Hudson	13 South Molton Street
Issey Miyake	52 Conduit Street
Ivory	104 New Bond Street
Jigsaw (& Jigsaw Junior)	126-127 New Bond Street
John Smedley	24 Brook Street
Jones the Bootmaker	15 South Molton Street
Joseph	23 Old Bond Street
Joseph	28 Brook Street
Karen Millen	46 & 57 South Molton Street
Krizia	24-25 Conduit Street
Kurt Geiger	65 South Molton Street
Lanvin	108 New Bond Street
Laurèl	105 New Bond Street
Leather Rat Classics	37 South Molton Street
L.K.Bennett	31 Brook Street
Loewe	130 New Bond Street
Louis Féraud	73 New Bond Street
Louis Vuitton	17-18 New Bond Street
Marina Rinaldi	39 Old Bond Street
MaxMara	153 New Bond Street
Miss Selfridge	36-38 Great Castle Street
Miu Miu	123 New Bond Street
Moschino	28-29 Conduit Street
Mulberry	41-42 New Bond Street
Nicole Farhi	158 New Bond Street
Nine West	9 South Molton Street
Nitya	118 New Bond Street
Office	55 South Molton Street
Petit Bateau	62 South Molton Street
Pied à Terre	19 South Molton Street
Pleats Please: Issey Miyake	20 Brook Street
Poste	10 South Molton Street
Prada	16-18 Old Bond Street
Press & Bastyan	22 South Molton Street
Proibito	94 New Bond Street
Proibito	42 South Molton Street
Ralph Lauren	1 New Bond Street
Ralph Lauren (children)	143 New Bond Street
Reiss	78-79 New Bond Street
Rigby & Peller	22a Conduit Street
Robina	68 New Bond Street
Ronit Zilkha	34 Brook Street
Ruco Line	64 South Molton Street
Russell & Bromley	24-25 & 109-110 New Bond Street
Samsonite	49-50 New Bond Street
Senso	6 South Molton Street
Sergio Rossi	15 Old Bond Street

SpaceNK	45-47 Brook Street
Stella McCartney	30 Bruton Street
Tartine et Chocolat	66 South Molton Street
Thierry Mugler	134 New Bond Street
Timberland	72 New Bond Street
Ventilo	70 New Bond Street
Versace	113-115 New Bond Street
Vertice Uomo	16 South Molton Street
Vivienne Westwood	44 Conduit Street
Voyage	50 Conduit Street
Wardrobe	42 Conduit Street
Wolford	3 South Molton Street
Yohji Yamamoto	14-15 Conduit Street
Yves Saint Laurent: Rive Gauche	137 New Bond Street

Camden Town (NW1)

Anna	126 Regent's Park Road
Buffalo Boots	190 Camden High Street
Camden Market	Camden High Street
Graham & Green	164 Regent's Park Road
Marks & Spencer	143 Camden High Street
Offspring	221 Camden High Street
Swear	6 Stables Market, Chalk Farm Road

Canary Wharf (E14)

Austin Reed	Cabot Place East
Dorothy Perkins	24 Canada Place
French Connection	18 Canada Place
Gap Kids	Cabot Place East
Jones the Bootmaker	Cabot Place East
Monsoon	21-22 Canada Square
Next	Cabot Place East
Oasis	19 Canada Square
Phase Eight	Cabot Place East
SpaceNK	Cabot Place West
Thomas Pink	Cabot Place East
Warehouse	14 Canada Square

City

See map page 207

Austin Reed	1-2 Poultry, EC2
Austin Reed	13-23 Fenchurch Street, EC3
Austin Reed	1-14 Liverpool Street, EC2
Bodas	29 Lime Street, EC3
Cecil Gee	153 Fenchurch Street, EC3
Charles Tyrwhitt	43 Bow Lane, EC4
Ede & Ravenscroft	93 Chancery Lane, WC2
Emmett Shirts	4 Eldon Street, EC2
Episode	Bishopsgate Arcade, 137 Bishopsgate, EC2
Ermenegildo Zegna	12-13 The Courtyard, Royal Exchange, EC3

Gap	1 Poultry, EC2
Gordon Scott	119 Cannon Street, EC4
Hackett	19 Eastcheap, EC3
Hermès	2-3 Royal Exchange, EC3
Hobbs	64-72 Leadenhall Market, EC3
Hobbs	Bishopsgate Arcade, 137 Bishopsgate, EC2
Hope + Glory	Broadgate Link, EC2
Jigsaw	31 Leadenhall Market, EC3
Jigsaw	44 Bow Lane, EC2
Jones the Bootmaker	15 Cullum Street, EC3
Jones the Bootmaker	70-71 Watling Street, EC4
Karen Millen	Bishopsgate Arcade, 137 Bishopsgate, EC2
Louis Vuitton	5-6 Royal Exchange, EC3
Monsoon	87 Gracechurch Street, EC3
Moss Bros	4 Blomfield Street, EC2
Moss Bros	83 Cheapside, EC2
Natural Blue	52-54 Artillery Lane, E1
Oasis	85/86 Old Broad Street, EC2
Oasis	4 Queen Victoria Street, EC4
Paul Smith	7 The Courtyard, Royal Exchange, EC3
Pickett	6 Royal Exchange, EC3
Prada	1 The Courtyard, Royal Exchange, EC3
Roderick Charles	31 Blomfield Street, EC2
Roderick Charles	25 Lime Street, EC3
Roderick Charles	52 Bow Lane, EC4
Roderick Charles	78-80 Chancery Lane, WC2
SpaceNK	Bishopsgate Arcade, 137 Bishopsgate, EC2
START	59 Rivington Street, EC2
T.M.Lewin	34-36 Lime Street, EC2
T.M.Lewin	32-33 Blomfield Street, EC2
T.M.Lewin	67 Moorgate, EC2
T.M.Lewin	85 Cheapside, EC2
T.M.Lewin	77 London Wall, EC2
T.M.Lewin	9-9a Cullum Street, EC3
T.M.Lewin	59 Ludgate Hill, EC4
T.M.Lewin	49 Bow Lane, EC4
T.M.Lewin	27a Chancery Lane, WC2
T.M.Lewin	9a Chichester Rents, WC2
Thomas Pink	2 Bow Lane, EC4
Thomas Pink	16 Blomfield Street, EC2
Timothy Everest	32 Elder Street, E1
Warehouse	26 Blomfield Street, EC2

Covent Garden (WC2)

See map pages 204–205

Accessorize	22 The Market
Ad Hoc	10-11 Moor Street
Adolfo Dominguez	15 Endell Street
agnès b.	35-36 Floral Street
Aldo	3-7 Neal Street
Angels	119 Shaftesbury Avenue

Aquaint	38 Monmouth Street
Base	55 Monmouth Street
Bertie	25 Long Acre
Birkenstock	37 Neal Street
Blackout II	51 Endell Street
Blunauta	69-76 Long Acre
Boxfresh	2 Shorts Gardens
Buffalo Boots	65-67 Neal Street
Burro	29 Floral Street
Camper	39 Floral Street
Carhartt	56 Neal Street
Cecil Gee	47 Long Acre
Cenci Rags	31 Monmouth Street
Claire's Accessories	120 Long Acre
Cyberdog	9 Earlham Street
Diesel	43 Earlham Street
Diesel Style Lab	12 Floral Street
Dockers	Unit 8, North Piazza
Dr. Marten Department Store	1-4 King Street
Due Passi	15 The Market
Duffer of St. George	29 & 34 Shorts Gardens
East	16 The Piazza
Egoshego	76 Neal Street
Ellis Brigham	30-32 Southampton Street
Fat Face	13 Thomas Neals Centre
Field & Trek	42 Maiden Lane
Foot Locker	30-32 Neal Street
Fred Perry	14 The Piazza
French Connection	11 James Street
French Connection	99-103 Long Acre
Gamba	3 Garrick Street
Gap	2-3 James Street
Gap	30-31 Long Acre
Gap Kids	121-123 Long Acre
H&M	27-29 Long Acre
High Jinks	25 Thomas Neals Centre
Hobbs	17 The Market
Hobbs	124 Long Acre
Hope + Glory	17-19 Thomas Neals Centre
Hope + Glory	30 Nottingham House, Shorts Gardens
I Love Voyage	33 Monmouth Street
Jigsaw	21 Long Acre
Jones	13-15 Floral Street
Jones the Bootmaker	16 New Row
Jones the Bootmaker	7-8 Langley Court
Jungle	21 Earlham Street
Karen Millen	22-23 James Street
Key Largo	19 Shelton Street
Koh Samui	65-67 Monmouth Street

Kookaï	Covent Garden Market
Kookaï	39 Long Acre
Levi's	117a Long Acre
L.K.Bennett	130 Long Acre
The Loft	35 Monmouth Street
Maharishi	19a Floral Street
Mango/MNG	8-12 Neal Street
Mexx	112-115 Long Acre
Miss Sixty	39 Neal Street
Monsoon	23 The Piazza
Monsoon	5-6 James Street
Morgan	36 Long Acre
Moss Bros	27 King Street
Muji	135 Long Acre
The Natural Shoe Store	21 Neal Street
Next	15-17 Long Acre
Nigel Hall	18 Floral Street
Nine West	1 James Street
Oasis	13 James Street
Office	57 Neal Street
Offspring	60 Neal Street
O'Neill	9-15 Neal Street
Paul & Joe	33 Floral Street
Paul Smith	40-44 Floral Street
Pineapple	6a Langley Street
Pop Boutique	6 Monmouth Street
Poste Mistress	61-63 Monmouth Street
Question Air	38 Floral Street
Quiksilver	12 North Piazza
Quiksilver	1 & 23 Thomas Neals Centre
Reiss	116 Long Acre
Robot	37 Floral Street
Shellys	14-18 Neal Street
Size?	17-19 Neal Street
Sole Trader	72 Neal Street
SpaceNK	4 Thomas Neals Centre
Stüssy	19 Earlham Street
Super Lovers	64 Neal Street
Swear	61 Neal Street
Sweatshop	9a Endell Street
Ted Baker	1-4 Langley Court
Ted Baker	9-10 Floral Street
Warehouse	24 Long Acre
Whistles	20 The Market
William Hunt	68 Neal Street
Woodhouse	138 Long Acre
Zara	52-56 Long Acre

Fulham / Parsons Green (SW6)

Angela Stone	257 New King's Road
Blooming Marvellous	725 Fulham Road
Cath Kidson	668 Fulham Road
CCO'	273 New King's Road
CCO'	307 Fulham Road, SW10
Crew Clothing Co	62 New King's Road
e.g. Butterfly	70 New King's Road
Eskandar	134 Lots Road
Fat Face	827 Fulham Road
Harriet Gubbins	813b Fulham Road
Iceblu	24a New King's Road
Jacqueline Hogan	640 Fulham Road
Jenesis	52 New King's Road
Kit Clothing/Twentieth Century Frox	614 Fulham Road
Laura Tom	Redloh House, 2 Michael Road
Pantalon Chameleon	28 & 187 New King's Road
Phase Eight	54 New King's Road
Phillipa Lepley	494 Fulham Road
Pollyanna	811 Fulham Road
Sally Parsons	610 Fulham Road
Serafina	Redloh House, 2 Michael Road
Sweaty Betty	833 Fulham Road
T&G Clothing	783 Fulham Road
Thailandia	222 Munster Road
Tim Little	560 King's Road
White Stuff	845 Fulham Road

Green Park / Piccadilly (W1) *See map pages 202–203*

Accessorize	1 Piccadilly Circus
Anna Molinari Blumarine	11a Old Bond Street
Bally	30 Old Bond Street
Berk	6 & 46-49 Burlington Arcade
Bianchi	10 Vigo Street
Camper	8-11 Royal Arcade, 28 Old Bond Street
Chanel	26 Old Bond Street
Charles Jourdan	27 New Bond Street
Church's	58-59 Burlington Arcade
Claire's Accessories	13 Coventry Street
Crichton	7 Sackville Street
DKNY	27 Old Bond Street
Daks	10 Old Bond Street
Dolce & Gabbana	6-8 Old Bond Street
Dormeuil	35 Sackville Street
Ede & Ravenscroft	8 Burlington Gardens
Edward Green	12-13 Burlington Arcade
Elégance	14a Grafton Street
Etro	14 Old Bond Street
Fallan & Harvey	7 Sackville Street

Favourbrook	19 Piccadilly Arcade
Fortnum & Mason	181 Piccadilly
Gap (& Gap Kids)	1-7 Shaftesbury Avenue
Georgina von Etzdorf	1-2 Burlington Arcade
Georgina Goodman	12-14 Shepherd Street
Gérard Darel	31 Old Bond Street
Gina	9 Old Bond Street
Gucci	34 Old Bond Street
House of Cashmere (Barbour)	8-9 Burlington Arcade
Jil Sander	7 Burlington Gardens
Joseph	23 Old Bond Street
Kokon to Zai	57 Greek Street
Lillywhites	24-36 Lower Regent Street
Louis Vuitton	17-18 New Bond Street
Marina Rinaldi	39 Old Bond Street
Neil Cunningham	28 Sackville Street
N.Peal	37 & 71-72 Burlington Arcade
Orvis	36a Dover Street
Ozwald Boateng	9 Vigo Street
Paule Ka	13a Grafton Street
Pickett	32-33 & 41 Burlington Arcade
Prada	16-18 Old Bond Street
Pringle	111-112 New Bond Street
Ralph Lauren	1 New Bond Street
Shop	4 Brewer Street
Stephane Kélian	13 Grafton Street
Tanner Krolle	3 Burlington Gardens
Travelling Light	35 Dover Street

Hammersmith (W6)

J.W.Beeton	121 Shepherd's Bush Road
Marks & Spencer	27 King Street

Hampstead (NW3)

agnès b.	58-62 Heath Street
French Connection	29 Hampstead High Street
Jigsaw (& Jigsaw Junior)	58-62, 83 Heath Street
Monsoon	1 Hampstead High Street
Nitya	19 Hampstead High Street
Oasis	58-62 Heath Street
Reiss	52-54 Heath Street
Ronit Zilkha	17 Hampstead High Street
Whistles	2-4 Hampstead High Street

Hyde Park Corner (SW1)

See map pages 200–201

Bradleys	57 Knightsbridge
Egg	36 & 37 Kinnerton Street
Emma Somerset	69 Knightsbridge
Harvie & Hudson	55 Knightsbridge

Jacques Azagury	50 Knightsbridge
Joseph Azagury	73 Knightsbridge
Patricia Roberts	60 Kinnerton Street
Please Mum	85 Knightsbridge
Zibba	61 Knightsbridge

Islington (N1)

See map page 205

Broadway	152 Upper Street
Clusaz	56 Cross Street
Diverse	286 & 294 Upper Street
Emma Hope	33 Amwell Street, EC1
Gotham Angels	23 Islington Green
Noa Noa	146 Upper Street
Oasis	10 Upper Street
Phase Eight	211-212 Upper Street
scorah pattullo	137 Upper Street
Sefton	196 & 271 Upper Street
Whistles	135 Upper Street
White Stuff	12-14 Essex Road

Jermyn Street (SW1)

See map pages 202–203

Bates Gentleman's Hatter	21a Jermyn Street
Charles Tyrwhitt	92 Jermyn Street
Church's	108-110 Jermyn Street
Coles the Shirtmakers	101 Jermyn Street
Crockett & Jones	69 Jermyn Street
Crombie	99 Jermyn Street
Daks	32 & 34 Jermyn Street
Dunhill	48 Jermyn Street
Emma Willis	66 Jermyn Street
Fabri	75 Jermyn Street
Favourbrook	55 Jermyn Street
Favourbrook	19 Piccadilly Arcade
Fortnum & Mason	181 Piccadilly
Foster & Son	83 Jermyn Street
Hackett	87 Jermyn Street
Harvie & Hudson	77 & 97 Jermyn Street
Hawes & Curtis	23 Jermyn Street
Henry Maxwell	83 Jermyn Street
Herbert Johnson	54 St. James's Street
Herbie Frogg	18-19 & 21 Jermyn Street
Hilditch & Key	37 & 73 Jermyn Street
John Bray	78-79 Jermyn Street
John Lobb	88 Jermyn Street
John Lobb	9 St. James's Street
Jones the Bootmaker	112 Jermyn Street
Lock & Co	6 St. James's Street
New & Lingwood	53 Jermyn Street
Roderick Charles	90 Jermyn Street

Russell & Bromley	95 Jermyn Street
Swaine Adeney Brigg	54 St. James's Street
T.M.Lewin	106 Jermyn Street
Thomas Pink	85 Jermyn Street
Tricker's	67 Jermyn Street
Turnbull & Asser	71-72 Jermyn Street
Van Heusen	112 Jermyn Street

Kensington (W8)

See map page 206

Accessorize	123a Kensington High Street
Atticus	14 Kensington Church Street
Barkers of Kensington	63 Kensington High Street
Bonpoint	17 Victoria Grove
The British Hatter	36b Kensington Church Street
Cecil Gee	172 Kensington High Street
Claire's Accessories	169 Kensington High Street
Designer Bargains	29 Kensington Church Street
Diesel	38a Kensington High Street
Dune	66 Kensington High Street
East	143 Kensington High Street
Eda Lingerie	173 Kensington High Street
French Connection	168-170 Kensington High Street
Gap Kids	99-101 Kensington High Street
H&M	365 Kensington High Street
Hobbs	63 Kensington High Street
Jauko	34c Kensington Church Street
Jigsaw	65 Kensington High Street
Jones the Bootmaker	26 Kensington Church Street
Karen Millen	4 Barkers Arcade, Kensington High Street
Knickerbox	Kensington Arcade, Kensington High Street
Kookaï	123d Kensington High Street
Laura Ashley	96b Kensington High Street
Marks & Spencer	113 Kensington High Street
Miss Selfridge	42-44 Kensington High Street
Miss Sixty	42 Kensington High Street
Monsoon	5 Barkers Arcade, Kensington High Street
Morgan	88-90 Kensington High Street
Muji	157 Kensington High Street
Musa	31 Holland Street
Next	54-56 Kensington High Street
Nine West	155 Kensington High Street
Pegaso	275 Kensington High Street
River Island	124-126 Kensington High Street
Robinson Valentine	4 Hornton Place
Seraphine	28 Kensington Church Street
Shellys	40 Kensington High Street
Sisley	129-131 Kensington High Street
Skin Machine	25 Kensington Church Street
Sole Trader	96a Kensington High Street

SpaceNK	3 Kensington Church Street
Sweaty Betty	5 Kensington Church Street
Top Gun	23 Kensington High Street
United Colors of Benetton	147-153 Kensington High Street
Urban Outfitters	36-38 Kensington High Street
Wallis	42-44 Kensington High Street
What Katy Did	49 Kensington Church Street
Woodhouse	141 Kensington High Street
Zara	48-52 Kensington High Street

King's Road (SW1, 3 & 10) *See map pages 200–201*

Accessorize	102 King's Road, SW3
Ad Hoc	153 King's Road, SW3
Aftershock	194 King's Road, SW3
agnès b	31-32 Duke of York Square, SW3
Allegra Hicks	4 Cale Street, SW3
American Classics	398-400 King's Road, SW10
Antoine et Lili	40a King's Road, SW10
Atticus	64 King's Road, SW3
Audley	72 Duke of York Square, SW3
Aware	182 King's Road, SW3
Bally	92 King's Road, SW3
Blue Velvet	174 King's Road, SW3
Bodas	74 Duke of York Square, SW3
Brora	344 King's Road, SW3
cm Store	121 King's Road, SW3
Calvin Klein	68 King's Road, SW3
Cath Kidston	8 Elystan Street, SW3
Cathryn Grosvenor	3 Elystan Street, SW3
Chloé	152-152 Sloane Street, SW1
Claire's Accessories	55 King's Road, SW3
Coccinelle	13 Duke of York Square, SW3
Collette Dinnigan	26 Cale Street, SW3
The Corridor	309a King's Road, SW3
Couverture	310 King's Road, SW3
Crew Clothing Co	Unit 6, B Block Duke of York Square, SW3
Daisy & Tom	181-183 King's Road, SW3
Dune	33b King's Road, SW3
East	105 King's Road, SW3
Eda Lingerie	132 King's Road, SW3
Emma Hope	53 Sloane Square, SW1
Emmett Shirts	380 King's Road, SW3
Escapade	141 King's Road, SW3
Essence	317 King's Road, SW3
Fly	352 King's Road, SW3
French Connection	140-144 King's Road, SW3
French Sole	6 Ellis Street, SW1

Furla	17 King's Road, SW3
Gap (& Gap Kids)	122 King's Road, SW3
Gieves & Hawkes	33 Sloane Square, SW1
Graham & Green	340 King's Road, SW3
Hackett	136-138 Sloane Street, SW1
Harvest	136 King's Road, SW3
Hobbs	88 King's Road, SW3
Iana	186 King's Road, SW3
iBlues	23 King's Road, SW3
Jaeger	145 King's Road, SW3
Jigsaw	126 King's Road, SW3
Jigsaw Junior	124 King's Road, SW3
Joanna's Tent	289b King's Road, SW3
John Smedley	19 King's Road, SW3
Jones the Bootmaker	57-59 King's Road, SW3
Joseph	53 King's Road, SW3
Joseph	Unit E1, Duke of York Square, SW3
Karen Millen	33e King's Road, SW3
Kenneth Cole	33 King's Road, SW3
King's Road Sporting Club	38-42 King's Road, SW3
Knickerbox	28 Sloane Square, SW1
Kookaï	124 King's Road, SW3
L.K.Bennett	83 & 239 King's Road, SW3
La Scala	39 Elystan Street, SW3
Lucy in the Sky	178a King's Road, SW3
Lulu Guinness	3 Ellis Street, SW1
Mandy	139 King's Road, SW3
Manolo Blahnik	49 Old Church Street, SW3
Marks & Spencer	85 King's Road, SW3
MiMi	309 King's Road, SW3
Monsoon	33c-33d King's Road, SW3
Naf Naf	13-15 King's Road, SW3
The Natural Shoe Store	325 King's Road, SW3
Nine West	90 King's Road, SW3
Oasis	76-78 King's Road, SW3
Office	100 King's Road, SW3
One Night Stand	8 Chelsea Manor Studios Flood Street, SW3
Pantalon Chameleon	50 Duke of York Square, SW3
Paola Tregemini	137 King's Road, SW3
Patrick Cox	129 Sloane Street, SW1
Peter Jones	Sloane Square, SW1
Peter Werth	184 King's Road, SW3
Petit Bateau	106-108 King's Road, SW3
Phase Eight	97 Lower Sloane Street, SW1
Phase Eight	34 Duke of York Square, SW3
Phlip	191 King's Road, SW3
Pickett	149 Sloane Street, SW1
Pleats Please	313 King's Road, SW3

Pringle	141-142 Sloane Street, SW1
R.Soles	109a King's Road, SW3
Reiss	114 King's Road, SW3
Ronit Zilkha	21 King's Road, SW3
Shellys	124b King's Road, SW3
Sign of the Times	17 Elystan Street, SW3
Size?	104 King's Road, SW3
Sox Kamen	394 King's Road, SW10
SpaceNK	307 King's Road, SW3
SpaceNK	27 Duke of York Square, SW3
Steinberg & Tolkien	193 King's Road, SW3
Strada	63 King's Road, SW3
Sukie's	285 King's Road, SW3
Tabio	94 King's Road, SW3
Ted Baker	75-77 King's Road, SW3
Thomas Pink	74 Sloane Street, SW1
Thomas Pink (W)	161 Sloane Street, SW1
Tops & Bottoms	3 Cale Street, SW3
Trésor	13 Cale Street, SW3
Trotters	34 King's Road, SW3
V.I.P.	155 King's Road, SW3
The Vestry	120 King's Road, SW3
Via Venise	163 King's Road, SW3
Vivienne Westwood	430 King's Road, SW10
Warehouse	96 King's Road, SW3
Whistles	31 King's Road, SW3
Woodhouse	97 King's Road, SW3

Knightsbridge / Belgravia (SW1, 3 & 7)

See map pages 200–201

9 London	4 Beaufort Gardens, SW3
Accessorize	61 Brompton Road, SW3
Agent Provocateur	16 Pont Street, SW1
Ajanta	21 Motcomb Street, SW1
Alberta Ferretti	205-206 Sloane Street, SW1
Ananya	4a Montpelier Street, SW7
Anya Hindmarch	15-17 Pont Street, SW1
Belinda Robertson	4 West Halkin Street, SW1
Ben de Lisi	40 Elizabeth Street, SW1
Bonpoint	35b Sloane Street, SW1
Boyd	42 Elizabeth Street, SW1
Browns	6c Sloane Street, SW1
Burberry	2 Brompton Road, SW1
Camper	35 Brompton Road, SW3
Chanel	167-170 Sloane Street, SW1
Chanel	278-280 Brompton Road, SW3
Christian Dior	31 Sloane Street, SW1
Church's	143 Brompton Road, SW3
Coach	8 Sloane Street, SW1
Crichton	34 Elizabeth Street, SW1

Dolce & Gabbana	175 Sloane Street, SW1
Elspeth Gibson	7 Pont Street, SW1
Emma Somerset	69 Knightsbridge, SW1
Emporio Armani	191 Brompton Road, SW3
Escada	194-195 Sloane Street, SW1
Favourbrook	11 Pont Street, SW1
Fogal	3a Sloane Street, SW1
Fratelli Rossetti	196 Sloane Street, SW1
Freak Naughty	64 Brompton Road, SW3
French Connection	44 Brompton Road, SW3
Gant USA	47-49 Brompton Road, SW3
Gianfranco Ferré	29 Sloane Street, SW1
Gina	189 Sloane Street, SW1
Giorgio Armani	37 Sloane Street, SW1
Gucci	17 Sloane Street, SW1
Harrods	87-135 Brompton Road, SW1
Harvey Nichols	109-125 Knightsbridge, SW1
Herbie Frogg	13 Lowndes Street, SW1
Hermès	179 Sloane Street, SW1
High & Mighty	81-83 Knightsbridge, SW1
Hobbs	37 Brompton Road, SW3
Hugo Boss	190 Sloane Street, SW1
iBlues	161 Brompton Road, SW3
Jacques Azagury	50 Knightsbridge, SW1
Jaeger	16-18 Brompton Road, SW1
Jane Norman	59 Brompton Road, SW3
Jigsaw	31 Brompton Road, SW3
Jitrois	6f Sloane Street, SW1
Jones the Bootmaker	187 Brompton Road, SW3
Joseph	26 Sloane Street, SW1
Joseph Azagury	73 Knightsbridge, SW1
Karen Millen	33 Brompton Road, SW3
Kenneth Cole	3 Sloane Street, SW1
Kenzo	15 Sloane Street, SW1
Koh Samui	28 Lowndes Street, SW1
Kookaï	5-7 Brompton Road, SW3
La Perla	163 Sloane Street, SW1
Lacoste	20 Brompton Road, SW1
The Library	268 Brompton Road, SW3
Liza Bruce	9 Pont Street, SW1
Loro Piana	47 Sloane Street, SW1
Louis Vuitton	198-199 Sloane Street, SW1
Louise Kennedy	11 West Halkin Street, SW1
Marni	16 Sloane Street, SW1
MaxMara	32 Sloane Street, SW1
Mexx	75 Brompton Road, SW3
Monsoon	29 Brompton Road, SW3
Mulberry	171-175 Brompton Road, SW3

Nicole Farhi	193 Sloane Street, SW1
Ninivah Khomo	4a Motcomb Street, SW1
Oilily	9 Sloane Street, SW1
Patricia Roberts	60 Kinnerton Street, SW1
Paul & Joe	309 Brompton Road, SW3
Philip Treacy	69 Elizabeth Street, SW1
Please Mum	85 Knightsbridge, SW1
Prada	43-45 Sloane Street, SW1
Rachel Riley	14 Pont Street, SW1
Ricci Burns	25 Lowndes Street, SW1
Rigby & Peller	2 Hans Road, SW3
Russell & Bromley	45 Brompton Road, SW3
Russell & Haslam	(private design studio in SW1)
Salvatore Ferragamo	207 Sloane Street, SW1
Semmalina	225 Ebury Street, SW1
Shanghai Tang	6a/b Sloane Street, SW1
Stephane Kélian	48 Sloane Street, SW1
Stewart Parvin	14 Motcomb Street, SW1
Thomas Pink	74 Sloane Street, SW1
Tod's	35-36 Sloane Street, SW1
Tommy Hilfiger	6 Sloane Street, SW1
Uniqlo	163-169 Brompton Road, SW3
United Colors of Benetton	23 Brompton Road, SW3
Valentino	174 Sloane Street, SW1
Versace	183-184 Sloane Street, SW1
Young England	47 Elizabeth Street, SW1
Yves Saint Laurent: Rive Gauche	33 Sloane Street, SW1
Zibba	61 Knightsbridge, SW1

Little Venice (W9)

Golden Glow	1 Lanark Place
Hels Bels	3 Clarendon Terrace
Joujou Lucy	32 Clifton Road

Marble Arch (W1)

See map pages 202–203

Bally	472 Oxford Street
Clarks	476 Oxford Street
Gap (& Gap Kids)	473 Oxford Street
H&M	481 Oxford Street
High & Mighty	145-147 Edgware Road, W2
Jimmy Choo (couture)	18 Connaught Street, W2
Laura Ashley	449-451 Oxford Street
Marks & Spencer	458 Oxford Street
Next	508-520 Oxford Street
Ritva Westenius	28 Connaught Street, W2
Sharon Cunningham	23 New Quebec Street
Wallis	532-536 Oxford Street

Marylebone / North of Oxford Street (W1)

See map pages 202–203

agnès b.	40-41 Marylebone High Street
Bang Bang	21 Goodge Street
Bare	8 Chiltern Street
Brora	81 Marylebone High Street
Due Passi	27 James Street
Gap	93-94 Marylebone High Street
Gary Anderson	36 Chiltern Street
Ghost	14 Hinde Street
Jesus Lopez	69 Marylebone High Street
Johanna Hehir	10-12 Chiltern Street
Ken Smith Designs	6 Charlotte Place
Long Tall Sally	21-25 Chiltern Street
Margaret Howell	34 Wigmore Street
Monsoon	96 Marylebone High Street
Parallel	22 Marylebone High Street
Parallel Intimo	85 Marylebone High Street
Philip Somerville	38 Chiltern Street
Rachel Riley	82 Marylebone High Street
Robert Clergerie	67 Wigmore Street
Ronit Zilkha	107 Marylebone High Street
SpaceNK	83a Marylebone High Street
Texier	6 New Cavendish Street
Whistles	1 Thayer Street

Mayfair *(excluding Bond Street)* (W1)

See map pages 202–203

Comme des Garçons	59 Brook Street
Douglas Hayward	95 Mount Street
Elégance	14a Grafton Street
Formes	33 Brook Street
Golden Glow	31 Avery Row
Herbie Frogg	16 Brook Street
Holland & Holland	31-33 Bruton Street
James Purdey & Sons	57-58 South Audley Street
John Smedley	24 Brook Street
Joseph	28 Brook Street
L.K.Bennett	31 Brook Street
Orvis	36a Dover Street
Paule Ka	13a Grafton Street
Pleats Please: Issey Miyake	20 Brook Street
Ronit Zilkha	34 Brook Street
Sonia Rykiel	27-29 Brook Street
SpaceNK	45-47 Brook Street
Stephane Kélian	13 Grafton Street
Thomas Pink	18 Davies Street
Travelling Light	35 Dover Street
Vivienne Westwood	6 Davies Street

Notting Hill / Ladbroke Grove / Portobello (W2, 10 & 11)

See map page 206

295	295 Portobello Road, W10
The 1920s-1970s Crazy Clothes Connection	134 Lancaster Road, W11
Accessorize	237 Portobello Road, W11
agnès b.	233-235 Westbourne Grove, W11
Aimé	32 Ledbury Road, W11
Ann Wiberg	63a Ledbury Road, W11
The Antique Clothing Shop	282 Portobello Road, W10
Bill Amberg	10 Chepstow Road, W2
Bodas	38b Ledbury Road, W11
Bonpoint	197 Westbourne Grove, W11
Cath Kidston	8 Clarendon Cross, W11
Catherine Buckley	302 Westbourne Grove, W11
Clementine	73 Ledbury Road, W11
Coco Ribbon	21 Kensington Park Road, W11
The Cross	141 Portland Road, W11
Debonair Debonair	281 Portobello Road, W10
The Dispensary	200 Kensington Park Road, W11
Dolly Diamond	51 Pembridge Road, W11
Ember	206 Portobello Road, W11
Emma Hope	207 Westbourne Grove, W11
Euforia	61b Lancaster Road, W11
Euforia	281 Portobello Road, W10
Feathers	176 Westbourne Grove, W11
Gap	132-136 Notting Hill Gate, W11
Ghost	36 Ledbury Road, W11
Graham & Green	4,7 & 10 Elgin Crescent, W11
Heidi Klein	174 Westbourne Grove, W11
The Hive	3 Lonsdale Road, W11
Il Piacere Donna	185 Westbourne Grove, W11
JC's Boutique (was The Dispensary)	29 Pembridge Road, W11
J&M Davidson	42 Ledbury Road, W11
J.W.Beeton	48-50 Ledbury Road, W11
The Jacksons	5 All Saints Road, W11
Jane Brown	189 Westbourne Grove, W11
Jigsaw (& Jigsaw Junior)	190 Westbourne Grove, W11
Joseph	61 Ledbury Road, W11
Justin Kara	253 Portobello Road, W11
The L Boutique	28 Chepstow Corner, W2
Laundry Industry	186 Westbourne Grove, W11
Marilyn Moore	7 Elgin Crescent, W11
Matches	60-64 Ledbury Road, W11
Myla	77 Lonsdale Road, W11
The Natural Shoe Store	181 Westbourne Grove, W11
Nick Ashley	57 Ledbury Road, W11
Nicole Farhi	202 Westbourne Grove, W11
Nothing	230 Portobello Road, W11

Office	217 Portobello Road, W11
Offspring	217 Portobello Road, W11
Olivia Morris	355 Portobello Road, W10
Olowu Golding	367 Portobello Road, W10
One of a Kind	253 & 259 Portobello Road, W11
Paul & Joe	39-41 Ledbury Road, W11
Paul Smith	122 Kensington Park Road, W11
Phase Eight	164 Notting Hill Gate, W11
Portobello Market	Portobello Road, W11
Preen	281 Portobello Road, W10
Question Air	229 Westbourne Grove, W11
Rellik	8 Golborne Road, W10
Sasti	281 Portobello Road, W11
scorah pattullo	193 Westbourne Grove, W11
Sheila Cook	283 Westbourne Grove, W11
The Shirtsmith	2a Ledbury Mews North, W11
Sigerson Morrison	184 Westbourne Grove, W11
Size?	200 Portobello Road, W11
Skins	232 Portobello Road, W11
So aei kei	357 Portobello Road, W10
SpaceNK	127-131 Westbourne Grove, W2
Still...	61d Lancaster Road, W11
Sub Couture	204 Kensington Park Road, W11
Titri	1 Denbigh Road, W11
Trudy Hanson	25 All Saints Road, W11
Vent	178a Westbourne Grove, W11
Virginia	98 Portland Road, W11
West Village	35 Kensington Park Road, W11
White Stuff	66 Westbourne Grove, W2
Wigwam	25 Kensington Park Road, W11
Willma	339 Portobello Road, W10

Oxford Street (W1)

See map pages 202–203

Accessorize	293 & 386 Oxford Street
Aldo	309 Oxford Street
Ann Harvey	266 Oxford Street
Cecil Gee	170 & 287 Oxford Street
The Changing Room	10a Gees Court
Claire's Accessories	108 Oxford Street
Clarks	15 & 260 Oxford Street
Debenhams	334-348 Oxford Street
Dorothy Perkins	189 & 379 Oxford Street
Dorothy Perkins	118-132 New Oxford Street, WC1
Dune	The Plaza, 120 Oxford Street
Expensive!	221-223 Oxford Street
Faith	192-194 Oxford Street
Foot Locker	363-367 Oxford Street
French Connection	396 Oxford Street
Gap	118, 223-235 & 315 Oxford Street

Gap Kids	315 & 376-384 Oxford Street
H&M	174-176 Oxford Street
High & Mighty	The Plaza, 120 Oxford Street
House of Fraser	318 Oxford Street
Jeans West	5 Harewood Place
Jeans West	The Plaza, 120 Oxford Street
Jigsaw	St. Christopher's Place
John Lewis	278-306 Oxford Street
Kookaï	257-259 & 399 Oxford Street
La Senza	162 Oxford Street
Mango/MNG	225-235 Oxford Street
Marks & Spencer	173 Oxford Street
Mash	73 Oxford Street
Miss Selfridge	214 Oxford Street
Miss Sixty	31-32 Great Marlborough Street
Monsoon	264 Oxford Street
Morgan	270 & 391-393 Oxford Street
Moss Bros	229 Oxford Street
Muji	187 Oxford Street
Muji	6 Tottenham Court Road
Mulberry	11-12 Gees Court
New Look	175-179 Oxford Street
Next	201-205 & 325-329 Oxford Street
Niketown	236 Oxford Street
Oasis	The Plaza, 120 Oxford Street
Osprey	11 St. Christopher's Place
Paddy Campbell	8 Gees Court
Ravel	184-188 Oxford Street
Reiss	14-17 Market Place
River Island	283 Oxford Street
Selfridges	400 Oxford Street
Shellys	159 Oxford Street
Top Shop/Top Man	214 Oxford Street
United Colors of Benetton	415-419 Oxford Street
Warehouse	The Plaza, 120 Oxford Street
Whistles	12 St. Christopher's Place
Woodhouse	28-32 St. Christopher's Place
Zara	242-248 & 333 Oxford Street

Regent Street / Carnaby Street (W1)

See map pages 202–203

Adolfo Dominguez	129 Regent Street
Agent Provocateur	6 Broadwick Street
Aquascutum	100 Regent Street
Austin Reed	103-113 Regent Street
Bally	260 Regent Street
Barker Shoes	215 Regent Street
Beau Monde	43 Lexington Street
Blunauta	171-173 Regent Street

Burberry	165 Regent Street
Carhartt	13 Newburgh Street
Church's	201 Regent Street
Claire's Accessories	49-63 & 187 Regent Street
Clarks	101 & 203 Regent Street
Dickins & Jones	224-244 Regent Street
Diesel	24 Carnaby Street
The Dispensary	8 & 9 Newburgh Street
Esprit	178-182 Regent Street
Expensive!	154 Regent Street
French Connection	249 Regent Street
French Connection	10 Argyll Street
Gap	146 Regent Street
Gap Kids	208 Regent Street
H&M	261-271 Regent Street
Hackett	143-147 Regent Street
Henri Lloyd	48 Carnaby Street
High Jinks	13-14 Carnaby Street
Hugo Boss	184-186 Regent Street
Jaeger	200-206 Regent Street
Jigsaw	9 Argyll Street
Jones the Bootmaker	15 Foubert's Place
Karen Millen	262-264 Regent Street
Knickerbox	281a Regent Street
Laura Ashley	256-258 Regent Street
Levi's	174-176 & 269 Regent Street
Liberty	210-220 Regent Street
Liz Claiborne	211-213 Regent Street
Mango/MNG	106-112 Regent Street
Moss Bros	88 Regent Street
Muji	41 Carnaby Street
Next	160 Regent Street
Oasis	292 Regent Street
Oasis	12-14 Argyll Street
O'Neill	527 Carnaby Street
Pepe Jeans	42 Carnaby Street
Peter Werth	10 Foubert's Place
The Pineal Eye	49 Broadwick Street
Puma	52-55 Carnaby Street
R.M.Williams	223 Regent Street
Racing Green	195 Regent Street
Reiss	172 Regent Street
Savage London	14a Newburgh Street
Shellys	266-270 Regent Street
Size?	31 Carnaby Street
Souvenir	47 Lexington Street
Swear	22 Carnaby Street
Talbots	115 Regent Street
Ted Baker	5-7 Foubert's Place

Uniqlo	84-86 Regent Street
United Colors of Benetton	255-259 Regent Street
Viyella	179-183 Regent Street
Warehouse	19-21 Argyll Street
Zara	118 Regent Street

St. John's Wood (NW8)

Gap Kids	47-49 St. John's Wood High Street
Joseph	21 St. John's Wood High Street
SpaceNK	73 St. John's Wood High Street
Whistles	51 St. John's Wood High Street

Savile Row (W1)

See map pages 202–203

40 Savile Row	40 Savile Row
Anderson & Sheppard	30 Savile Row
Anthony J. Hewitt/Airey & Wheeler	9 Savile Row
Davies & Son	38 Savile Row
Dege & Skinner	10 Savile Row
Gary Anderson	34-35 Savile Row
Gieves & Hawkes	1 Savile Row
Hardy Amies	14 Savile Row
Henry Poole & Co	15 Savile Row
Huntsman	11 Savile Row
James Levett	13 Savile Row
Kilgour French Stanbury	8 Savile Row
Maurice Sedwell	19 Savile Row
Paraboot	37 Savile Row
Richard James	29 Savile Row
Scabal	12 Savile Row
Welsh & Jefferies	20 Savile Row
William Hunt	41 Savile Row

South Kensington / Fulham Road (SW3, 7 & 10)

See map pages 200–201

agnès b.	111 Fulham Road, SW3
Amanda Wakely	80 Fulham Road, SW3
Anne Fontaine	151 Fulham Road, SW3
Beatrice von Tresckow	273 Fulham Road, SW10
Bertie Wooster	284 Fulham Road, SW10
Betty Jackson	311 Brompton Road, SW3
Butler & Wilson	189 Fulham Road, SW3
Camilla Ridley	339 Fulham Road, SW10
Caramel Baby & Child	291 Brompton Road, SW3
Catherine Walker	46 Fulham Road, SW3
The Chelsea Collections	90 Fulham Road, SW3
Claudia Sebire	136 Fulham Road, SW10
East	192 Fulham Road, SW10
Gap (& Gap Kids)	145-149 Brompton Road, SW3
Great Expectations	78 Fulham Road, SW3

Issey Miyake	270 Brompton Road, SW3
Jigsaw	91-95 Fulham Road, SW3
Jigsaw Junior	97 Fulham Road, SW3
Joseph	77 & 299 Fulham Road, SW3
Joseph	74 Sloane Avenue, SW3
Joseph	315 Brompton Road, SW3
Kenzo	70 Sloane Avenue, SW3
Kim Davis	84 Fulham Road, SW3
The Library	268 Brompton Road, SW3
Neisha Crosland	137 Fulham Road, SW3
Nicole Farhi	115 Fulham Road, SW3
Night Owls	78 Fulham Road, SW3
Paul Smith	84-86 Sloane Avenue, SW3
Phase Eight	345 Fulham Road, SW10
Ralph Lauren	105-109 Fulham Road, SW3
Sally Parsons	15a Bute Street, SW7
Shirin Guild	241 Fulham Road, SW3
SpaceNK	307 Brompton Road, SW3
Sweatshop	188 Fulham Road, SW10
Tatters	74 Fulham Road, SW3
Thomas Starzewski	14 Stanhope Mews West, SW7
Whistles	303 Brompton Road, SW3

South of the River (SW11, 13, 15, & 21)

Alice Berrill	31 Lavender Hill, SW11 (Battersea/Clapham)
Jigsaw	114 Putney High Street, SW15 (Putney)
Lilli Diva	32 Lavender Hill, SW11 (Battersea/Clapham)
Monsoon	25 Putney Exchange Shopping Centre SW15 (Putney)
Parallel	23 Putney Exchange Shopping Centre SW15 (Putney)
Question Air	86 Church Road, SW13 (Barnes)
Question Air	85-87 Dulwich Village, SE21 (Dulwich Village)
White Stuff	49 Northcote Road, SW11 (Battersea/Clapham)
Wild Swans	70 Battersea Rise, SW11 (Battersea/Clapham)

The Strand (WC2)

Jigsaw	449 The Strand
Moss Bros	92-93 The Strand

Victoria (SW1)

Christiana Couture	53 Moreton Street
Cornucopia	12 Upper Tachbrook Street
Dorothy Perkins	Victoria Station
La Senza	8 Kingsgate Parade, Victoria Street
New Look	Victoria Station

Whiteley's Shopping Centre, Queensway (W2)

Gap (& Gap Kids)
H&M
Jigsaw

Knickerbox
Nine West
Oasis

Wimbledon / Wimbledon Village (SW19)

Jaeger	27 High Street, Wimbledon Village
Joseph	64 High Street, Wimbledon Village
Matches (5!)	34, 37, 38, 39 & 56b High Street Wimbledon Village
Monsoon	Centre Court Shopping Centre
New Look	Centre Court Shopping Centre
Phase Eight	31 High Street, Wimbledon Village
Question Air	77 & 78 High Street, Wimbledon Village
Rodier	4 Church Road

Stores by Category

Women's

Men's

Children's

Tweens

Women's Accessories

Accessorize
Claire's Accessories
Fenwick
Georgina von Etzdorf
Golden Glow
Harrods
Harvey Nichols
The Jacksons
Liberty
Lucy in the Sky
Mulberry
Neisha Crosland
Net-a-porter
Ninivah Khomo
Selfridges
So aei kei
Tabio
Top Shop
Willma

Women's Activewear

Crew Clothing Co
Ellis Brigham
Fat Face
Field & Trek
Foot Locker
Fred Perry
Gamba
Harley-Davidson
Heidi Klein
Henri Lloyd
Holland & Holland
Jungle
Key Largo
King's Road Sporting Club
Lacoste
Lillywhites
Liza Bruce
Loro Piana
O'Neill
Orvis
Puma
Quiksilver
R.M.Williams
Sweatshop
Sweaty Betty
T&G Clothing
Timberland
Travelling Light
White Stuff

Women's Bridal

Amanda Wakely
Angela Stone
Anello and Davide
Bruce Oldfield
Caroline Holmes
Catherine Buckley
Christiana Couture
Eda Lingerie
Harriet Gubbins
Isabell Kristensen
Jacqueline Hogan
Kruszynska
Neil Cunningham
Phillipa Lepley
Ritva Westenius
Russell & Haslam
Serafina
Sharon Cunningham
Stewart Parvin
Trudy Hanson

Women's Cashmere/Knitwear

Ballantyne Cashmere
Belinda Robertson
Ben de Lisi
Berk

Brora
Cashmere London
Cathryn Grosvenor
Caz

Gigi
House of Cashmere
John Smedley

Krizia
Liola
Loro Piana
Louise Kennedy

M-A-G
Marilyn Moore
N.Peal
Oilily

Patricia Roberts
Rodier
Shi Cashmere

Women's Casual

Blunauta
Broadway
Episode
Eskandar

Esprit
French for Less
Gap
J.W.Beeton

Justin Kara
Kit Clothing/Twentieth Century Frox
Laundry Industry

Laura Tom
Levi's
Muji

Naf Naf
Pantalon Chameleon
Pepe Jeans
Phase Eight

Phlip
Racing Green
Sally Parsons
Sisley

Ted Baker
Tops & Bottoms
Uniqlo
United Colors of Benetton

Wall
White Stuff
Wild Swans

Women's Classic

40 Savile Row
Adolfo Dominguez
Aquascutum
Armand Basi

Beau Monde
Betty Jackson
Burberry
Catherine Walker

Caroline Charles
CCO'
Cerruti 1881
Claudia Sebire

Daks
Elégance
Emanuel Ungaro
Emma Somerset

Feathers
Fenwick
Galerie Gaultier
Gigi

Hobbs
iBlues
J&M Davidson
Jaeger

Women's Classic *(continued)*

Laura Ashley
Louise Kennedy
Mulberry
Paddy Campbell
Pantalon Chameleon
Paule Ka
Press & Bastyan
Spaghetti
Talbots

Women's Contemporary

à la mode
Aimé
Ajanta
Alice Berrill
Allegra Hicks
Ann Wiberg
Anna
Antoine et Lili
Aquaint
Arté
Bare
Ben de Lisi
Betsey Johnson
Browns Focus
Butler & Wilson
The Changing Room
Charlotte Smith
Clusaz
The Cross
Coco Ribbon
Debonair Debonair
Designer Club
Diverse
e.g. Butterfly
Egg
Essence
Euforia
Gotham Angels
Graham & Green
Heidi Klein
The Hive
Il Piacere Donna
The Jacksons
Joanna's Tent
Jones
Justin Kara
Kenneth Cole
Kim Davis
Koh Samui
Kokon to Zai
Lilli Diva
L.K.Bennett
Matches
Marilyn Moore
MiMi
Musa
Noa Noa
Nothing
The Pineal Eye
Preen
Proibito
Question Air
Rachel Riley
Samsonite
Sefton
Shirin Guild
Shop
So aei kei
Sub Couture
Tashia
Tokïo
Ventilo
Voyage
Wardrobe
West Village
Wild Swans
Willma

Women's Department Store* & High Street Chains

Austin Reed
*Debenhams
Dickins & Jones
Dorothy Perkins

East
*Fenwick
*Fortnum & Mason
French Connection

Gap (& Gap Kids)
H&M
*Harrods
*Harvey Nichols

Hobbs
House of Fraser
Jigsaw (& Jigsaw Junior)
*John Lewis

Karen Millen
Kookaï
*Liberty
*Lillywhites

Mango/MNG
Marks & Spencer
Miss Sixty
Monsoon

Morgan
Muji
New Look
Next

Oasis
*Peter Jones
Phase Eight
Reiss

Russell & Bromley
*Selfridges
SpaceNK
Top Shop

United Colors of Benetton
Wallis
Whistles
Zara

Women's Designer

agnès b.
Alberta Ferretti
Alexander McQueen
Amanda Wakely
Anna Molinari Blumarine

Anne Fontaine
Betsey Johnson
Bruce Oldfield
Calvin Klein

Céline
Chanel
Chloé
Christian Dior

Collette Dinnigan
Comme des Garçons
Dolce & Gabbana
Donna Karan

Elspeth Gibson
Emanuel Ungaro

Emporio Armani
Escada
Eskandar
Etro
Galerie Gaultier

Georgina von Etzdorf
Gérard Darel
Ghost
Gianfranco Ferré

Gibo
Giorgio Armani
Gucci
Hels Bels (discount)

I Love Voyage
Isabell Kristensen
Issey Miyake
Jacques Azagury

Jil Sander
Joseph

Women's Designer *(continued)*

Kenneth Cole
Kenzo
Kim Davis
Krizia
The L Boutique
Laurèl
Liz Claiborne
Liza Bruce
Louis Féraud
Louis Vuitton
Louise Kennedy
Maharishi
Marilyn Moore
Marni
MaxMara
Miu Miu
Moschino
Net-a-porter
Nicole Farhi
Olowu Golding
Paul & Joe
Paul Costelloe
Pleats Please: Issey Miyake
Plein Sud
Prada
Pringle
Ralph Lauren
Robinson Valentine
Ronit Zilkha
Shirin Guild
Sonia Rykiel
Stella McCartney
Thierry Mugler
Thomas Starzewski
Tommy Hilfiger
Tracey Boyd
Valentino
Versace
Vivienne Westwood
Voyage
Yohji Yamamoto
Yves Saint Laurent

Women's Ethnic (& Asian)

Ajanta
Ananya
East
Graham & Green
Jauko
Monsoon
Nitya
Noa Noa
Shanghai Tang
Sox Kamen
Thailandia
Titri
Wall
Wigwam

Women's Formalwear, Eveningwear & Special Occasions

Aftershock
Amanda Wakely
Angela Stone
Angels
Ann Wiberg
Beatrice von Tresckow
Betsey Johnson
Bruce Oldfield
Camilla Ridley
Cashmere London
Catherine Walker
The Chelsea Collections
Emanuel Ungaro
Emma Willis
Escada
Escapade
Favourbrook
Gianfranco Ferré
Isabell Kristensen
Joanna Hehir
Kit Clothing/Twentieth Century Frox
The L Boutique
One Night Stand
Ricci Burns
Robina
Robinson Valentine
The Shirtsmith
Tatters
Valentino
Wardrobe

Women's Handbags

Aldo
Alice Berrill
Anya Hindmarch
Bally
Bill Amberg
CCO'
Coach
Cocinelle
Fenwick
Furla
Georgina Goodman
Gigi
Gucci
Hermès
Karen Millen
Louis Vuitton
Lulu Guinness
Miu Miu
Mulberry
Pantalon Chameleon
Paola Tregemini
Pickett
Prada
Russell & Bromley
Tanner Krolle
Wild Swans

Women's Hats

Bates Gentleman's Hatter
(but women's, too)
The British Hatter
The Chelsea Collections
Fenwick
Harvey Nichols
Liberty
Philip Somerville
Philip Treacy
Selfridges

Women's Leathergoods

Bill Amberg
The Bridge
Coach
Connolly
Furla
Harley-Davidson
Hermès
Leather Rat Classics
Mulberry
Osprey
Pickett
Skin Machine
Texier
Top Gun

Women's Lingerie & Nightwear

Agent Provocateur
Bodas
Bradleys
Couverture
Eda Lingerie
Fogal (hosiery specialist)
Janet Reger
Knickerbox
La Perla
La Senza
Laurence Tavernier
Marks & Spencer
Monogrammed Linen Shop
Myla
Night Owls
Parallel Intimo
Rigby & Peller
Wolford (hosiery specialist)

Maternity

9 London
Blooming Marvellous
Formes
Great Expectations
Long Tall Sally
Seraphine

Women's Petite Sizes

Celia Loe
Dorothy Perkins
Jaeger
Liz Claiborne
Miss Sixty
Next
Talbots
Top Shop
Viyella
Wallis

Women's Plus Sizes (& tall women)

Ann Harvey
Base
Dorothy Perkins
Gordon Scott (for shoes)
Ken Smith Designs
Long Tall Sally
Marina Rinaldi

Women's Secondhand, Leftovers & Exchange

Bang Bang
Bertie Golightly
Browns Labels for Less
Blackout II
Cornucopia
The Corridor
Designer Bargains
La Scala
The Loft
One of a Kind
Proibito
Sign of the Times
Trésor

Women's Shirts

Anne Fontaine
Charles Tyrwhitt
Emma Willis
Louise Kennedy
The Shirtsmith
Thomas Pink
T.M.Lewin
Turnbull & Asser

Women's Shoes

Aldo
Anello & Davide
Atticus
Audley
Bally
Bertie
Bertie Golightly
Birkenstock
Blue Velvet
The Bridge
Buffalo Boots
Camper
Charles Jourdan
Christian Louboutin
Church's
Clarks
Clio
Dr. Marten Department Store
Due Passi
Dune
Egoshego
Eliot Zed
Emma Hope
F.Pinet
Faith
Foot Locker
Fratelli Rossetti
French Sole
Georgina Goodman
Gigi
Gina
Golden Glow
Hobbs
Hudson
Ivory
Jane Brown
Jesus Lopez
Jimmy Choo
John Lobb

Women's Shoes *(continued)*

Jones the Bootmaker
Joseph Azagury
Karen Millen
Kenneth Cole

Koh Samui
Kurt Geiger
L.K.Bennett
Manolo Blahnik

Miu Miu
The Natural Shoe Store
Niketown
Nine West

Offspring
Olivia Morris
Olowu Golding
Pantalon Chameleon

Paola Tregemini
Paraboot
Parallel

Patrick Cox
Pied à Terre
Poste Mistress

Puma
R.Soles
Ravel
Robert Clergerie

Robot
Ruco Line
Russell & Bromley
Salvatore Ferragamo

scorah pattullo
Senso
Sergio Rossi
Shellys

Sigerson Morrison
Size?
Sole Trader
Stephane Kélian

Strada
Sukie's
Swear

Tod's
Via Venise
Zibba

Women's Trend & Streetwear

Ad Hoc
American Classics
Boxfresh
Carhartt

cm Store
Cyberdog
Diesel
Diesel Style Lab

The Dispensary
Dockers
Expensive!
Fat Face

Fly
French Connection
High Jinks
Hope + Glory

Jane Norman
Jeans West
Jenesis
Jitrois

Kookaï
Mandy
Mango/MNG
Mash

Miss Selfridge
Miss Sixty
Morgan
Nara

New Look
Oasis
O'Neill
Pepe Jeans

Phlip
Pineapple
Pop Boutique
Quiksilver

River Island
Savage London
START
Stüssy

Tops & Bottoms
Urban Outfitters
V.I.P.
The Vestry

Warehouse
Whistles
Zara

Women's Vintage/Retro

The 1920s-1970s Crazy Clothes Connection
295
The Antique Clothing Shop
Bang Bang
Blackout II
Butler & Wilson
Camden Market
Cath Kidston
Cenci
Cornucopia
Dolly Diamond
Ember
Hels Bels
Musa
One of a Kind
Pop Boutique
Portobello Market
Rachel Riley
Rellik
Sheila Cook
Souvenir
Steinberg & Tolkien
Still...
Vent
Virginia

Men's Accessories

Aware
Coach
Dege & Skinner
Duffer of St. George
Dunhill
Gieves & Hawkes
New & Lingwood
Richard James
Tabio
Turnbull & Asser

Men's Activewear

Berluti
Ellis Brigham
Fat Face
Field & Trek
Foot Locker
Fred Perry
Harley-Davidson
Henri Lloyd
Holland & Holland
House of Cashmere
James Purdey & Sons
Jungle
King's Road Sporting Club
Lacoste
O'Neill
Orvis
Puma
Quiksilver
R.M.Williams
T&G Clothing
Timberland
Travelling Light
White Stuff

Men's Cashmere/Knitwear

Ballantyne Cashmere
Berk
Brora
Connolly
John Smedley
Loro Piana
N.Peal

Men's Casual

Armand Basi
Crew Clothing Co
Dockers
Duffer of St. George
Dunhill
Ermenegildo Zegna
Fabri
Fat Face
Gant USA
Hackett
John Bray
Key Largo
Lacoste
Natural Blue
O'Neill
Peter Werth
Quiksilver
Racing Green
Tommy Hilfiger
Urban Outfitters
Versace
White Stuff
William Hunt

Men's Classic

40 Savile Row
Adolfo Dominguez
Anthony J. Hewitt/Airey & Wheeler
Aquascutum
Avi Rossini
Bernini
Brioni
Browns
Canali
Cerruti 1881
Crombie
Daks
Davies & Son
Dege & Skinner
Dunhill
Ermenegildo Zegna
Gieves & Hawkes
Hackett
Henry Poole & Co
Herbie Frogg
Huntsman
James Levett
James Purdey & Sons
John Bray
Kilgour French Stanbury
Lanvin
Levi's
Maurice Sedwell
Mulberry
Pegaso
Roderick Charles
Welsh & Jefferies

Men's Contemporary

Browns Focus
Collezioni: Giorgio Armani
Egg
Hackett
Kilgour French Stanbury
The Library
Manucci
Maurice Sedwell
Nigel Hall
Olowu Golding
Pegaso
The Pineal Eye
Question Air
Richard James
Samsonite
Scabal
Sefton
Sox Kamen
Ted Baker
Thierry Mugler
Urban Outfitters
Vertice Uomo
William Hunt
Woodhouse
Yohji Yamamoto

Men's Department Store* & High Street Chains

Austin Reed
Cecil Gee
*Debenhams
Dickins & Jones
French Connection
Gap
H&M
*Harrods
*Harvey Nichols
House of Fraser
Jigsaw
*John Lewis
*Liberty
*Lillywhites
Marks & Spencer
Next
Office
*Peter Jones
Reiss
*Selfridges
Top Shop/Top Man
United Colors of Benetton

Men's Designer

Burberry
Calvin Klein
Comme des Garçons
Dolce & Gabbana
Donna Karan
Emporio Armani
Etro
Ghost
Giorgio Armani
Gucci
Hermès
Hugo Boss
Issey Miyake
Jil Sander
Joseph
Kenneth Cole
Kenzo
Krizia
Louis Vuitton
Maharishi
Moschino
Nicole Farhi
Ozwald Boateng
Paul & Joe
Paul Smith
Prada
Pringle
Ralph Lauren
Valentino
Versace
Yves Saint Laurent

Men's Formalwear & Special Occasions

Favourbrook
Gary Anderson
Hawes & Curtis
Moss Bros

Men's Hats

Bates Gentleman's Hatter
Douglas Hayward
Ede & Ravenscroft
Harvey Nichols
Herbert Johnson
Lock & Co
Skin Machine

Men's Leathergoods

Bill Amberg
The Bridge
Coach
Connolly
Dunhill
Leather Rat Classics
Mulberry
Proudfoot
Skin Machine
Texier
Top Gun

Men's Plus Sizes

Gordon Scott (for shoes)
High & Mighty

Men's Secondhand, Leftovers & Exchange

Bertie Wooster
Blackout II
Browns Labels for Less
The Loft
Proibito
Skins

Men's Shirts

Charles Tyrwhitt
Coles the Shirtmakers
Dege & Skinner
Dunhill
Emma Willis
Emmett Shirts
Ermenegildo Zegna
Gieves & Hawkes
Hackett
Harvie & Hudson
Hawes & Curtis
Henry Poole & Co
Hilditch & Key
Huntsman
John Bray
New & Lingwood
Richard James
Roderick Charles
T.M.Lewin
Thomas Pink
Turnbull & Asser
Van Heusen
William Hunt

Men's Shoes

Aldo
Audley
Bally
Barker Shoes
Berluti
Birkenstock
The Bridge
Buffalo Boots
Camper
Charles Jourdan
Church's
Clarks
Cleverley
Crockett & Jones
Dr. Marten Department Store
Edward Green
Eliot Zed
F.Pinet
Foot Locker
Foster & Son
Fratelli Rossetti
Gordon Scott
Ivory
John Lobb
Jones the Bootmaker
Kurt Geiger
The Natural Shoe Store
New & Lingwood
Nick Ashley
Niketown
Offspring
Paraboot
Patrick Cox
Pegaso
Poste
Puma
R.Soles
Ravel
Robert Clergerie
Robot
Ruco Line
Russell & Bromley
Salvatore Ferragamo
scorah pattullo
Sergio Rossi
Shellys
Size?
Sole Trader
Strada
Sukie's
Swear
Tim Little
Tod's
Tricker's
Via Venise

Men's Trend & Streetwear

American Classics
Boxfresh
Burro
Carhartt
Cyberdog
Diesel
Diesel Style Lab
The Dispensary
Fly
High Jinks
Hope + Glory
J.W.Beeton
Jones
Pepe Jeans
Phlip
Pop Boutique
River Island
Savage London
START
Stüssy

Men's Vintage/Retro

The 1920s-1970s Crazy Clothes Connection
295
The Antique Clothing Shop
Ember
Pop Boutique

Children's (* for Children's Shoes)

Ad Hoc
Blooming Marvellous
Bonpoint
Brora
Burberry
Butterscotch
*Caramel Baby & Child
*Catimini
*Clementine
*Cookie
Couverture
Crew Clothing Co
The Cross
*Daisy & Tom
Debenhams
*The Dispensary
*Dr. Marten Department Store
Field & Trek
*Foot Locker
*Gap Kids & Baby Gap
Gotham Angels
Gucci
Gymboree
H&M
*Harvey Nichols
Hermès
House of Fraser
Iana
*Jigsaw Junior
*Joanna's Tent
*John Lewis
*Joujou Lucy
Kit Clothing/Twentieth Century Frox
La Scala
Laura Ashley
Lillywhites
Maharishi
Marks & Spencer
*Mikihouse
Monogrammed Linen Shop
Monsoon
*Next
*Niketown
*Oilily
Patricia Roberts
Patrizia Wigan Designs
*Paul Smith
Petit Bateau
Please Mum
*Pollyanna
*Prada
*Rachel Riley
Ralph Lauren
R.Soles

Children's (* for Children's Shoes)

*Ruco Line
Sasti
Semmalina
Shellys
Shanghai Tang
*Tartine et Chocolat
*Timberland
*Tod's
*Trotters
*United Colors of Benetton
What Katy Did
Young England

Tweens (* for Tweens' Shoes)

Accessorize
*Atticus
*Bertie
*Blue Velvet
Boxfresh
Buffalo Boots
Camden Market
Camper
Carhartt
Claire's Accessories
cm Store
Diesel
Dorothy Perkins
*Dune
Esprit
Expensive!
*Faith
Fat Face
Fly
*Foot Locker
French Connection
Gap
H&M
Jauko
Jeans West
Knickerbox
Kookai
Levi's
Mandy
Mango
Marks & Spencer
Miss Selfridge
Miss Sixty
Morgan
Naf Naf
Nara
New Look
Next
Niketown
*Nine West
Oasis
*Office
Pepe jeans
Phlip
Portobello Market
Quiksilver
River Island
*Shellys
Sisley
*Size?
Stüssy
Sweaty Betty
Ted Baker
Top Gun
Top Shop/Top Man
Uniqlo
United Colors of Benetton
Urban Outfitters
V.I.P.
Zara

Health & Beauty

Barbers

Hair Salons

Hair Removal

Beauty Treatments

Manicures

Day Spas

Fitness Studios

Massage Therapists

Yoga, Pilates, Alexander technique

Tanning

Make-up Artists

Barbers

Adams London — **020 7499 9779**
12 St. George Street — tube: Oxford Circus/Bond Street
London W1 — Mon-Fri 9-8, Sat 10-6

Cuts — **020 7734 2171**
39 Frith Street — tube: Piccadilly Circus
London W1 — Mon-Fri 11-7, Sat 10-6

Flittner — **020 7606 4750**
86 Moorgate — tube: Moorgate
London EC2 — Mon-Fri 8-6 (Thurs 8-6:30)

Fourth Floor — **020 7405 6011**
4 Northington Street — tube: Chancery Lane
London WC1 — Mon-Fri 9-7, Sat 9-6

Fish — **020 7494 2398**
30 D'Arblay Street — tube: Oxford Circus/ Tottenham Court Road
London W1 — Mon-Thurs 10-7 (Fri 10-8), Sat 10-5

George F. Trumper — **020 7499 1850**
9 Curzon Street — tube: Green Park
London W1 — Mon-Fri 9-5:30, Sat 9-1

George F. Trumper — **020 7734 6553**
20 Jermyn Street — tube: Piccadilly Circus
London SW1 — Mon-Fri 9-5:30, Sat 9-5

The Refinery — **020 7409 2001**
60 Brook Street — tube: Bond Street
London W1 — Mon-Tues 10-7, Wed-Fri 10-9
Sat 9-6, Sun 11-5

Sadlers Wells Barbers Shop — **020 7833 0556**
110 Rosebery Avenue — tube: Angel
London EC1 — Mon-Sat 8-6

Truefitt & Hill — **020 7493 2961**
71 St. James's Street — tube: Green Park
London SW1 — Mon-Fri 8:30-5:30 (Thurs 8:30-6:30)
Sat 8:30-5

Urban Rites — **020 7352 6888**
151 Sydney Street — tube: Sloane Square/South Kensington
London SW3 — Mon-Sat 9:30-8

Hair Salons

Charles Worthington — **020 7631 1370**
7 Percy Street — tube: Tottenham Court Road
London W1 — Mon-Thurs 8-8, Fri 10:15-5:15, Sat 9:15-6

Charles Worthington — **020 7831 5303**
34 Great Queen Street — tube: Covent Garden/Holborn
London WC2 — Mon-Thurs 8-8, Fri 10-7, Sat 9-6

Charles Worthington — **020 7638 0802**
The Broadgate Club — tube: Liverpool Street
1 Exchange Place — Mon-Thurs 7-9
London EC2 — Fri 10:15-7, Sat-Sun 10-6

Charles Worthington **020 7317 6321**
The Dorchester tube: Hyde Park Corner/Marble Arch
Park Lane Mon-Thurs 9:30-8, Fri 9:30-7
London W1 Sat 10-6, Sun 10-5

Daniel Galvin **020 7486 9661**
58-60 George Street tube: Bond Street/Baker Street
London W1 Mon-Sat 9-6

Daniel Hersheson **020 7434 1747**
45 Conduit Street tube: Oxford Circus
London W1 Mon-Sat 9-6

Errol Douglas **020 7235 0110**
18 Motcomb Street tube: Knightsbridge
London SW1 Mon-Sat 9-6

Jo Hansford **020 7495 7774**
19 Mount Street tube: Bond Street
London W1 Tues-Sat 9-6

John Frieda **020 7636 1401**
75 New Cavendish Street tube: Oxford Circus
London W1 Mon-Sat 9-5

John Frieda at Claridge's **020 7499 3617**
54-55 Brook Street tube: Bond Street
London W1 Mon-Sat 9-5

John Frieda **020 7491 0840**
4 Aldford Street tube: Bond Street
London W1 Mon-Sat 9-5

Martyn Maxey **020 7629 6161**
18 Grosvenor Street tube: Bond Street/Green Park
London W1 Mon-Sat 9-6

Michaeljohn **020 7629 6969**
25 Albemarle Street tube: Green Park
London W1 Mon-Fri 8-7:30, Sat 8-6:30

Neville **020 7235 3654**
5 Pont Street tube: Sloane Square/Knightsbridge
London SW1 Mon-Sat 8:30-6

Nicky Clarke **020 7491 4700**
130 Mount Street tube: Bond Street/Green Park
London W1 Tues-Sat 9-6 (Thurs 9-8)

Real **020 7589 0877**
6-8 Cale Street tube: South Kensington/Sloane Square
London SW3 Mon-Sat 8:30-7

Hair Removal

Feré Parangi (hot wax) **020 7235 3654**
At Neville Hair & Beauty tube: Sloane Square/
5 Pont Street Knightsbridge
London SW1 Mon-Sat 9-6

Kamini Vaghela (threading) **020 7723 8838**
15 Wyndham Place tube: Baker Street/Marylebone
London W1 Mon 10-6, Tues 12-5
Wed-Fri 10-7, Sat 11-5

Shape 020 7724 3344/ 07710 171 493
(Lulu's waxing, men & women) tube: Warwick Avenue
500 Edgware Road (by appointment)
London W2

Martine Henry (electrolysis & laser) 020 7823 7882
at The Beauty Clinic tube: Knightsbridge
122 Knightsbridge Tues-Fri 9-7 (Wed 9-8), Sat 9-5:30
London SW1

Beauty Treatments

Bharti Vyas Therapy & Beauty Centre 020 7935 5312
24 Chiltern Street tube: Baker Street
London W1 Mon-Sat 9:30-6

Eve Lom 020 7935 9988
2 Spanish Place tube: Bond Street
London W1 Tues-Sat 9-5

Greenhouse 020 7486 6800
142 Wigmore Street tube: Bond Street
London W1 Mon-Fri 10-6, Sat 10-4

Pure Beauty 020 7836 4153
19-20 Long Acre tube: Covent Garden
London WC2 Mon-Sat 10-7 (Thurs-Fri 10-8)

Sophie Thorpe 020 7584 0321
2 Yeoman's Row tube: South Kensington/Knightsbridge
London SW3 Mon, Wed, Thurs (by appointment)

Vaishaly Patel 020 7224 6088
51 Paddington Street (by appointment)
London W1

Manicures

Bastien Gonzalez 020 7409 6565
Olympus Suite Spa at Claridge's tube: Bond Street
54-55 Brook Street Mon-Fri 6:30-9
London W1 Daily 8-8

Chelsea Nail Studio 020 7225 3889
5 Pond Place tube: South Kensington
London SW3 Mon-Fri 10-8, Sat 10-6

The Country Club 020 7731 4346
101 Moore Park Road tube: Fulham Broadway
London SW6 Mon-Tues, Sat 10-6, Wed-Fri 10-8

Nails Inc 020 7499 8333
41 South Molton Street tube: Bond Street
London W1 Mon, Fri-Sat 10-7, Tues-Thurs 9-8
Sun 12-5

Nails Inc 020 7382 9353
46 Bishopsgate tube: Liverpool Street
London EC1 Mon-Fri 8-7

Nails Inc at Fenwick of Bond Street **020 7491 1155**
63 New Bond Street tube: Bond Street
London W1 Mon-Sat 10-6:30 (Thurs 10-8)

Nails Inc at House of Fraser **020 7529 4798**
318 Oxford Street tube: Oxford Circus
London W1 Mon-Fri 10-8 (Thurs 10-9), Sun 12-6

Nails Inc **020 7519 1669**
1 Canada Square tube: Canary Wharf
London E14 Mon-Fri 9-7, Sat 10-6, Sun 11-5

Rene Rainbird **020 7434 1747**
at Daniel Hersheson tube: Oxford Circus
45 Conduit Street Mon-Sat 9-6
London W1

Scarlet **020 7499 5898**
37 Maddox Street tube: Oxford Circus
London W1 Mon-Tues, Sat 10-7, Wed-Fri 10-8

Scarlet **020 7224 5898**
38 Marylebone High Street tube: Baker Street
London W1 Mon, Sat 10-7, Tues-Fri 10-8

Scarlet **020 7376 9376**
7 Kensington Church Street tube: High Street Kensington
London W8 Mon, Sat 10-7, Tues-Fri 10-8, Sun 10:30-6

Scarlet **020 7229 4321**
118 Westbourne Grove tube: Notting Hill Gate
London W2 (opening times as above)

Super Nails of Los Angeles **020 7723 1163**
101 Crawford Street tube: Baker Street
London W1 Mon-Thurs 9-8, Fri 9-6, Sat 9-5:30

Day Spas

Agua **020 7300 1414**
The Sanderson tube: Oxford Circus/
50 Berners Street Tottenham Court Road
London W1 Daily 9-9

The Aveda Urban Retreat **020 7759 7355**
174 High Holborn tube: Covent Garden/Holborn
London WC1 Mon-Fri 9:30-7, Sat 9-6:30

Bliss London **020 7584 3888**
60 Sloane Avenue tube: South Kensington/Sloane Square
London SW3 Mon-Fri 9:30-8, Sat 9:30-6:30

The Dorchester Spa **020 7495 7335**
The Dorchester tube: Hyde Park Corner/Marble Arch
Park Lane Daily 7-9
London W1

Elemis Day Spa **020 7499 4995**
2-3 Lancashire Court tube: Bond Street
London W1 Mon-Sat 10-7 (Thurs-Fri 10-9), Sun 10-6

Elizabeth Arden Red Door 020 7629 4488
Hair & Beauty Spa tube: Bond Street
29 Davies Street Mon-Tues, Fri 10-7, Wed-Thurs 10-8
London W1 Sat 9-7, Sun 11-5

The Hale Clinic 020 7631 0156
7 Park Crescent tube: Regents Park/Great Portland Street
London W1 Mon-Fri 8:30-9, Sat 9-5

Olympus Suite Spa at Claridge's 020 7409 6565
54-55 Brook Street tube: Bond Street
London W1 Mon-Fri 6:30-9, Sat-Sun 8-8

The Parlour 020 7729 6969
3 Ravey Street tube: Old Street/Liverpool Street
London EC2 Mon-Fri 10-8, Sat 10-5

The Sanctuary 08700 630300
12 Floral Street tube: Covent Garden
London WC2 Mon-Fri 9:30-6, Sat-Sun 10-7
Wed-Fri Evening Spa (5-10)

The Spa Illuminata 020 7499 7777
63 South Audley Street tube: Bond Street
London W1 Mon-Fri 10-8, Sat 10-6

The Spa at Mandarin Oriental 020 7838 9888
Mandarin Oriental Hyde Park tube: Knightsbridge
66 Knightsbridge Daily 7:30-10
London SW1

Spa NK 020 7727 8002
127-131 Westbourne Grove tube: Notting Hill Gate
London W2 Mon 11-7, Tues-Thurs 9-9, Fri-Sat 9-7, Sun 10-5

The Temple 020 7229 2828
22 Powis Terrace Mon-Fri 6:30-9:30pm
London W11 Sat 8-5, Sun 11-5

Fitness Studios

The Berkeley Health Club & Spa 020 7235 6000
The Berkeley tube: Knightsbridge/Hyde Park Corner
Wilton Place Mon-Fri 6:30-10, Sat-Sun 8-8
London SW1

The Circle Health Club 020 7722 1234
41 Mackennal Street tube: St. John's Wood
London NW8 Mon-Fri 7-10, Sat-Sun 10-7

Lotte Berk 020 7385 2477
465 Fulham Road tube: Fulham Broadway
London SW6 (call for class timetable)

The Peak Health Club 020 7858 7008
Carlton Tower tube: Knightsbridge
Cadogan Place Mon-Fri 6:30-10
London SW1 Sat-Sun 7:30-9

The Third Space 020 7439 6333
13 Sherwood Street tube: Piccadilly Circus
London W1 Mon-Fri 6:30-10:30, Sat-Sun 8:30-8:30

Massage Therapists

Amanda Birch — **020 7629 6969**
Michaeljohn Ragdale Clinic — tube: Green Park
25 Albemarle Street — Mon, Sat 8-6:30
London W1 — Tues-Fri 8-8

Clarins at Fenwick — **020 7493 1901**
60 New Bond Street — tube: Bond Street/Oxford Circus
London W1 — Mon-Sat 10-6:30
(The Clarins general number is 0800 036 3558)

Kannika Parker — **020 7409 6565**
Olympus Suite Spa at Claridge's — tube: Bond Street
54-55 Brook Street — Mon-Fri 6:30-9
London W1 — Sat-Sun 8-8

Micheline Arcier Aromatherapy — **020 7235 3545**
7 William Street — tube: Knightsbridge
London SW1 — Mon-Fri 9-6, Sat 9-5

Nari Sadhuram — **020 7328 5452**
(call to arrange home visit)

Terry Kingscote — **020 7835 0400**
7 Stanhope Mews — tube: South Kensington/ Gloucester Road
London SW7 — (by appointment)

Yoga, Pilates, Alexander technique

Breath of Life — **020 7371 3224**
with Andrea Levinson (yoga) — (by appointment)

Danceworks — **020 7629 6183**
16 Balderton Street — tube: Marble Arch/Bond Street
London W1 — Mon-Fri 8:30-10, Sat-Sun 9-6

The Life Centre — **020 7221 4602**
15 Edge Street — tube: Notting Hill Gate
London W8 — Mon-Fri 7:30-9:30, Sat 8:30-8, Sun 9-7

Lynne Pinette — **020 7580 4400**
Portland Hospital (pregnancy & post-natal yoga)
234 Great Portland Street — tube: Oxford Circus
London W1 — Tues 10-11:30, Thurs 12:30-1:45
Sat 10:30-11:45 (by appointment)

Triyoga Centre — **020 7483 3344**
6 Erskine Road — tube: Chalk Farm
London NW3 — Mon-Fri 6:30-9, Sat-Sun 9-8:30

Noel Kingsley (Alexander technique) — **020 7491 3505**
19 Cavendish Square — tube: Oxford Circus
London W1 — (by appointment)

Pilates off the Square — **020 7935 8505**
4 Mandeville Place — tube: Bond Street
London W1 — Mon-Fri 8-8:30, Sat 9-5

Stephanie Wright (Kum Nye) **020 7881 5800**
Eden Medical Centre tube: Sloane Square
63a King's Road Mon-Fri 8-8, Sat 10-6
London SW3

Tanning

Aesthetique **020 7823 2023**
36 Knightsbridge tube: Knightsbridge/Hyde Park Corner
London SW1 Mon-Thurs 9-8, Fri 9-6, Sat 10-6

Golden Glow (one-minute mist-on tans) **020 7495 7677**
31 Avery Row tube: Bond Street
London W1 Mon-Sat 9:30-6:30

Golden Glow **020 7286 4033**
1 Lanark Place tube: Warwick Avenue
London W9
(opening times as above)

St. Tropez at House of Fraser **020 7529 4792**
318 Oxford Street tube: Bond Street/Oxford Circus
London W1 Mon-Sat 10-8 (Thurs 10-9), Sun 12-6
(The St. Tropez general number is 0115 983 6363)

Make-up artists

Jackie Hamilton-Smith **020 7434 3202**
Untitled Management tube: Piccadilly Circus
72 Wardour Street (by appointment)
London W1

Jemma Kidd's school **07743 487 557**
For those aiming at the very top, supermodel Jemma (sister of supermodel Jodie) is now an international make-up specialist. She and Ginni Bogardo run 6-week courses (fee £8,500) at their make-up school on everything from how to make up for your wedding to cutting-edge fashion make-up techniques. Okay, the runway doesn't feature in your life and you weigh more than 100 pounds, but it could be worth a call—somebody there must have the answer to your question. www.jemmakiddmakeupschool.com

Katherine Saunders **020 8249 7508/077 8857 8767**
(by appointment)

Valentine Gotti **020 7300 1414**
The Sanderson tube: Oxford Circus/Tottenham Court Road
50 Berners Street (by appointment)
London W1

Repairs & Services

Dry Cleaners

Mending, Alterations & Custom Tailoring

Shoe Repair

Trimmings

Personal Shoppers

Dry Cleaners

Blossom & Brown Sycamore 020 7727 2635
73a Clarendon Road tube: Holland Park
London W11 Mon-Fri 8:30-5:30 (Thurs 8:30-4:30)
Sat 8:30-3 (closed for lunch 1-2)

Buckingham Dry Cleaners 020 7499 1253
83 Duke Street tube: Bond Street
London W1 Mon-Fri 8-6, Sat 9:30-12:30

Cashmere Clinic 020 7584 9806
9 Beauchamp Place tube: Knightsbridge
London SW3 /South Kensington
Mon-Fri 10-4

Celebrity Cleaners 020 7437 5324
(wedding dress specialists) tube: Oxford Circus
30 Brewer Street Mon-Fri 8:30-6:30
London W1

Chalfont Dryers & Cleaners 020 7935 7316
222 Baker Street tube: Baker Street
London NW1 Mon-Fri 8:30-6, Sat 9-1

Concorde of Knightsbridge 020 7584 0784
3 Motcomb Street tube: Knightsbridge
London SW1 Mon-Fri 8-6, Sat 9-5

Elias 020 7589 5851
85 Walton Street tube: South Kensington
London SW3 Mon-Fri 7:30-5:30, Sat 7:30-5

Elias 020 7584 1246
16-17 Glendower Place tube: South Kensington
London SW7 Mon-Sat 8-5:30

Elias 020 7722 2212
68 St. John's Wood High Street tube: St. John's Wood
London NW8 Mon-Sat 8-6, Sun 11-4

Jeeves of Belgravia 020 7235 1101
8-10 Pont Street tube: Knightsbridge/Sloane Square
London SW1 Mon-Fri 8:30-7, Sat 8:30-6

Jeeves of Belgravia 020 7589 9229
123 Fulham Road tube: South Kensington
London SW3 Mon-Fri 8:30-7, Sat 8-6

Jeeves of Belgravia 020 7262 0200
59 Connaught Street tube: Marble Arch
London W2 Mon-Fri 8-7, Sat 8-6

Jeeves of Belgravia 020 7603 0484
271 Kensington High Street tube: High Street Kensington
London W8 Mon-Fri 8:30-5:30, Sat 8:30-5

Jeeves of Belgravia 020 7491 8885
54 South Audley Street tube: Bond Street
London W1 Mon-Fri 8-7, Sat 8:30-5

Jeeves of Belgravia 020 7794 4100
11 Heath Street tube: Hampstead
London NW3 Mon-Fri 8:30-5:30, Sat 8:30-5, Sun 11-3

Lilliman & Cox **020 7629 4555**
34 Bruton Place tube: Green Park/Bond Street
London W1 Mon-Fri 8:30-5:30

Lilliman & Cox **020 7730 1234**
Harrods tube: Knightsbridge
Knightsbridge Mon-Sat 10-7
London SW1

Perkins Dry Cleaners **020 7935 3072**
28 Thayer Street tube: Bond Street
London W1 Mon-Fri 8:30-7 (Thurs 8:30-6), Sat 8:30-3

Peters & Falla **020 7731 3255**
281 New King's Road tube: Parsons Green
London SW6 Mon-Fri 8:30-6:15, Sat 9:30-2

Peters & Falla **020 7731 5114**
179 New King's Road tube: Parsons Green
London SW6 Mon-Fri 8:30-6, Sat 9:30-2

Seven Dials **020 7240 9274**
37 Monmouth Street tube: Covent Garden
London WC2 Mon-Fri 8-6, Sat 9-2

Valentino Dry Cleaners **020 7240 5879**
(suede & leather specialists) tube: Tottenham Court Road
125 Shaftesbury Avenue Mon-Fri 8:30-6, Sat 9-1
London WC2

Mending, Alterations & Custom Tailoring

The Alterations Station **020 7627 0167**
29 The Pavement tube: Clapham Common
London SW4 Mon-Fri 8-6:30, Sat 10-4

Bob Tailoring **020 7495 4099**
58 Maddox Street tube: Bond Street/Oxford Circus
London W1 Mon-Fri 10-6, Sat 10-3

British Invisible Mending Service **020 7935 2487**
32 Thayer Street tube: Bond Street
London W1 Mon-Fri 8:30-5:30, Sat 10-1

Celebrity Cleaners **020 7437 5324**
(invisible mending specialists)
30 Brewer Street tube: Oxford Circus/Piccadilly Circus
London W1 Mon-Fri 8:30-6:30

First Tailored Alterations **020 7730 1400**
(leather, suede & sheepskin specialists)
85 Lower Sloane Street tube: Sloane Square
London SW1 Mon-Sat 9-6

General Leather Company **020 7935 1041**
56 Chiltern Street tube: Baker Street
London W1 Mon-Fri 10-6, Sat 10-5

George the Tailor **020 7437 6876**
83-84 Berwick Street tube: Oxford Circus/Piccadilly Circus
London W1 Mon-Fri 6-6:30, Sat 6-2, Sun 6-12

KS Tailoring Service **020 7437 9345**
13 Savile Row tube: Piccadilly Circus/Oxford Circus
London W1 Mon-Fri 9:30-5:30, Sat 10-2

Mike Mandalia Tailors **020 7629 4021**
22 South Molton Street tube: Bond Street
London W1 Mon-Fri 9-6, Sat 11-5:30

Roland Lilley & Co **020 7734 4300**
Suite 24, Grafton House tube: Piccadilly Circus
2-3 Golden Square Mon-Fri 9-6, Sat 9-1
London W1

Stitchcraft **020 7629 7919**
7 South Molton Street tube: Bond Street
London W1 Mon-Fri 9-5, Sat 10-4

Shoe Repair

The Complete Cobbler **020 7636 9040**
26 Tottenham Street tube: Goodge Street
London W1 Mon-Fri 8-6, Sat 9:30-1

Fifth Avenue Shoe Repairs **020 7636 6705**
41 Goodge Street tube: Goodge Street
London W1 Mon-Wed 8:30-6:30, Thurs-Fri 8:30-7, Sat 10-6

The Heel Bar **020 7580 6024**
35 Tottenham Street tube: Goodge Street
London W1 Mon-Fri 9-6:30, Sat 9:30-1

Special Footwear & Orthotics **020 7486 4664**
12 New Cavendish Street tube: Bond Street
London W1 Mon-Fri 9-6, Sat 10-2

Trimmings

Allans of Duke Street (fabrics) **020 7629 3781**
75 Duke Street tube: Bond Street
London W1 Mon-Fri 9:30-6, Thurs 10-7, Sat 10-5:30

The Button Queen **020 7935 1505**
19 Marylebone Lane tube: Bond Street
London W1 Mon-Wed 10-5, Thurs-Fri 10-6, Sat 10-4

Ells & Farrier (beads) **020 7629 9964**
20 Beak Street tube: Oxford Circus/Piccadilly Circus
London W1 Mon-Fri 9-5:15, Sat 10-5

Joel & Son (fabrics) **020 7724 6895**
75-83 Church Street tube: Edgware Road
London NW8 Mon-Sat 9-5

John Lewis **020 7629 7711**
278 Oxford Street tube: Oxford Circus/Bond Street
London W1 Mon-Sat 9:30-7 (Thurs 10-8)

Liberty **020 7734 1234**
210-220 Regent Street tube: Oxford Circus
London W1 Mon-Wed 10-6:30, Thurs 10-8
Fri-Sat 10-7, Sun 12-6

MacCulloch & Wallis **020 7629 0311**
25 Dering Street tube: Oxford Circus/Bond Street
London W1 Mon-Fri 9-6 (Thurs 9-7), Sat 10:30-5

Soho Silks **020 7434 3305**
22 D'Arblay Street tube: Oxford Circus/
London W1 Tottenham Court Road
Mon-Sat 9:30-6

V V Rouleaux (ribbons) **020 7730 3125**
54 Sloane Square tube: Sloane Square
London SW1 Mon-Sat 9:30-6

V V Rouleaux (ribbons) **020 7224 5179**
6 Marylebone High Street tube: Bond Street
London W1 Mon-Sat 9:30-6

Personal Shoppers

Charlotte Wilson **020 7385 2001**

Personal Allies **0780 829 9492**
www.personalallies.com Charlie@personalallies.com
Arranges personal shopping itineraries, as well as corporate events and private parties.

Mary Young **020 7350 1877**
The Shopping Service PO Box 31329
London SW11 www.vipshoppinglondon.com
Will take clients out on a tailor-made shopping spree with special appointments at each store.

Fashion Speak

Avant-garde: forward-thinking or advanced. When referring to art or costume, sometimes implies erotic or startling. Derived from the French for "advance guard".

Bridge collection: a collection that is priced between designer and mass market.

Couture: French word used throughout fashion industry to describe the original styles, the ultimate in fine sewing and tailoring, made of expensive fabrics, by designers. The designs are shown in collections twice a year—spring/summer and fall/winter.

Custom-made/tailor-made, also called bespoke: garments made by tailor or couture house for an individual customer following couturier's original design. Done by either fitting a model form adjusted to the customer's measurements or by several personal fittings.

Diffusion line: a designer's second and less expensive collection.

Ensemble: an entire costume, including accessories, worn at one time. Two or more items of clothing designed and coordinated to be worn together.

Fashion trend: direction in which styles, colors and fabrics are moving. Trends may be influenced by political events, films, personalities, dramas, social and sporting events or indeed any human activity.

Faux: false or counterfeit, imitation: used in connection with gems, pearls and leathers. Faux fur (fake fur) is commonplace today, as is what is sometimes known as "pleather" (plastic leather). Artificial gems, especially pearls, are often made from a fine kind of glass known as "paste", and are accordingly sometimes called "paste" for short.

Haberdashery: a store that sells men's apparel and furnishings.

Knock-off: trade term for the copying of an item of apparel, e.g. a dress or a coat, in a lower price line. Similar to piracy.

Made-to-measure: clothing (dress, suit, shirt etc) made according to individual's measurement. No fittings required.

One-off: a unique, one-of-a-kind item that will not be found in any other store or produced again in the future, e.g. a customized denim skirt or a rare vintage cocktail dress. Can also refer to made-to-measure and couture garments designed for a particular person and/or event, such as a dress for the Oscars.

Prêt-à-porter: French term which literally means ready-to-wear, i.e. to take (or wear) straight out of the shop.

Ready-to-wear (rtw): apparel that is mass-produced in standard sizes. Records of the ready-to-wear industry tabulated in the U.S. Census of 1860 included hoop skirts, cloaks, and mantillas; from 1890 shirtwaists and wrappers were added; and, after 1930, dresses.

Notes

Notes

Notes